D1061756

Slums

SLUMS

Edited by
S. Martin Gaskell

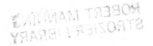

Leicester University Press
(a division of Pinter Publishers)
Leicester, London and New York

© Editor and Contributors 1990

First published in Great Britain in 1990 by Leicester University Press
(a division of Pinter Publishers)

Editorial offices
Fielding Johnson Building, University of Leicester, University Road,
Leicester LE1 7RH, England

Trade and other enquiries
25 Floral Street, London, WC2E 9DS, England

British Library Cataloguing in Publication Data

A CIP catalogue record for this book
is available from the British Library.
ISBN 0-7185-1293-6

Library of Congress Cataloging-in-Publication Data

CIP Data available from the Library of Congress

Typeset by Mayhew Typesetting, Bristol, England
Printed and bound in Great Britain by
Biddles Ltd, Guildford and King's Lynn

Contents

List of figures

Introduction

S. Martin Gaskell

The slum, according to E.R. Dewsnup at the turn of the century, was the physical embodiment of the housing evil;[1] as such it had become the subject of frontal attack in terms of extensive slum demolition. As an environmental reality, however, it had always been much more difficult to isolate and quantify; everyone has always seemed to know with certainty when they were in a slum, but why is less clear and is the matter of the debate which these studies address. The dividing line with respectability could be both sharp and indefinable.

It is, therefore, appropriate that this introduction should be written from an office in Houndsditch in the City of London which on one side looks out to the unparalleled wealth and high technology of the City and on the other surveys the dereliction of Middlesex Street leading through Spitalfields to Brick Lane with their present-day response of inner-city regeneration to the plight of immigrant poverty. For that stark and shaming contrast not only is intrinsic to the slums' identity, but in this particular context was highlighted by Blanchard Jerrold in his commentary to Gustave Doré's *London*, which can still stand as the text for a study on slums:

The West End Londoner is as completely in a strange land as any traveller from the Continent. A saunter through the extensive vegetable market of Spitalfield; a turn in Houndsditch, by Bishopsgate church; a pause where Whitechapel joins Aldgate . . . and so out upon the tea and colonial grandees of America Square and Mincing Lane—will reveal a new world of London to many a Cockney who thought he knew the great city well. The grandest and noblest spectacles of commerce, touch the basest and most heart-breaking . . .[2]

Thus in the heart of London were established and existed those features which created and reinforced slum conditions throughout the country in the course of the nineteenth and twentieth centuries. Though cheek by jowl with wealthy and respectable neighbourhoods, the slums were isolated and physically cut off from them in a way which reinforced their basic characteristics of terrible housing, foul drainage and inadequate sewerage, abundance of bugs and dirt, extreme unhealthiness and populations of transients, criminals and the unskilled living in extremely insecure and impoverished circumstances.

The reality of such areas was to make them a 'problem' because they persisted as a source of shame within otherwise beautiful and improving cities. As a problem, those in authority have had to explain their existence in terms of the characters of the slum-dwellers or the limitations of building. The result that Barnes identified in the 1930s was the continually sounding antiphons of environment and character.[3] The one embraces the collective activity that arises out of the organised will of the people and rests on their collective resources, the other comprises the ethical and emotional agencies which have as their common function the elevation of individual character. That dichotomy means that in practice the slum by definition can be dependent for its existence on lack of either moral qualities or material possessions. It is the persistence of that debate and the continuance of that conflict that impart to the slum as a phenomenon its unique challenge to the moral, social, economic and aesthetic mores of civilised societies.

Such a challenge persists today in the Third World where the post-war urban explosion replicates the problems and pressures of European industrialisation and urbanisation. In those cities of recent expansion two-thirds of the growth is attributable to immigration and much of that increased population lives in shanty towns. These perhaps contain between a quarter and a half of the population of such cities as Manila, Djakarta, Mexico City, Ankara and Lima, with the slum populations often growing at twice the growth rates of the cities as a whole. As elsewhere the opportunities seen to exist in the city far outweigh those apparent in the rural areas, and migration comes from all corners of the different countries, with a preponderance from adjacent areas. Such an influx of population tends to be too poor to purchase land and build a house, and is unable, and perhaps unwilling, to find a room for the family in older, decaying property. In such circumstances the migrant is impelled towards illegal occupation and to squat in shacks constructed of waste materials on vacant land. Such squatter camps and shanty towns are the latter-day slums of the Third World. In these, as in their European predecessors, the population is transitory, with people given the availability of permanent employment moving out, and with constant influxes of new migrants. The poverty of the populace is thus reflected in the quality of slum housing. As a result, as Peter Lloyd has characterised it:

Emotionally we contrast the squalor of the slums, negating all our own standards of privacy and cleanliness, with an image of idyllic rural life in which disease resulting from such factors as inadequate water supply, fears of witchcraft caused by interpersonal tensions, are conveniently excluded. We feel guilty that man should have fallen so low. We fear the spread of diseases from the insanitary shanties to the decorous suburbs.[4]

Such emotive reaction is no new response to the phenomenon of the slums. Indeed, it is the essence of the slum that it summons forth such sensibilities. It is part of the interest and importance of the slum that it was through its very existence as a term that the *housing problem* as such was identified, while the use of the term indicates changing attitudes to the phenomenon itself. The origins of the term and its semantic evolution have been analysed by Dyos.[5] Appearing in general usage in the 1840s, he has shown how the semi-slang expression became synonymous with 'rookeries', 'feverdens', 'little hells', 'devil's acres', and 'dark purlieus'. The slum was a sensation. What had existed for centuries and what had been a reality of the Industrial Revolution and the early urbanisation of Great Britain was now to be seen as something spectacular. They had an unreality and a sense of danger for those outside them and who only read of them. It was this, as much as the manner of presentation of slum life and environment, that gave the slum its emotive power and impact. The facts about slums were thus both unpalatable and unavoidable.

It is a remarkable feature of the slum as an historical phenomenon that its impact lessened little over a hundred years and its characterisation changed hardly at all. In 1933, when Howard Marshall wrote his book *Slum*, having followed many earlier social explorers in the experience of living incognito in a slum, he sought to emphasise the other-world experience that continued to mark off the slum from 'civilised society'. Having described for his readers what they might expect to find in any slum, he wrote:

. . . it is difficult for most of us to see the other point of view. The slum-dwellers look upwards: the rest of us look down. We look down such a long way that we can only see black dots swarming around the foot of the ladder. It does not occur to us immediately that these dots are human beings, and we turn our heads away, and leave the swarming heaps to the sanitary inspector.[6]

The slum was thus not only physically separate, but its inhabitants were a race apart whose characters were judged akin to the most primitive form of humankind, or, worse, to assume the nature of the animals with whom they shared their existence. Thus James Grant, in his third account of London life in 1842, described how 'whole families messed together as if they were so many pigs'.[7] In Arthur Morrison's *A Child of the Jago*, the people are unreservedly described as rats.[8] They are not likened unto rats but are literally described as such, creeping in and out of their rat holes. The expression may not be just but it is significant, and that significance is explained in detail and in practice by Green and Parton. The first writings of the 1840s to reveal both the reality and the threat of the slums were destined to contribute only slowly and piecemeal to the building-up of factual information; they were, however, stripping away the veneer of stark ignorance, with their shocking accounts of 'occular proof' removing all question of the possibility of doubt. Dr Arnott's account of Glasgow slums in 1842, for instance, contributed to this dossier:

There were no privies or drains there, and the dungheaps received all the filth which the swarm of wretched inhabitants could give; and we learnt that a considerable part of the rent of the houses was paid by the produce of dung heaps. Thus, worse off than wild animals, many of which withdraw to a distance and conceal their ordure, the dwellers in these courts have converted their shame into a kind of money by which their lodging was to be paid.[9]

'Worse off than wild animals' was to epitomise one set of attitudes. At the same time, another note has also been struck: the sensationalism that was to be taken up by journalism in the middle years of the nineteenth century, as the populist cause of anti-urban sentiment fed on the fear of retrogression in society despite economic progress. Such sensationalism was not simply cheap journalism, but was often genuinely devoted to establishing awareness, disseminating information and persuading people to take action. As George Godwin wrote in *Town Swamps and Social Bridges* in 1859, 'The first step towards obtaining a remedy is to make existence of the disease known'.[10] To that end he moved from the broad canvas of slum characterisation to the detailed dissection of particular identifiable areas. Thus of Charlotte's Buildings in the Clerkenwell district of London:

When we examined it a few days ago it was, still, in an abominable condition. The atmosphere throughout the court was unbearable: the broken pavement was reeking with rotting matter: the houses are in ruins; the inhabitants in misery. What the minds *must* be that are formed in such a mould, the world should by this time know.[11]

Those consequences were increasingly spelt out as the century progressed in terms of the medical, moral and social consequences. In the 1850s Sir John Simon began to draw attention to what few people were paying attention to at the time, that is that the incidence of certain dangerous diseases varied widely between places characterised by very different physical conditions. So the death rate from fever was always high where there was overcrowding, and, as a consequence, the extreme wastefulness of this had to be set against the 'cheapness of filthy residences and ditch-drawn drinking water'.

Although moral considerations had been associated with concern for physical welfare in the 1850s and before, it was subsequently that the concern for the moral and spiritual well-being of the poor became more marked. This was partly a consequence of the considerable concern for morality explicit in mid-Victorian society; it also resulted from the greatly increased knowledge of slums and slum life. The journalistic forays into the working-class districts of the country, and particularly the capital, had resulted in a realisation of the missionary task on society's own doorstep. Between 1850 and 1888 the slums consequently became the object of a veritable moral and spiritual crusade. General Booth was characteristically blunt on the hypocrisy involved: 'What a satire it is upon our Christianity and our civilisation that the existence of these colonies of heathens and savages in the heart of our capital should attract so little attention! It is no better than a ghastly mockery.'[12] But, though the emphasis was changing, the image of the slum remained essentially the same with its constant reference to an 'abyss' at the edge of society. As a result, that element of class fear, which results from the fear of contagious disease or revolution, is never entirely absent, and as the century progresses it is heightened by despair at the worsening social situation and the apparent inability of existing institutions to deal with the problem.

Below the level of 'deserving poor' was what were generally known as the 'criminal classes' inhabiting the slums. This was the underworld of the dosser, shifting in and out of work. It was a world which has been significantly neglected in housing history, but a world which infected the public conscience of the later nineteenth century. Of course Dickens brought the connection between slums and crime before a very large audience. His descriptions of parts of London made them forever the haunt of the outcast and fed a view of the slums as places threatening danger that was best encapsulated in Lord Shaftesbury's observation, 'Who would wonder that in these receptacles, nine-tenths of the great crimes, the burglaries, and murders, and violence, that desolated society, were conceived and hatched'.[13]

The connection between crime and the teeming slum suggested itself naturally. But if the increasing evidence of crime worried the Victorians, so too did the possibility of mass protest. Revolution and social upheaval were the fears that provoked the cry for improvement or destruction of the slums. As the connection between bad housing and national weakness began to take on Darwinian tones, the slum was transformed from an affront to a threat to the human race. As such, it had to be removed in a twentieth-century world that was to be 'fit for heroes'. From being unpalatable it moved to being unacceptable.

By the 1920s it was increasingly apparent that long awareness of the slum problem and repeated efforts to deal with it had had in effect little or no impact on the real condition of the poor. This is evident from Jim Yelling's study of London where, despite all the efforts to enhance factual appreciation of the problem, there was still widespread conviction that slums were the consequence of failings in the inhabitants and that slum-dwellers constituted a special order of society that was undisciplined, thriftless, dangerous and intemperate. It still needed the social investigators and the medical officers of health to restate and re-affirm the reality of those conditions. Their reports read little differently from those of their predecessors of nearly a century before. The litanies recited lack of sanitation, faulty sewerage, broken buildings, dampness and infestation, overcrowding and total lack of facilities, leading to an unhealthy and discontented population. Throughout the country in every town and city were hundreds and thousands of tenemented houses where families lived in one or two rooms of decayed buildings, sharing one lavatory and one tap between fifty people or more.

The problem persisted; what was new was the benchmark by which it was judged. For the question of slums was always one of relativities. It had never been a precise term; it never had a clear technical meaning definable by law. The basis on which a house is 'unfit for habitation' is one of judgement. And in the post-First World War period, despite all the political vicissitudes pertaining to housing policy, a new standard of working-class housing had been set. As E.D. Simon characterised the position by 1929: 'A family of children growing up in any of the million new houses has, so far as the house is concerned, as good a chance of health and strength as the child of a millionaire.'[14] Thus what it felt like to live in a slum, or perhaps more importantly what it was thought to feel like to live in a slum, depended to a degree on what it might feel like to live in a new suburb. Against that standard are to be judged the facts of the 1931 census that only 37 per cent of London families had a house or flat of their own, and a third of London's population lived at a density of more than three people to two rooms. As a result, the level of unfitness for habitation soared in the 1930s, due both to the failure to deal with the problem over the past hundred years and to the resolve to reform.

It was totally appropriate that ultimately the standard of the slum should be defined in terms of the number of obsolescent houses which a local authority could claim rather than the level of the houses involved. The slum, as the origins of the term betray, was the consequence of the desire to reform and replace. Though this volume is not of itself directed to the question of the resolution of the slum problem, it cannot avoid the solution to the extent that the solution creates or confirms the problem.

The slums were the test-beds of social theories and social policies. It was the conviction that such an environment would directly inform the habits and characters of the populace which made surveys of the conditions of the slums a *sine qua non* for the statisticians of early Victorian Britain. The collection of valuable data and the detailed measurement of social conditions resulted in a more realistic view of the relationship between poverty and degradation. The shock of exposure of the human misery collected in the slums provoked amongst men of scientific interest an intellectual reaction to the emotional basis of so much public health campaigning hitherto. Hard facts collected in an irreproachable manner could not be ignored. The statistical societies ensured that no one could henceforth justifiably claim ignorance of slum conditions.

To set out the scale of the problem was to stress the physical and moral dangers of overcrowding. To do so was to establish the slum as the laboratory of social reform. In the period between the 1830s and the 1870s there was a transition from the first investigations raising public concern about the slums to realisation of the manifest need for action and a public housing policy. The pioneering literature of empirical sociology combined fact-finding and analysis with protest, comment and reform. The result of the exposure of the casualties of urbanisation was a gradual change in the values, attitudes and assumptions of the middle classes towards their environment and their consequent demand for improvement in the quality of urban life.

The vast literature which prompted and promoted such change was in itself a transition from the work of the social explorer to that of the professional sociologist. Out of the attempts to come to terms with this new and strange society, which the slums represented, developed a distinctive literature in which, as Peter Keating has established: '. . . one class consciously sets out to explore, analyse and report upon, the life of another class lower on the social scale than his own . . .'[15]

The slums satisfied the curiosity of the social explorer, and the study of Bath by Graham Davis shows that such exploration was not restricted to the metropolis. Slums everywhere provided a challenge and an adventure that was enhanced by the frequent adoption of disguise to enter this unknown and thus unsafe world. The consequence of such an approach is inevitably to be found in the semiology of the slum: 'An abyss still contains enough sense of distance to be attractive to the social explorer, but it carries with it an eeriness which replaces the most exotic associations of travel. You don't journey to an abyss: you descend or fall into it.'[16] In the twentieth century, following the examples set by Booth and Rowntree, the terminology changes, but exploration of the slum remains the source of the new science of sociological investigation. The slums continue to exercise the power to shock and to disturb the equilibrium of established society. The extent of poverty and the realisation that slums were not restricted to London or large industrial cities meant that in the inter-war years the Anti Slum Campaign became one of the first social issues to make a national impact in terms of a mass publicity campaign. Its interest and appeal added to the journalism and evangelism of the previous century the stimulus of broadcast accounts and the mobilisation of Church and royalty on behalf of the cause.

The corollary of the slum was thus slum clearance as both Gordon Mingay and Jim Yelling articulate in their contributions. From the moment that the slum was identified it was isolated as a problem and the very nature of a problem is that it seeks a solution. The slum was to be 'improved', 'removed', 'destroyed' or 'replaced'. It was by definition transient. Its very characteristics were defined as ills in society, factors to be remedied: obsolescence; overcrowding; unfit for habitation; criminal; insanitary; unhealthy. From the time when the problem was clearly perceived, the slum formed the subject of national debate. It became the point of reference for most of the important Housing Acts and it helped to forge a national housing policy. It was in the context of the slum that the housing question was most precisely defined and subjected to the closest analysis of most prolonged and searching political discussion. And it was around the slum that attempted remedies received most attention and their inadequacies were most strikingly expressed. The continuing reality of the buildings that constituted slums and of the life that went on in them demonstrated the futility of adopting purely punitive legislation and action against overcrowding; the human dimension could not be solved by clearance orders unaccompanied by rehousing. The magnitude and the persistence of the problem identified the inadequacies of traditional methods of social amelioration.

The slum problem was therefore the housing problem, but it was not solely a problem about housing. The slum as an identifiable concept was much more than simply bad housing, and the deprivations which it encapsulated cannot be understood within such a restricted framework of reference. For many reformers throughout the nineteenth and early twentieth centuries, overcrowding, and thus the existence of slum property, was definable as a moral problem; in particular it has been argued that poor accommodation sheltering the unskilled classes was the consequence of an unregenerate race sacrificing household comfort to alcohol. There was no doubt that bad housing related to low income and that the correlation between quality of housing and income sharpened towards the bottom of any income table, with those earning least paying the greatest proportion of their income on housing. Cause and effect between overcrowding and patterns of moral and social behaviour are less easy to determine. There is, however, some element of truth in the argument that bad housing cannot be divided from other quantifiable hallmarks of poverty.

These characteristics which became implied in the term slum certainly predate the urban poverty of the nineteenth century. Gordon Mingay's important corrective to the traditional view of the slum demonstrates that it was in the slums of rural Britain that the moral dangers of over-crowding were first articulated. Report after report of conditions in agricultural villages in the late eighteenth and early nineteenth centuries recall pictures of dilapidated hovels in which large families and even lodgers were crowded into one bedroom, and in which whole families lay ill of fever in the same room. When the Rev. James Frazer reported on the situation in Norfolk to the *Royal Commission on the Employment of Children, Young Persons and Women in Agriculture* in the 1860s, he summarised the perceived moral problems of the slums in a way that remained as true when transferred to the centre of the city: 'It is imposs-ible to exaggerate the ill-effects in every respect, physical, social, economical, moral, intellectual . . . modesty must be an unknown virtue, decency an unimaginable thing . . .'[17]

If morality caused the greatest concern for some in society, in the urban slum, poverty, crime, ill health and heavy mortality were the conditions most commonly found together with overcrowding and con-gestion. Of course, criminal areas in cities have a long tradition; what was new was the scale and concentration of such activities. To a large extent, crime, be it petty pilfering or prostitution, was dependent on the casual activities of the inhabitants and was associated with their drunken condition. Inevitably to outsiders this world of crime was feared as violent and often perceived as undeserving of help and consideration. Such fears were fed in turn by latent xenophobia, with the tendency of poor immigrants to congregate in inner-city slums, especially in London. In 1901 Whitechapel's population was 31.8 per cent alien, compared to 2.9 per cent for London as a whole. The Irish, followed by the Jewish exodus from the European pogroms between 1881 and 1914, swelled the ranks of the urban poor in London and to a lesser extent in Leeds, Manchester, Liverpool and other large provincial cities. Unlike most British migrants who, as Gareth Stedman Jones has shown, tended to settle more in the suburbs and to avoid the inner industrial districts, those with no choice self-selected the slums.[18]

In this volume this aspect of slum society is dealt with most particularly by Green and Parton in relation to London and Birmingham. It would be wrong, however, to characterise the slums at any point in their history as places of unitary culture or static society. For they were always places of appreciably changing structure. As Dyos analysed in his classic account of Sultan Street in Camberwell, successive censuses of the late nineteenth century showed a big turnover of inhabitants, resulting by the 1890s in a community that was distinctly older than it would have been if the young people who had gone there at the start had stayed.[19] In this volume Graham Davis has taken that analysis forward in relation to Bath where, just as irresistibly as in metropolitan London, poverty continually forced families to move as part of the struggle for existence.

The result within working-class areas was one of striking variations across very small areas of social and economic identities. Robert Tressall in *The Ragged Trousered Philanthropist* identified the class gradations down to social isolation,[20] while working-class Londoners, confronted by a constantly shifting and socially amorphous population, took particular pains in drawing their social boundaries, relying not just on wages and employment patterns, but also on race and religion. In Roberts's 'classic slum' in Salford, an area of some thirty streets, there were enough diverse elements from artisan to unskilled labourers to require a classification and categorisation of neighbourhoods in terms of every street. The slum did not just contain the submerged tenth. The shock literature of the nineteenth century had subsumed the heterogeneity of working-class life and it took Charles Booth to demonstrate that misery was not all-pervasive. In his survey of East London completed between 1889 and 1902, he estimated that those living substandard lives and in chronic want constituted no more than 30 per cent. Those categories contained those with small regular earnings and intermittent earnings. Only some 1.25 per cent of the population was made up of the 'degenerate and incorrigible class' which comprised 'occasional labourers, street sellers, loafers, criminals and semi-criminals'.[21] Earlier unsupportable generalisations failed to take account of the sense of kinship which for many inhabitants of slum housing continued to make their lives at all bearable. As such districts became entrenched in the urban fabric they ceased to be solely, or indeed primarily, the haunts of unneighbourly transients.

While fluctuating within particular areas of towns, the populace developed ties to a locality. As Michael Young and Peter Wilmott analysed in their famous survey, *Family and Kinship in East London*, a network of family relationships spread across the neighbourhood giving shape and substance to its life.[22] In this volume Green and Parton have examined those relationships in the context of occupation and ownership patterns in the rookeries of St Giles. Thus slums developed their own momentum and their own intrinsic characteristics. They shared in common, however, certain factors which, in variable combinations, accounted for their condition and their creation as wynds and rookeries. Whether they were erected as slums or whether they descended rapidly into that state, the reasons for their situation were indubitably a mixture of human and environmental pressures which consequently locked an area into an unalterable cycle of deprivation. What could be afforded and who could afford it were inevitable corollaries in the housing experience of the poor.

Casual labour, for a start, always gravitated towards the central parts of large towns and the riverside areas of ports where the worst property was located. For these were the areas where casual labour had the best chance of securing employment. To meet that market demand speculators erected, prior to any bye-law control, insanitary courts and 'back' houses commonly bereft of any basic amenity. So on grounds of cost and location, the poor sought out the back-to-back houses and decayed tenements on the banks of the Tyne in Newcastle or the enclosed courts and cellars of the old parish of Liverpool.

It was as a result of the casual basis of employment that working men were obliged to live within reasonably close walking distance of their work. This was a situation exacerbated when the number of jobs available in any location could vary considerably from day to day and when such uncertainty affected not only the unskilled but also many skilled trades. While some working men tramped several miles to and from work, particularly in semi-rural areas, in large cities there was much closer tying to the workplace. Thus the area of 'Old Nichol' in Bethnal Green was one of irregular and poorly paid employment. There brick-yards and market-gardens, pushed ever further out by the spreading streets, needed seasonal supplies of low-skilled labour which could be laid off when not needed. Also it was within walking distance of the huge, ever fluctuating, market for casual labour in and around the docks and shipyards. As a result, development was not a matter of chance; rather it was, arguably, the most grossly obvious instance of social morbidity affecting a whole urban zone. In such places the connection between the worker's home and workplace had to be extremely close and it was in the circumstances of sweated labour and of insecure and poorly paid employment that, '. . . creeping congestion either made a district ready for the complete descent into slum or more indelibly confirmed a condition that had already been sketched in'.[23]

The lowest paid workers were, therefore, those who were forced by the circumstances of their employment to spend the highest proportion of their income on rent. Given the uncertainty of the employment market and the insecurity of life at the economic margins of society, it was not surprising that throughout the nineteenth century slum-dwellers resorted to a variety of strange trades in order to preserve even an existence. The nature and practice of those trades added much to the lurid folklore of the slums: '. . . occupations are forged which in civilised parts are never dreamt of, except it be in exceptionally bad dreams. One does not like even to hint at the way in which scores of poor wretches in the locality pick up a living . . .'[24]

Even if trades such as cat-flaying or collection of dog ordure for tanning were the exception, and solely the preserve of the submerged tenth, the fact remained that for the majority of slum-dwellers there was a necessity to make ends meet through such trading and such domestic activity as they could manage. Life, even for those who aspired to some degree of respectability, was always lived at the margins, right through into the twentieth century. It was thus difficult for such families to devote more than small sums towards basic furnishing. According to Mrs Pember Reeves's analysis of labourers' budgets in Lambeth in 1913, the homes of the unskilled were still characterised by few chairs, limited table space, no wardrobes, unsatisfactory cooking utensils, and an inadequate supply of beds.[25] In this the links between the early and late nineteenth century and the mid-twentieth century remain strong. The slum conditions of the buildings were mirrored in the slum conditions of their interiors; the economic realities of life in the slums depressed their situation and worsened their prospects.

Various conditions of property could thus be brought down to what was recognisable as a slum in terms of the quality of life. It took, however, different physical and environmental circumstances to create the essential pre-requisites for a slum. According to Williams, writing about *London Rookeries and Colliers Slums* in 1893, in addition to ignorance, the other two main causes that went to produce the slums were greed and prosperity.[26] The former accounted for the overbuilding of gardens and small plots of land; the latter created the slums and shanties around coal-pits and blast-furnaces. In addition, in the more fashionable areas of cities, where housing speculation could go awry, builders over-reached themselves, the expected middle class demand did not materialise and originally prepossessing houses still had to be subdivided into tenements. Such are the well-documented slums of Victorian Kensington.[27] In a variety of forms there were custom-built slums, often erected on the land of corporate bodies, public charities, deans and chapters and public schools, but dependent on the speculator who broke the relationship between the lessor and lessee and engrossed the bulk of profit to himself. Such properties were the product of complicated patterns of letting and sub-letting, which are analysed in detail in both Birmingham and London by Green and Parton. Throughout their history, strong vested interests in any area deterred interference with the rights or interests of private property. Meanwhile, prior to any effective control of building standards and planning requirements (which only began to take hold in urban areas in the third quarter of the nineteenth century and after 1875 in rural areas), builders had the freedom to skimp on structures and erect the physically sub-standard. The nature and the quality of building construction set the prerequisites for social inferiority, as Chadwick reported in 1842:

An immense number of small houses occupied by the poorer classes in the suburbs of Manchester are of the most superficial character . . . new cottages are erected with a rapidity that astonishes persons who are unacquainted with their flimsy structure. They have certainly avoided the objectionable mode of forming underground dwellings, but have run into the opposite extreme, having neither cellar nor foundation. The walls were only half-brick thick of what the bricklayers call 'brick-noggin', and the whole of the materials are slight and unfit for the purpose . . . they are built back-to-back; without ventilation or drainage: and, like a honeycomb, every particle of space is occupied.'[28]

Such shoddiness of construction was exacerbated by the nature of the localities in which the housing of the poor was set. Inevitably, these gravitated towards the worst parts of towns and cities, which were either low-lying and ill-drained swamps close to rivers or the neighbourhoods of noxious trades and industries. The poor were assigned to the most notorious plague spots of cities—the Bank District of Leeds, Little Ireland in Manchester, the Central Wynds of Glasgow and Exchange Ward in Liverpool. In these areas water supplies were deficient, drainage was rudimentary and the air was stale and stagnant.

These were the physical foundations of the slums; their development and decline were frequently hastened by subsequent urban development which served to isolate and to fossilize the slum as a district.[29] In particular, the driving through of the railways in Victorian cities was perhaps the most important single agency in that transformation. Districts divided and confined by the railway tended to develop similar patterns of shabby mixed zoning and gross residential overcrowding. The barrier effects of both railway lines and areas of sidings and goods yards created what were referred to at the time as 'walled cities', while competing lines often squeezed areas of inner cities and cut off streets and houses into separate islands.

At the same time the coming of the railways and the construction of great termini and stations by the different railway companies often entailed destruction of the houses of the poor without any alternative accommodation being provided. This was followed by the wide-scale demolition of houses for street improvements and commercial expansion. Prior to 1885, there was no legislative requirements to re-house people so displaced and as a result Dyos has established that between 1850 and 1900 railway building in London alone displaced about 80,000 people and that its effect was first to increase overcrowding in central areas and later, when saturation density was reached, to extend it to adjacent 'overspill' districts. The consequence in terms of overcrowding and the herding of people together in the oldest and poorest districts was replicated in most provincial cities. But even more disastrous to the short-term interests of the slums was the intervention of local authorities in the housing field. Such intervention only slowly intensified after 1850 and was intermittent in terms of application, nevertheless whenever it happened it tended to be accompanied by a lack of foresight which meant that driving the poor from their existing slums only forced them into other inferior and ill-conditioned dwellings. As slum clearance progressed and became more extensive in scope after 1870, the scale of destruction of existing houses was greater and forced even more overcrowding in equally objectionable locations. As a result, overcrowding was increasing in the later-nineteenth century city, especially in London and other large cities which were affected by slum clearance.

'Filtering up' did not, in fact, affect the housing standards of the poorer working class in any significant way, since such people were not mobile either physically or economically. Those on the margins of the economy could not move out of the slums, where at least they had some modicum of shelter, because they could devote no more money to rent. It was the realisation of the ineffectiveness of such policies hitherto that resulted by 1930, with the Greenwood Act, in a slum clearance policy that related to the numbers displaced and the numbers rehoused.[30] The loopholes in that legislation were considerable and the inadequacies of its application were persistent; it did, however, signal the beginning of the end, and in recognising the interdependence of slums and slum clearance highlighted the slum as both a symptom and symbol of poverty.

That fundamental connection encouraged those in authority, who had failed to remove the slums, to block them out of consciousness as a justification for lack of action. This was particularly the case as both the expectations of civic pride and the standards of urban expansion were raised in the later nineteenth century and consistently throughout the twentieth century. As a result, instead of exposing and dealing with that fundamental equation at the heart of the slum problem, authority continually fell back on explanations which reverted to the character of slum-dwellers or the lack of building regulations. Acceptance of low standards and bad conditions was, however, a consequence of the apathy bred by the slums rather than a cause. As Howard Marshall found when he journeyed through the slums of London and Tyneside in 1933:

... I wondered why the people in their wretched insanitary hovels were so apathetic, so resigned, so lacking in bitterness. I must admit that I had expected anger and violent feelings; instead, the women shrug their shoulders, and the men stare into the fire, and slowly I realise that they were too hungry and wretched to care. It was far worse, this dull resignation, than any resentment or abuse, and the exceptions to it were rare and startling.[31]

Furthermore, low-amenity, high-density housing influenced the physical deficiencies of slum dwellers, which could not be ignored by the beginning of the twentieth century. The relationship between health and housing pointed to high land values in city-centre districts and the pressure on the working classes as the fundamental causes of poor health. Thus in Liverpool by the turn of the century, it was concluded that it could not be an accident that boys from two-roomed houses should be 11.7 lbs lighter than boys from four-roomed houses and 4.7 inches smaller. Neither was it considered an accident that girls from one-roomed houses were on average 14 lbs lighter and 5.3 inches shorter than girls from four-roomed houses.[32] As Charles Booth had concluded, overcrowding remained the great cause of degeneracy.[33] Though, overall, there was less overcrowding than earlier in the century, owing to higher standards of requirement, the evil now seemed greater in some places, usually due to clearance making things worse in surrounding streets. This difficulty thus remained inherent in the whole question of the slums.

Surveying then the period from the end of the eighteenth century to the outbreak of the Second World War, one is struck by the way in which observers of the slums repeatedly came away from their surveys of such areas depressed, not only by the monotony of what they saw, but also by the hopelessness of doing much to change what they kept seeing. The problem remains, however, that given such evidence one must handle it cautiously. It is always mediated through middle-class eyes and sensibilities. Yet if we examine recollections of life in the slums, they do not recall a world of unrelieved grimness. Life went on despite the appalling conditions and within their homes the inhabitants of the slums sought to beautify them with prints and ornaments:

Let us in a parenthesis, by way of relief from the unpleasantness of the details we are forced to go into, here refer to the love of 'art' which is often exhibited in the most miserable quarters, in the shape of plaster casts and little prints,—not of very refined character, it is true, but still agreeable and cheering as evidence of a striving upwards. The painted parrots and spotted cats, and red-and-blue varnished prints, which not many years ago *decorated* homes of great pretence, have found a resting-place lower down in the social scale.[34]

The accommodation of the slums in which it was impossible for a family to maintain health and decency was nevertheless often kept clean, and with major efforts children were well brought up. There was more to the slums than merely a struggle which was brutalising. There was an unselfishness in the standards of home life and in the way the poorest people helped one another through difficulties. In the end, there was a recognition of the courage which enabled men and women to endure the slums and preserve their self respect.

This then, in conclusion, is the problem of generalisation. For over a century social observers and reformers visited the slums, they even went to live in them as urban anthropologists. From one specific area conclusions were derived and dubiously applied across a city and indeed a country. Yet what is apparent is the uniqueness of each individual slum within certain common characteristics. The slums of both industrial and rural Britain range from apartments formed within superior houses built originally for single-family occupancy to purpose built hovels, to municipally-owned or employer-owned tenements. Some owe their characters to lengthy periods of decline and were long established, others were recent accretions. Similarly, the characteristics of the inhabitants varied equally widely—recent immigrants, second or third generation, skilled, semi-skilled, 'respectable', 'deserving', 'undeserving', criminal, degenerate.

For some the slum was a place from which to rise to better surroundings and higher social aspirations; for many more the slums were the resort of despair. Given such disparity, conclusions deriving from a few small areas seem dubiously valid. Yet the establishment and expansion of slum districts as part of the urban revolution of industrial Britain was generated by factors which were common and not restricted to particular cities. The character of the slums and the slum-dwellers, as these studies identify, have many features in common. It is tempting in summary, therefore, to present a picture of a 'typical' or 'model' slum as a generalisation against which the deviations of others may be measured. This, however, is not the intention of this book; the purpose of these studies is to present a variable, out of which it is possible, as this introduction has sought to suggest, to distil a number of factors which are of continuing significance in terms of presenting the slum-dwellers' view of their world. That world is complex and any single dimensional explanation is inadequate. The slums do not lend themselves to a comprehensive and balanced view; their half-hidden world requires both the pursuit of the experience of slum life and of attitudes towards slums, as well as the examination of the reasons for the existence and survival of those slums. This volume concentrates historically on the phenomenon for the first time, and continues the process of social exploration of a world that is distant yet on the doorstep: '. . . a world where you've never set foot before, even though it's always existed underneath your nose'.[35]

Notes

1. E.R. Dewsnup, *The Housing Problem in England: Its Statistics, Legislation and Policy*, Manchester, 1907, p.227.
2. Gustave Doré and Blanchard Jerrold, *London*, London, 1872, pp.124-5.
3. H. Barnes, *The Slum. Its Story and Solution*, London, 1932, p.xiv.
4. P. Lloyd, *Slums of Hope? Shanty Towns of the Third World*, Manchester, 1979, p.31.
5. H.J. Dyos, 'The Slums of Victorian London', *Victorian Studies*, xi (1967-68), pp.7-10.
6. H. Marshall (in collaboration with Miss Alice Trevelyan), *Slum*, London, 1933, p.32.
7. J. Grant, *Lights and Shadows of London Life*, 2 vols., London, 1842, I, pp.163-5.
8. A. Morrison, *A Child of the Jago*, London, 1896, p.273.
9. P.P. 1842, Lords, xxvi, p.24.
10. G. Godwin, *Town Swamps and Social Bridges*, London, 1859, p.12.
11. Ibid., p.7.
12. W. Booth, *In Darkest England and the Way Out*, London, 1890, p.16.
13. *Hansard*, third series, cxv (1851), pp.1259, 1260.
14. E.D. Simon, *How to Abolish the Slums*, London, 1929, p.2.
15. P. Keating (ed.), *Into Unknown England 1866-1913*, Glasgow, 1976, p.13.
16. Ibid., p.20.
17. P.P. 1867-68, xvii, *Commission on the Employment of Children, Young Persons, and Women in Agriculture (1867)*, Appendix Part I, p.35, para.116.
18. G.S. Jones, *Outcast London*, Oxford, 1971, pp.127-51.
19. H.J. Dyos, op. cit., pp.29-34.
20. R. Tressall, *The Ragged Trousered Philanthropist*, London, 1955, p.79.
21. C. Booth, *Life and Labour in London*, 17 vols., London, 1889, I, pp.37-8.
22. M. Young and P. Wilmott, *Family and Kinship in East London*, rev. ed., Harmondsworth, 1962, pp.76-88.
23. H.J. Dyos and D.A. Reeder, 'Slums and Suburbs' in *The Victorian City: Images and Realities*, 2 vols., ed. H.J. Dyos and M. Wolff, London, 1973, II, p.369.
24. J. Greenwood, *Low Life Deeps*, London, 1876, p.137.
25. M.S. Pember Reeves, *Round About a Pound a Week*, London, 1913, pp.49-56.
26. R. Williams, *London Rookeries and Colliers Slums*, London, 1893, pp.13, 14.

27. P.E. Malcolmson, 'Getting a Living in the Slums of Victorian Kensington', *The London Journal*, i, 1975, pp.28–55.
28. Lords Sessional Papers (1842), xxvii, p.240.
29. H.J. Dyos, 'Railways and Housing in Victorian London', *Journal of Transport History*, ii, 1955–56, pp.14–18. H.J. Dyos and D.A. Reeder, 'Slums and Suburbs', in *The Victorian City: Images and Realities*, 2 vols., ed. H.J. Dyos and M. Wolff, London, 1973, ii, pp.365–7.
30. The Housing Act, 1930, 20 & 21 Geo. V, c.39.
31. H. Marshall, op. cit., pp.8–9.
32. Lord Leverhulme, *The Six-Hour Day and other Industrial Questions*, London, 1918, p.171–5.
33. C. Booth, *Life and Labour in London*, 3rd ed., London, 1902, Series 3, Vol III, pp.170–8.
34. G. Godwin, op. cit., p.18.
35. C. MacInnes, *City of Spades*, Harmondsworth, 1964, p.75.

1 Slums and slum life in Victorian England: London and Birmingham at mid-century

David R. Green and Alan G. Parton

The great mass of the metropolitan community are as ignorant of the destitution and distress which prevails in large districts of London . . . as if the wretched creatures were living in the very centre of Africa.

(Grant, 1842, p.164–5)

There are some things about urban life that the historians can never tell . . . sometimes the images speak and we hear what they have to say. They tell us how the various urban containers were made and a little of what went into them, and we get in consequence a more solid sense of form, if not of substance.

(Dyos, 1969, p.33)

Introduction

There is on the surface no apparent shortage of information on the lives of the poor in mid-nineteenth century British cities. From the 1830s statistical societies, parliamentary investigations, the sanitary movement, the Poor Law Commission and the Office of the General Registrar began to shower the public with facts relating to life from the lower depths. Newspaper reports and social novels focusing on the 'condition of England question' added sensationalism and a fictional gloss to this emerging factual basis. But in each case the lives of the poor were remarked upon from the outside: the internal structure and social organisation of slum life in major cities remained largely obscured to all but those who resided in such areas. Indeed, the filth and stench of the slums were so thoroughly offensive to the senses that only the most dedicated and determined middle-class visitor remained for long in the courts and homes of the poor. Consequently, the inner life of the urban underclass, that substratum described variously at the time as perishing, decaying or just dangerous, was known to contemporaries only in fragments and from the outside: as an object for debate and reform but rarely as a subject worthy of investigation and understanding in its own right.

The growth of urban history in more recent years has helped to focus attention on the slum as a physical rather than as a social entity. Since the topic was first examined by Dyos, much effort has been directed towards investigating the material conditions of slum life, particularly relating to housing conditions and slum clearance. (Chapman, 1971; Dyos, 1967; Dyos and Reeder, 1973; Taylor, 1974; Wohl, 1977; Yelling, 1986.) Though most research has concentrated on London, other cities have also received a share of the attention. (Chapman, 1971; Forster, 1972; Robb, 1983.) But whilst the slum as a physical entity has received much attention, the same is not true of its social aspects. Those works which have discussed the social organisation of slum life have tended either to concentrate on specific ethnic groups, notably the Irish, or to have been narrowly focused on local studies based on oral evidence drawn from the late nineteenth and early twentieth century. (Finnegan, 1982; L. Lees, 1969; L. Lees, 1979; Richardson, 1968; Roberts, 1971; Ross, 1983; Sponza, 1988; White, 1980; White, 1986).

An understanding of the social order of the mid-nineteenth century slum, however, must set out from a different point of departure, both in terms of the issues posed and the data sources used. First, the internal complexity of slum life, of which ethnicity was but one dimension, needs to be treated as a whole. The slum was far more than just an ethnic enclave and as such needs to be seen primarily in its wider role as a concentration of the urban poor. Its inhabitants reflected other social distinctions relating to poverty, such as age, occupation and gender, which deserve greater attention than they have hitherto received. Nor should such distinctions be conceived as separate, for it is clear that each was related to the other. Secondly, without oral evidence any attempt to probe into the subtle complexities of slum life is beset with severe problems relating to data sources. Conventional sources of evidence, such as the census and reports from local government and medical officers of health, are blunt tools with which to gauge the fluidity of life in the lower depths and it is imperative, therefore, to consult wherever possible data arising from direct contact with the poor. In this respect, poor law records, notably those devoted to investigating the condition of applicants for relief and those which recorded the decisions, are of immense value. Though not without their problems, such data sources have the advantage of being derived primarily in the context of slum life. If the challenge of laying bare the social order of the slum, and of replacing form with substance, is to be met, what is needed above all then is an approach that unravels the internal complexity of slum life as a whole based primarily on data relating directly to the poor. The aim here is to cast light on what has hitherto remained in shade, namely life in the lower depths of mid-nineteenth century urban society. The life of the residuum or lumpenproletariat—that section of the working class which remained on the fringes of wage labour, such as street sellers, prostitutes, beggars and thieves—is our primary concern. The intention is not to replicate descriptions of slum conditions at the time but to illuminate the lived world of the poor by examining the resources available to slum communities, the rhythms of poverty they faced and the relationships of reciprocity that emerged to cope with the problems of daily life. Though every city of the period contained to a greater or lesser extent concentrations of the poor, detailed attention here is confined to Birmingham and London, the first as a city without a reputation for squalor and slums and the second as a city whose reputation for both was second to none. The main period covered is defined by the great surge of urbanisation that occurred in the middle part of the century and during which concern over the social condition of cities reached its height. Indeed, a significant element in developing an understanding of slum life at this time is an awareness of contemporary concern about the slum as a social problem. The starting point for analysis, therefore, is contemporary consciousness of the slum and the urban underclass.

Poverty and the urban underclass: discovery and reaction

Few periods of English history excited as much social concern as did the 1830s and 1840s. Set against a background of sharp economic fluctuations, worsening conditions in cities and working-class political radicalism, the period brought to the fore an intense disquiet over the nature of urban industrial society (A. Lees, 1985). As the rapid growth of London and other cities testified, the crucible in which new forms and relations of society were being shaped was above all the large city. But it was becoming equally clear that the forces which threatened progress gathered strength in precisely the same places (Vaughan, 1843). The biological threat to life arising from worsening urban conditions fuelled bourgeois fear of the city whilst the breakdown of identifiable communities under the impact of rapid urban growth, coupled with growing levels of class separation as a result of increasing residential segregation, made the maintenance of social order more difficult. Slums or 'rookeries', in particular, never defined in detail but described in general terms as 'beds of pestilence', 'rendezvous of vice', 'nurseries of felons' and 'haunts of pauperism', came to embody many of the anxieties of mid-nineteenth-century bourgeois society (Beames, 1850, p.119). Living like animals, it was argued, how could the poor be anything but animals, subject to the unrestrained passions and savage appetites pertaining to their conditions of life. Fears regarding the threats of contagion and social disorder focused increasingly on the slums and their inhabitants. Such fears lent urgency to middle-class flight to the suburbs and, in turn, growing spatial separation of the classes encouraged the development of imagery and terminology which viewed the poor as a race apart, distinguished both by physiognomy and culture from the civilised portion of society. In such a way the underclass came to be portrayed as a race apart; devoid of culture, society and even humanity. The commercial crisis of 1825 heralded the onset of a prolonged period of relative economic stagnation which lasted with minor interruptions until mid-century (Kondratieff, 1935, p.111; Mandel, 1980, p.7). Although cyclical fluctuations interrupted the pattern, and real wages rose, nevertheless at certain times and amongst specific groups of workers distress was severe (Flinn, 1974; Gayer, Rostow and Schwarz, 1953; O'Brien and Engerman, 1981, pp.169–70; Tucker, 1936). In London construction stagnated and by 1831 it was estimated that at least 12,000 carpenters were unemployed (Cairncross and Weber, 1956–57, pp.291–2; *Poor Man's Guardian*, 13 August 1831; Shannon, 1934, pp.305–9; Sheppard, Belcher and Cottrell, 1979, pp.194–6). Silk weaving in the capital also received its final dénouement whilst clothing manufacture and shoemaking survived by absorbing downward pressure on costs through increases in outdoor work and 'sweating' (Green, 1984, pp.152–3, 226–9). The story was the same elsewhere. Reports from Manchester and the surrounding towns spoke of poor trade and short-time working in cotton manufacturing whilst in Birmingham it was claimed that in some districts workers had no more than three days' employment per week (BPP, 1833 VI, q.4585–8, 9107, 10975, 11474–8).

Prosperity returned briefly in the early 1830s but another downturn later in the decade which lasted until 1842 brought renewed reports of distress. In Nottingham, William Felkin remarked that destitution had risen as a result of falling wages in stocking- and lace-making (Felkin, 1837, pp.3–8). Similar stories were repeated elsewhere. In the textile districts cyclical downturn exacerbated the structural decline of handloom weaving and many weavers, a large number of whom were Irish, were said to be destitute and near starvation (Adshead, 1842; Poor Law Commission, 1842, p.4). Indeed, although few in number, deaths from starvation in London and elsewhere were reported in the newspapers at the time (Lhotky, 1844; *The Times*, 10 February 1840). Distress also occurred in the capital where the number of destitute persons rose alarmingly. During the winter of 1841 the number of applications to the Mendicity Society rose from 12,000 to 27,000 whilst similar pressure was felt by the metropolitan poor law unions (Society for the Suppression of Mendicity, 1841, p.22; *The Times*, 25, 28 November 1843; Poor Law Commission, 1843, pp.9–10). Some respite was afforded by a brief recovery during the middle of the decade but the commercial crisis of 1847 accompanied by the mass influx to major cities of poverty-stricken Irish fleeing the famine only helped to worsen conditions amongst the urban poor. In 1842 and again in 1848 over one in ten of the population of England and Wales was in receipt of poor relief, and although between those dates matters improved considerably, nevertheless the experience of urban poverty was widespread (Poor Law Commission, 1843; Poor Law Board, 1848).

Economic downturn was matched by deteriorating public health conditions in large towns, brought to light in the 1830s and 1840s as a result of the numerous investigations undertaken by Parliament, the Poor Law Commission and the Health of Towns Association. Edwin Chadwick's

Table 1.1: Housing and Urban Growth 1801–51

	Number of houses built in England and Wales (excluding Middle-sex) (000)	Percent-age Change	Number of houses built in Middlesex (000)	Percent-age Change	Urban Population in England and Wales (000,000)	Percent-age Change
1811	199	–	16.9	–	3.7	–
1821	284	42.7	25.4	50.3	4.8	29.1
1831	408	43.7	34.6	36.2	6.2	28.1
1841	493	20.8	22.6	– 34.7	7.7	25.0
1851	282	– 42.8	33.7	49.1	9.7	25.9

Sources: Caincross, A.K. and B. Weber, 1956–57; Lawton, R., 1978

Report on the Sanitary Condition of the Labouring Population of Great Britain made clear the extent to which working-class districts in all major cities were characterised by high rates of overcrowding, insanitary conditions and outbreaks of disease (BPP 1842, XXVI). In Liverpool, one fifth of the population lived in cellars and in Manchester the figure was one in ten (BPP 1840, XI, q.2377-9; BPP 1842, XXVI, pp.284-5; BPP 1845, XVIII, pp.323-4; Engels, 1973, pp.85-90). Streets covered with filth, cesspools that remained unemptied and houses which rotted before they were repaired were commonplace throughout working-class local-ities. Outbreaks of epidemic disease erupted with monotonous regularity in these uncleansed and unsewered districts with typhus and cholera hugging the same courts and houses from one generation to the next. 'In the sewer district there is a most remarkable absence of fever', remarked Dr Southwood Smith, 'and in the fever district a most remarkable absence of sewerage' (BPP 1840, XI, q.9). That the problem of public health in cities had worsened was due in large part to the differential rates of housing construction and population growth. Following the crisis of 1825 the rate of house-building slowed throughout the country, and particularly in London, only recovering in the late 1840s (Cairncross and Weber, 1956-57, p.292). At the same time, however, as Table 1.1 illustrates, the rate of urban growth continued to rise, thereby placing severe pressure on housing in major cities throughout the country. Chad-wick had remarked on the housing shortage in 1842 when he stated that 'The evidence received from every part of the country . . . attest[s] that the dwellings of large numbers of the labouring population are over-crowded, and from many districts that the overcrowding has increased' (BPP 1842, XXVI, p.121). In Birmingham and Leeds the rate of increase in the number of families was above that of new houses and in Liverpool the rate of increase was nearly two-fold (BPP 1842, XXVI, p.324). In Glasgow the failure of house-building in the 1830s to keep pace with the rapid increase of population was blamed for a rise in the level of mortality (Cowan, 1840, pp.268–9). During the 1840s surveys carried out by the Statistical Society of London showed that one-room living was the norm for working-class families, particularly in wealthier districts in which rents were high (Rawson, 1843, p.44; Statistical Society of London, 1848b, p.211; Weld, 1843, p.20). Everywhere, then, in each of the major cities, pressures on housing mounted during the 1830s and 1840s resulting in severe overcrowding and the rapid formation and expansion of slums.

Realisation of the extent of urban poverty and the existence of a large substratum of urban poor, however, did not come solely as a result of economic downturn or overcrowding. What was perhaps of equal significance was the fact that the period witnessed an upsurge in popular radicalism associated mainly but not exclusively with Chartism. Middle-class fear of radicalism in the 1830s was made all the more real by virtue of the fact that examples of urban insurrection were close to hand. Had not the Parisian crowd rebelled in 1830 and were not the reform bill riots in England in 1831 a portent of things to come? Radical meetings, such as that in Copenhagen Fields in 1834 in support of the Dorchester labourers, attracted many thousands of supporters.

But it was Chartism, described by Carlyle as 'bitter discontent grown fierce and mad', that crystallised middle-class fears of a conjuncture of political radicals and the urban underclass (Carlyle, 1840, p.2). Whilst respectable artisans were prominent in the movement, the mass rallies and forceful speeches attracted a more disparate following. As Henry Mayhew discovered in his investigations for the *Morning Chronicle*, London costermongers and rubbish carters also claimed to be Chartists, though at times their sights were set on more mundane matters than political reform (Mayhew, 1861, I, p.20; II, p.225). Nevertheless, their support for the Chartist cause was sufficient confirmation for the bourgeoisie of the existence in London and other major cities of a reckless and impoverished population easily led astray by political demagogues.

Fear of class conflict and social disorder arising in the slums and from there spreading outwards to engulf the city was real. With morality debased, religion neglected and the bonds of domestic life destroyed, middle-class observers were convinced that conditions in the slums were conducive to the spread of insurrection. In Manchester in 1832 James Kay warned of:

. . . a turbulent population, which, rendered reckless by dissipation and want,— misled by the secret intrigues and excited by the inflammatory harangues of demagogues, has frequently committed daring assaults on the liberty of more peaceful portions of the working classes, and the most frightful devastations on the property of their masters.

(Kay, 1832, p.26.)

It was in London, however, that fears were expressed with greatest conviction. In 1831 Edward Wakefield struck a note of common concern when he warned against the possibility of an alliance between Huntite and Owenite 'political desperadoes' and the London poor (Wakefield, 1831). Thomas Beames echoed this concern in 1850 when he claimed that indifference to religion and a sullen discontent born of squalor provided fertile ground for the spread of disaffection. Pointing ominously to the spectre of revolution in France and conjuring up an image in which the supporters of Chartism and the most riotous elements of the masses were recruited from the slums, Beames focused attention on the creation of rookeries and the dangers they represented for the social order: 'Our argument is that Rookeries are among the seeds of revolution; that taken in connection with other evils, they poison the minds of the working classes against the powers that be, and thus lead to convulsions' (Beames, 1850, p.198).

Anxiety over the political volatility of slum-dwellers and the conditions of the slums themselves prompted the start of detailed investigation into the social condition of the urban working class. The factual basis that emerged was remarkable for its breadth and scope. In most large cities, statistical societies were formed in the 1830s and 1840s to inquire into the social conditions of the labouring classes: the Manchester society was founded in 1833 and its counterpart in London was formally established in the following year (see Cullen, 1975). The scope of their investigations was impressive. In Manchester a house-to-house survey of the poor in 1835 and 1836 covered over 4,000 families (Statistical Society of London, 1837–38, p.2). Extensive surveys were also carried out in London: an investigation of conditions amongst the working class in St John and St Margaret, Westminster, in 1840 covered over 5,000 families and that was followed in 1845 by a detailed household survey of nearly 2,000 working-class families in St George-in-the-East (Statistical Society of London, 1840, pp.14–24; 1848b, pp.193–249). Other surveys covered the poor in St George, Hanover Square, St Giles, Grays Inn, Soho, St Marylebone and Southwark (Edgell, 1838; Statistical Society of London, 1840, 1848a; Weld, 1843).

Similarly impressive was parliamentary concern with the collection of statistical material relating to the condition of the people. The establishment in 1834 of the Poor Law Commission and in 1837 of the General Register Office, together provided an annual record of vital statistics relating to the health and prosperity of the nation. The volume of social inquiry undertaken by Parliament itself was equally impressive: pauperism, factory reform, children's employment, health and housing were major concerns of the period. During the 1840s no less than four investigations into sanitary conditions were initiated, including two Royal Commissions and Edwin Chadwick's far-reaching report on the *Sanitary Condition of the Labouring Population of Great Britain*. The Health of Towns Association, founded in 1843, also did much to publicise facts about conditions in the major cities. If the mass of facts proved indigestible there were still the opinions of social investigators such as James Kay or Peter Gaskell, or the social novels of Dickens, Disraeli or Mrs Gaskell. If even these failed to attract notice then social reportage, such as that undertaken at mid-century by Henry Mayhew and others for the *Morning Chronicle*, remained available. In one form or another, then, the social conditions of the urban working class were brought into full view to an extent hitherto unknown to contemporaries (Gauldie, 1974, pp.101-12; Himmelfarb, 1984).

The discovery that a vast underclass of slum-dwellers—a chaotic and volatile substratum cut adrift from the cultural norms of bourgeois society and marginal to its economic functioning—existed in London and other major cities came as a profound shock to the urban middle class. Prior to the 1830s the urban poor were not seen as a threat to the stability of society. Images of the poor portrayed them more as individual subjects for caricature, as in the sketches and drawings by Thomas Rowlandson, John Smith or George Scharf, than as a threatening rabble bent on the destruction of civilised society. Mendicancy and street-begging rather than poverty and the slums were seen as the most pressing problems. From the 1830s and 1840s, however, a more alarmist vision of the poor began to circulate, alongside which developed a new terminology with which to describe this urban underclass.

The twin themes of political volatility and moral contagion were reflected in the frequent use of the term 'dangerous classes' to describe the poor (Himmelfarb, 1984, pp.371-99). The term itself referred, according to one author, 'not only [to] criminals, paupers and persons whose conduct is obnoxious to the interests of society, but [to] that proximate body of people who are within reach of its contagion and continually swell its number' (Symmons, 1849, p.1.) The theme of moral contagion and decay was well illustrated at the time; Marx described the urban poor as 'The "dangerous class", the social scum, that passively rotting mass thrown off by the lowest layers of old society' (Marx and Engels, 1968, p.44). In making a distinction between the 'dangerous class' and the 'perishing class', Mary Carpenter also drew on the theme of moral contagion, emphasising how the honest poor, forced to live cheek by jowl in squalor with criminals, paupers and beggars, could not but help suffer demoralisation and thus sink into crime and depravity (Carpenter, 1851, p.2). Moral contagion was also uppermost in Alexander Thompson's view of the base layers of society which he described as consisting of: '. . . an unstable agglomeration of mixed materials, often decaying and rotting away, whose corrupting influences are perpetually spreading upwards and whose material is perpetually receiving increase from the masses next above being crushed down into its bosom' (Thompson, 1853, p.18). If the political and moral imagery of the urban poor as the 'dangerous classes' emerged at this time, so too did a new racial terminology to describe slum-dwellers. The Irish in particular were stigmatised as wild and uncivilised, little different in habits and appetites, according to the more xenophobic observers, from the pigs with which they sometimes shared a residence (Carlyle, 1840, pp.28-32; Garwood, 1853, pp.245-62; Kay, 1832, p.7). Attitudes towards the Irish, however, touched on deeper concerns than just those associated specifically with one ethnic group. In a more general sense, the urban poor became viewed almost as a separate race, with a particular moral culture and physiognomy that distinguished them from bourgeois society. For Henry Mayhew the floating mass of London poor was indeed distinct:

. . . there is a greater development of the animal than of the intellectual or moral nature of man . . . they are all more or less distinguished for their high cheekbones and protruding jaws—for their use of slang language—for their lax ideas of property—for their general improvidence—their repugnance to continuous labour—their love of cruelty—their pugnacity—and their utter want of religion.

(Mayhew, 1861, I, p.3.)

For John Hollingshed, the poor were steeped in 'barbarous ignorance', 'herded together' in 'lurking nests of dwellings' and crammed into 'rookeries'. Little wonder that in the eyes of such observers the poor were metamorphosed into something subhuman; 'half human rats' with 'weasel-like offspring' (Hollingshed, 1986).

The social order of the slum

To most bourgeois commentators of the period slum-dwellers represented an undifferentiated mass of humanity; a 'lumpenproletariat' in Marx's view or just a chaotic mix of brutality, ignorance and filth in the opinions of others (Marx and Engels, 1968, p.136; Parker, 1853, p.193). The social ordering and culture of the slums were understood primarily as a negative and disordered reaction to a marginal position in urban society rather than as a creative attempt to cope with and understand the context of slum life by those forced to endure the conditions. More recently, however, urban anthropologists and sociologists have challenged this perspective, choosing instead to view slum life in a more positive vein as an ordered and creative response to a marginal position in urban society.

Based largely on participant observation, this reappraisal has followed two interrelated themes. First, the social structure of slum communities is interpreted as being both complex and internally differentiated or stratified, based largely around the dimensions of age, sex, race and ethnicity (Liebow, 1967; Suttles, 1968). Amongst such groupings differentiation is expressed not only in the symbolism of appearance and language but also in terms of territoriality and the control of space, making slum neighbourhoods the stage on which such distinctions are paraded (Ley, 1974). These 'inside' observations of slum life, therefore, emphasise the symbolism and territoriality that reflects sharp internal stratification within poor urban neighbourhoods.

The second aspect of this reappraisal is the suggestion by Oscar Lewis that slum-dwellers possess a distinctive 'culture of poverty' (Lewis, 1965, 1970). As initially defined by Lewis, the concept attempts to understand the adaptation and reactions of the poor to their marginal position in a class-stratified and individualistic society. The basic features include a lack of effective participation and integration of the poor into the major institutions of society at large, stemming from poverty, lack of education and a distrust of authority; a minimum of formal organisation beyond the level of the family and occasional informal groups; the existence of a sense of community, based frequently on ethnic, kinship or territorial links; loose ties of marriage and an absence of childhood as a prolonged stage of growth, and finally a sense of fatalism arising from individual feelings of marginality and helplessness. Criticisms of the concept have questioned its generality, claiming that the dominant ethic of slum-dwellers is not one of fatalism but of individual hard work and initiative, coupled with a degree of political consciousness. Doubts have also been expressed over Lewis's narrow emphasis on the household as the basic unit of study and the overall use of the concept to explain the perpetuation of poverty (Valentine, 1968, pp.63–5). Though few historians have adopted the concept of a culture of poverty in any consistent manner, nevertheless, together with the ideas described above concerning the social order of the slum, it provides a set of useful guidelines with which to unravel some of the complexities of slum life in the mid-nineteenth century (Himmelfarb, 1973).

Occupational stratification: ethnicity, gender and age

'The working classes are composed of strata', argued John Parker, 'differing in appearance and density, yet imperceptibly gliding into and blending with each other'. He continued, 'At the bottom we have the less, at the top the more highly educated and intellectual; but there is a great substratum, a chaotic mass, in which brutality, sensuality, filthiness, and ignorance are conspicuously present' (Parker, 1853, p.193). Charting this substratum revealed a certain uniformity of occupations and conditions: costermongers, hawkers, charwomen, sweeps and casual labourers were ever present together with those of more dubious callings, such as prostitutes, beggars and thieves, and those artisans and their families employed in declining or 'dishonourable' branches of trade. These were not the regularly employed skilled artisans but rather the residuum of casual workers forced to scrape a living as best they could and often not even achieving that. The common experiences of crushing poverty and continual uncertainty imposed a uniformity of conditions on the lives of those forced to inhabit the slums. But despite these similarities in occupations and circumstances, the poor were far from being an undifferentiated mass. As Henry Mayhew perceptively remarked in relation to the street trades, 'Among street folk there are as many distinct characters of people—people differing as widely from each other in tasks, habits, thoughts and creeds, as one nation from another' (Mayhew, 1861, I, p.7). Distinctions of age, gender, ethnicity, not to mention occupation and income, singly or in combination served to divide a seemingly undifferentiated mass into specific groups and sub-groups, creating in the process a social ordering or stratification that was of the utmost importance for those who lived in the slums.

Of all contemporary observers of the poor, none got so close or achieved a depth and range of knowledge as did Henry Mayhew. His investigations in 1849 and 1850 as metropolitan correspondent for the *Morning Chronicle* brought him into close and prolonged contact with the urban working class and in particular with its poorest substratum (Himmelfarb, 1971, 1984; Humphreys, 1977; Thompson, 1967; K. Williams, 1981; Yeo, 1973). One of the underlying themes which recurs throughout his work is the complex division within the working class and nowhere is this better illustrated than with reference to the street trades. The patterers who recited and sold broadsides and cheap literature were the 'haristocracy of the street' (Mayhew, 1861, I, p.213). Next came the ubiquitous costermongers, who in turn considered themselves a cut above street entertainers and old clothes sellers. Those dealing with the detritus of society, such as chimney-sweeps, sewer-hunters and pure finders, were firmly rooted at the bottom of the hierarchy. Nor did the distinctions stop there. Each group contained its own internal stratification. Mayhew observed, for instance, that 'compared to an acute costermonger the mere apple seller is but as the labourer to the artisan' (Mayhew, 1861, I, p.105). Even Italian barrel-organ grinders and hurdy-gurdy players were distinguished according to the type of instrument they played and whether or not they could lay claim to a regular round (Mayhew, 1861, III, p.176).

Ethnicity was also vitally important as a means of stratifying the labour force, not only in terms of specialised niches carved out and defended by specific groups but also in relation to patterns of segregation. Occupational specialisation frequently followed ethnic groupings, particularly where competition for employment was fierce. English costermongers, for example, resisted the intrusion of Irish into the trade and turned public occasions, such as Guy Fawkes processions, into patriotic displays of an anti-Irish, 'No-Popery' nature (*The Times*, 6 November 1850; Mayhew, 1861, I, p.104; III, pp.65–9). In contrast, by mid-century the Irish had supplanted Jewish hawkers in the sale of cheaper food items (Mayhew, I, pp. 107, 115–18). In St Giles, the Irish living around Seven Dials monopolised the secondhand shoe trade, or 'translating' as it was known, whilst the Jews in Whitechapel had control of the old clothes trade (Mayhew, 1861, II, pp.26–35). Barrel-organ grinding was dominated by Italians who formed a close-knit community in and around Saffron Hill (Sponza, 1988).

Ethnicity itself, however, was cross-cut by other lines of stratification, notably that of gender. In the street trades the more remunerative branches, such as the sale of stationery, books, popular eatables or heavier items, were monopolised by men whilst women were confined to the sale of less profitable items, such as flowers, apples or oranges. On the other hand the most abject group of street finders, such as bone-grubbers, rag-gatherers or pure finders were comprised mostly of men

(Mayhew, 1861, II, pp.136–8). But even gender divisions were cross-cut by age and ethnicity. Irish women, for example, took the lowest and hardest of the street trades, such as the sale of apples and oranges, whilst their English counterparts sold lighter and more profitable items, such as flowers, combs or laces. Age, too, helped to stratify the workforce with the very young and old restricted to the sale of small items, such as matchboxes and boot and stay laces (Mayhew, 1861, I, p.458; II, pp.103, 111).

Gender roles and behaviour

The differentiation of gender roles within the slum, though of crucial importance, is nevertheless far more difficult to establish than the occupational stratification discussed above. Broadly speaking men and women participated in separate spheres of activity with the former associated more closely with the public sphere of the street and the beer shop, and the latter with the private sphere in and around the home (Mayhew, 1861, I, p.43; II, pp.122, 175–7; White, 1986). From an early age girls were more tightly and spatially constrained than boys (Mayhew, 1861, I, p.122). The constraints continued in later life as frequent pregnancies and domestic duties tied women closely to the home (see Black, 1915; Pember Reeves, 1912; Ross, 1982). Traditional female occupations, including needlework and washing, further reinforced the tendency for women in the slums to remain in the home (Alexander, 1983).

In contrast the male sphere of activity was relatively unconstrained, with boys given more freedom than girls, and men being able to experience a wider range of settings and patterns of behaviour outside the home (White, 1986). Within the slums gambling, drinking and fighting—all of which were performed largely in public—were typically male activities. Starting at an early age, boys were initiated into gambling as look-outs for their elders and by the time they reached adulthood they were well versed in the art of betting (Mayhew, 1861, I. p.18). Away from the moralising gaze of the 'blue devils', frequently behind taverns or in the back courts, dog fights and rat killing were common. Fighting in public amongst men was also commonplace but served several functions in addition to being merely an occasion to lay a bet. Whilst it would be tempting to view public violence in the slums as mainly gratuitous, or as the result of intoxication, this interpretation omits the functional role of fighting and physical prowess as a means of stratification within the male sphere (White, 1986, pp.95–6). As outcasts from artisan culture, adult male slum-dwellers replaced skill with physical prowess as an additional form of stratification. Amongst juvenile gangs physical daring or prowess provided a clear means of establishing an internal hierarchy (Mayhew, 1861, II, pp.498–505). Learning the art of pugilism was considered to be an essential part of every coster boy's education (Mayhew, 1861, I, p.15). Fighting for a beer or just a 'lark' was one means of amusement for men but over and above its immediate rewards a good pugilist also received status and admiration from his peers (Mayhew, 1861, I, p.15). Violence, particularly that directed at an external threat such as the police, also served the purpose of binding together those groups that had shared experiences of persecution.

Political culture

Barriers against the incorporation of slum-dwellers into the formal political institutions of the urban working class were many. Antagonism between skilled and unskilled workers hindered the latter's membership of trade unions whilst shortage of time and money further limited the opportunities for participation. The outcome, as both Marx and Mayhew realised, was a total lack of class-consciousness within the slums. For Marx, the lumpenproletariat had little concept of politics and its members were as likely to act as the bribed tool of reactionary intrigue than to take part in any revolutionary activity (Marx and Engels, 1968, pp.136-7). Mayhew's opinion that: 'The artisans are almost to a man red-hot politicians . . . The unskilled labourers are as unpolitical as footmen', appeared to confirm this state of affairs (Mayhew, 1861, II, p.150). But lack of an institutional framework with which to express a political culture did not mean that such a culture did not exist. In the case of slum-dwellers daily experience rather than any abstract analysis of class relations informed political culture and directed the pattern of activity.

The lives and homes of the poor were subject to constant surveillance and inspection and as such hostility towards the agents of the state was commonplace. Police and sanitary inspection of lodging-houses was a constant reminder of the power of local authorities to delve into the lives of the poor, and lay agents and religious tract distributors who visited lodging-houses and who were suspected of being spies received rough treatment (Mayhew, 1861, I, p.249; Joseph Oppenheimer Diary, 2 September, 29 October 1861, 5 February 1862). But the greatest hostility was reserved for the police, known variously as 'crushers' or 'blue devils', whose job it was to enforce the regulations concerning the control of the streets.

Not surprisingly, for those struggling to make a living on the streets, the immediate problem of government regulations concerning hawking and troublesome interference by police and the courts was of greater urgency than the issue of political reform. Costermongers, for example, objected bitterly to Richard Martin's Cruelty to Animals Act of 1822 which they interpreted as being directed against their use of donkeys and carts. Even more objectionable to them were the attempts by the Metropolitan Police to enforce a new and more rigid discipline of the streets. Under the 1839 Police Act obstructions or annoyance by hawkers in any public thoroughfare in the Metropolitan Police District became an offence. Police were instructed to enforce the 'move on' system, which prevented any hawker from remaining stationary on the streets, and evidence from London and elsewhere suggests that it was used with increasing frequency during the 1850s (Green, 1982, pp.138–46). As agents of what was considered to be such unjust repression, the 'blue devils' soon became the immediate objects of hostility and for coster-mongers, nearly all of whom professed to be Chartists, to 'serve out a crusher' was considered to be the height of heroism (Mayhew, 1861, I, pp.16–20; II, pp.176–7, 225, 369–70).

Sabbatarianism was also a source of irritation to the urban poor. Sunday was the main shopping day of the poor and as such sabbatarian legislation was widely resented, particularly by street traders, as an attack on their customs and livelihood. During the 1840s, evangelical zeal in reforming the habits of the poor resulted in an upsurge of interest in sabbatarianism. Three parliamentary select committees investigated the problem between 1847 and 1851, eventually leading to Lord Grosvenor's Sunday Trading Bill of 1855 which sought to prohibit marketing on a Sunday and which occasioned instead serious rioting in Hyde Park (Harrison, 1965). Popular street ballads reflected the mood of the time and took up the theme of Sunday trading, using it as an illustration of the way in which those in power oppressed the poor. One such ballad, entitled 'The Joys of an Englishman's Life', commented:

> Closed all day the butchers and bakers,
> To put a stop to the Sabbath breakers
> So the poor who got paid too late for Sunday,
> Must have gone with empty bellies to Monday.

Another, called 'The Moralising Chummies' ridiculed the attempt to stop chimney-sweeps from ringing bells on Sunday for fear of disturbing divine service (Chilton, 1965, pp.44, 48). Beneath both ballads, however, lay a common resentment of intrusive authority and it was that issue which was central to the political culture of the slums.

Beyond a general dislike of authority wider political reform was only remotely grasped. Chartism was but a dimly understood concept and merely provided a label upon which to hang a dislike of authority in general and a hatred of the police in particular. One dustman interviewed by Henry Mayhew stated, 'I cares nothing about politics neither; but I'm a Chartist' (Mayhew, 1861, II, p.225). Though at times a vaguely defined class antipathy towards the aristocracy was expressed, more immediate concerns regarding policing of the streets, harassment and removal of street traders, and regulation of lodging-houses, formed the political context of slum life. Consequently, where political views were expressed they were usually couched in strongly anti-authoritarian tones, directed for the most part against specific pieces of legislation or the immediate oppression of the police and the courts, rather than as a more abstract notion of class-based politics.

Community

Poverty acted both as a bond and a solvent on the stability of slum communities. As a solvent, its effects were twofold: first, by forcing frequent changes of residence to accommodate fluctuations in daily and weekly income, and, secondly, by exacerbating tensions within both the home and the wider community. The existence of extremely high rates of residential mobility amongst the poor at first sight appear to belie the possibility of a permanent community within slum districts (Dennis, 1977, 1984, pp.255–69; Dennis and Daniels, 1981; Pooley, 1979). In the 1840s the Statistical Society of London found that 62 per cent of working-class families in Westminster and 50 per cent of families in St-George-in-the-East had been in their residence for less than one year (Statistical Society of London, 1840, 1848b). In all slum areas there existed a shiftless substrata of tramps and vagrants who moved from place to place and lodging-house to lodging-house (Samuel, 1973). These people, however, moved through the community but remained outside it. For the rest, residential mobility took place often within tightly circumscribed spatial limits (Lawton and Pooley, 1975; Pooley, 1979). Commenting on this pattern in the 1880s, Charles Booth remarked in relation to the population of East London that migration 'rarely proceeds outside the little charmed circle of alleys where "old pals" reside' and how at the end of a series of moves a family may have ended in an adjacent home to the one it first left (Booth, 1902, first series, Poverty, I, p.31).

In a second way poverty also acted to disrupt social relations by exacerbating the tensions inherent in any social grouping both within and beyond the home. Communal violence between rival ethnic groups, notably but not exclusively between English and Irish, was common enough but probably of greater frequency were outbreaks of domestic violence, the catalyst for which was often shortages in the household budget (Gilley, 1973; Ross, 1982; White, 1986). In a contemporary street ballad entitled 'The Fuddling Day, or Saint Monday', for example, a wife bemoans the fact that:

> Saint Monday brings more ills about
> For when the money's spent
> The children's clothes gone up the spout
> Which causes discontent

(Holloway and Black, 1979, p.110)

Nor were such fears without foundation, as Ellen Ross has recently pointed out in relation to late nineteenth-century working-class households (Ross, 1982).

As a bond, however, shared poverty encouraged a degree of reciprocity and cooperation among neighbours and kin which served to bind the community together in a set of mutual, overlapping social obligations. In an age in which formal means of assistance to the poor were limited, social networks based around the workplace and neighbourhood were an integral part of working-class life. The day-to-day sharing of goods, services and money and the provision of accommodation and general emotional support by relatives and friends were important aspects of survival strategies within poor communities (Young and Willmott, 1957; Roberts, 1971; Anderson, 1971; L. Lees, 1976; Ross, 1983). Furthermore, needs were often sudden, unpredictable and pressing, calling for immediate response from those in the close vicinity. The neighbourhood community in this situation was the most likely source of help and focus of social exchange, and it was within this closed spatial unit that much of the daily life of the slums was conducted. In London, as Mayhew's interviews reveal, lending amongst the poor, cross-cut by ties of occupation, ethnicity, gender and proximity was commonplace. Costermongers without stock money were lent funds by fellow traders or beer-shop keepers, the latter of which expected a corresponding increase in custom as a result of their investment. Defaulters, of course, were dealt with harshly (Mayhew, 1861, I, pp.30–1). Ethnic ties amongst the Irish dictated not only that lodgings be provided for fellow migrants but also that money be lent by more prosperous neighbours (Mayhew, 1861, I, p.115; L. Lees, 1976). Similarly, raffles and whip-rounds were also frequently conducted to help colleagues fallen on hard times (Mayhew, 1861, I, pp.58, 115, 417; II, pp.121, 370). Finally, where decent burials had to be paid for it was not unheard of for neighbours to contribute to the costs (Saunders, 1844, p.83). 'It must be confessed', noted Thomas Nunns, a clergyman from Birmingham, 'that the virtues of "weeping with them that weep" and "dividing their bread with the hungry" are found to exist among the poor to a degree which will, I think, in vain be looked for in any other class'. (Nunns, 1842, p.30.)

In addition to the innumerable channels of informal assistance, more formal means were also available and acted to stabilise the local community. Credit networks within the community with shopkeepers, hawkers, tallymen, publicans and neighbours were common amongst the poor and helped to anchor them within a locality, though as Robert Roberts has pointed out, the very poorest were often excluded even from these credit relations (Roberts, 1971, p.105). For women in particular, on whose shoulders fell much of the daily business of borrowing, being known in the locality was of crucial importance (Tebbutt, 1983, pp.36–7; Johnson, 1985, pp.165–88). For the poorest and most transient population, however, no such credit relations were undertaken and they had to fend as best they could relying on other forms of help including the poor law, to tide them over in the manifold crises of poverty.

Conclusion: the social order of the slum

There is a dual danger in attempting to recreate the social order of the slum. On the one hand, it is all too easy to assume that because of the crushing burden of poverty all those who lived in the slum were tarred with the same brush. Important, though seemingly small differences existed amongst the occupations of the slum-dwellers. Age, ethnicity and gender added further dimensions to the internal complexity of slum communities. On the other hand, however, these differences probably did little to foster disruption of local ties. The overarching similarity of problems faced by the poor served to bind them together in circumscribed communities based mainly around locality, ethnicity and occupation, and were reinforced by reciprocity and a shared hostility towards outside interference. An inward looking political culture helped to define the world in clear-cut terms of oppressors and oppressed, and this in turn helped to clarify the position of the poor within the broader social framework. Though life in the slums was indeed brutish, then, those forced to endure the conditions did so not as brutes but as members of a social order which comprised not only a set of interlocking pressures, responses and outcomes but also a series of socially mediated patterns of behaviour and beliefs.

Slum formation

In parallel with the distinctions amongst the poor the slums themselves were distinguished by their location and the processes which formed them. The impression that all slums, however defined, developed in decaying and abandoned middle-class housing in central areas is an over-simplification. Outer-city shanties, sometimes jerry built and at other times constructed from little more than rubbish, vied with inner-city rookeries in terms of squalor. Both forms were created as an outcome of processes at work within nineteenth-century society. Investment could have been directed into improving working-class housing conditions, profits could have been reduced to allow wages to be increased—but they were not. Our concern here, however, is not with the underlying structural relationships between the slums and society as a whole but rather with the individual characteristics and local factors relating to slum formation.

The nineteenth century was a period of urban transformation associated with the internal reorganisation of city structure. In the first half of the century urban population growth exerted severe pressures on the supply of housing and land. The economic, social and political parameters, however, limited the form and extent of the response the market could make. Demand for cheap labour in inner districts, coupled with increased accessibility for the middle class resulting from improvements in public transport, permitted or indeed encouraged growing concentrations of the poor in central areas. Suburban flight resulted in the rapid decay of centrally located middle-class housing into slumdom, adding to the rookeries which had already been formed in previous periods. By the 1840s, as Engels described for Manchester and as the growing body of evidence confirmed for other cities, the pattern was set.

By far the most important form of slum housing in central areas was the court, and in Midland and Northern cities the back-to-back house

(Chapman, 1971). The court was an adapted building form which was suited to conditions of land shortage or small and fragmented land-holdings, both of which tended to occur primarily in central areas of cities. Courts and alleys, frequently built up over what had formerly been back gardens or open space, rapidly deteriorated into slums (R. Williams, 1893). Often without through ventilation or drainage and lacking adequate light, such courts were little more than nurturing grounds for disease. Acres of such dwellings were erected during the nineteenth century in the burgeoning industrial towns. Whilst later forms of this housing with open courts were not unacceptable, the enclosed and densely inhabited narrow court with shared privy and adjacent water taps, came close to and sometimes became slums.

Local factors could accentuate the problems. In Nottingham grazing land surrounded the town and made for incredibly high population densities as population expanded within a frame which could not accommodate it without overcrowding and appalling slum conditions: 'Nowhere else shall we find so large a mass of inhabitants crowded into courts, alleys and lanes as in Nottingham, and those too of the worst possible condition. Here they are so clustered upon each other, court within court, yard within yard and lane within lane, in a manner to defy description.' (BPP 1845, XVII, p.554.)

Pressure on central space found other expressions. In Leeds back-to-back housing was common from the start of the century, encouraged not only by population growth and the demand for cheap housing but also by the pre-existing field pattern (Fraser, 1980; Beresford, 1971). In discussing the reason why back-to-backs were so common in Leeds the Royal Commission considered the view that people actually liked them, that in some way they had become a part of the urban culture. A more realistic view is that of the Medical Officer of Health who replied 'yes' to the implied question: 'But owing to the value of the land and having regard to the fact that builders like to get the greatest value out of their land by setting out the streets close to each other, they build back-to-back houses in Leeds' (BPP 1884-5, XXX, p.425).

Opinions were not so divided about cellar dwellings and lodging-houses, both of which were roundly condemned on grounds of fostering disease, crime and immorality. Cellar dwellings had existed in major towns since at least the eighteenth century and possibly earlier, but in the nineteenth century they became more widespread (Burnett, 1986, p.59). In Liverpool the pressure of population upon the available housing was so great that in 1842, apart from an estimated 55,534 people living in court dwellings, another 20,000 occupied 6,294 inhabited cellars (BPP 1844, XVII, p.518). Though unique in the extent of its cellar population, Liverpool was by no means alone in having numerous underground dwellings, many examples of which also occurred in other northern towns such as Manchester and Preston (BPP 1845, XVIII, pp.323-4; Burnett, 1986, p.61).

Lodging-houses, perhaps even more than cellar dwellings, crystallised the fears of the urban bourgeoisie in a way that no other aspect of the slum ever did. For most middle-class observers and local authorities they were 'the foci of disease, hotbeds of crime and moral depravity'—a theme echoed with monotonous regularity (BPP 1842, XXVI, pp.356–68; BPP 1852–53, LXXVIII, p.525). They were, according to William Miles 'links in the chain of crime', whilst for Edwin Chadwick common lodgings were 'the great foci of poverty, vice and crime, as well as of disease' (Miles, 1839, p.53).

The inhabitants themselves were often but one step removed from the workhouse (White, 1986, pp.15–16). People who had fallen in society together with destitute families congregated with vagrants, beggars, thieves, prostitutes and hawkers, and Mayhew cited the common opinion on such places when he noted 'when a man's lost caste in society, he may as well go the whole hog, bristles and all, and a low lodgings house is the entire pig'. (Mayhew, 1861, I, p.255.)

Conditions in such housing were for the most part deplorable. Prior to, and even despite of, the introduction in 1851 and 1853 of regulations governing the number of people allowed per house, gross overcrowding was a fact of lodging-house life (Gauldie, 1974, pp.241–50). It was not uncommon for one family to share a room with another or with individual strangers and lodgers who were often packed two or more to a bed and ten or more to a room. In London at certain times of the year, such as before Greenwich Fair or the Epsom races, and during the winter season, overcrowding was at its worst (Mayhew, 1861, I, p.254). Indeed some extent of the overcrowding can be gauged from the fact that of the 1,224 summonses in the capital brought against lodging-house keepers under the Common Lodging House Acts up to 31 March 1854, the majority were for sub-letting rooms over and above the permitted levels (BPP 1854, XXXV, p.125).

As with other institutions of the poor, the location of lodging-houses accurately picked out the impoverished districts within the city and within those districts the poorest streets. In some cases the licensing of common lodgings in a street undoubtedly helped to hasten its descent into slumdom (White, 1986, pp.15–17). Most probably, however, lodgings were merely one stage in the general descent of an entire neighbourhood which saw other forms of tenure change occurring alongside (Hollingshed, 1986, p.29). Indeed, in a large number of instances the distinction between a lodging-house and a tenement was so fine as to be unimportant. In York, for example, Beddern, a nest of insanitary dwellings located close to the centre, was described thus in 1844: 'The latter (the poorer classes) principally occupy the larger houses and their outbuildings, formerly the mansions of the wealthy and now sublet as apartments . . . Beddern once a fashionable quarter is now sub-let in this manner. Of 98 families living there, 67 have only one room for all purposes' (BPP 1844, XVII, p.96). The 1851 Census reveals that the family often shared their one or sometimes two rooms with anything from three to eight lodgers; whilst the heads of households rarely described themselves as lodging-house keepers, they were that in all but name.

Whilst general processes relating to the timing and pattern of urban growth help to explain the broad geography of slum formation, local factors were also important. Not all localities in these inner districts were slums and not all slums were located in these inner districts. Low-lying and poorly drained areas, frequently physically isolated from neighbouring areas, were highly conducive to the creation of slums. In Manchester, Faucher described how the two worst concentrations of slum housing, Little Ireland and Gibraltar, were both low swampy areas cut off by the Medlock and Irk rivers respectively (Faucher, 1844, p.66). In York in 1813 Bigland described most of the city in glowing terms with the exception of the ill-drained areas to the south-east of which he wrote: 'These parts of the city are both disagreeably situated and thinly inhabited, and from the Foss Bridge on both sides of Walmgate as far as the bar, scarcely anything is seen but ill-built houses and gardens.' (Bigland, 1813, p.239.)

By 1844 the Walmgate and Hungate areas had been intensively built over and were identified as the districts with the worst housing in the city (BPP 1844, XVII). These low-lying areas, susceptible to flooding, became the foci for the very poor and in particular for the many Irish who settled in these districts after the famine (Finnegan, 1982).

London too had its share of ill-drained slums. The Potteries in Kensington, formerly a brickfield but by 1850 better described as a swamp, housed an extremely poor community of Irish (BPP 1851, XXIII, pp.12, 37; Malcolmsen, 1976). At the centre of the district lay the 'ocean', a putrid lake into which drained numerous pigsties and in which, Robert Grainger noted at the time of his visit, the dead animals were thrown (BPP 1851, XXIII, p.12). Life expectancy amongst the human population here was even lower than that in the poorest parts of Liverpool.

Structural features relating to poorly constructed dwellings and inadequate internal arrangements also contributed to the creation of slums. Subdivision of pre-existing property, discussed above, was a potent factor hastening the descent of once high status housing into slumdom within central districts. Similarly, however, the seeds of decay were also sown as a result of poor construction at the outset, stemming either from pressures to skimp on building costs or from the shanty-town nature of many dwellings. In London, in Agar Town, houses built of rubbish had within a decade of their construction already attained a justifiable reputation for squalor (BPP 1851, XXIII; Hollingshed, 1986, pp.70–2). In Bethnal Green, summer houses built of brick and wood and frequently without foundations had by the late 1840s become permanent and squalid residences for the host of poor to be found in that district (Gavin, 1848).

Whilst all working-class housing was not slum housing, its physical form, often its location and site meant that factors such as population growth or street clearances frequently resulted in such housing becoming slums, especially where there were few legislative controls to regulate the building process or to ensure the removal of nuisances.

Birmingham: slums and slum life

The development of the town and its industries

At the beginning of the nineteenth century Birmingham was already established as a commercial and industrial centre of national importance. With a population of 74,000 it had experienced a period of rapid expansion during the late eighteenth century based upon an ability to adapt its economic base to meet the changing demands of the market (Wise, 1948). Within the next sixty years there occurred far-reaching changes in the regional pattern of the town (Wise, 1948), which were expressed both in its urban form and in its industrial structure.

The physical expansion of the built-up area intensified in the first decades of the nineteenth century. Birmingham grew rapidly outwards as its population increased to 130,000 by 1831 and 232,000 twenty years later. The direction and form of this development was partly conditioned by the physical make-up of the surrounding terrain. To the east of the city poorly drained land beyond the Rea acted as a deterrent to housing development and so the earliest suburbs had been to the north of the city centre on the New Hall estate and to the south and west upon the fashionable Calthorpe estate (see Figure 1.1). However, by the early 1820s many streets were developed in Deritend and Digbeth, in the valley of the Rea, and with the introduction of drainage and sewerage schemes in the 1840s the eastward growth of the city, which has been a feature of Birmingham's development ever since, became firmly established. By 1850 there had been some expansion on every side (see Figure 1.1). To the north, building had extended beyond New John Street; to the east, housing had advanced to Garrison Lane and St Andrew's Street; to the south, the built-up area had reached Stratford Place; to the west, Five Ways and Hagley Road defined Birmingham's extremities (Gill, 1952). Around the edges of the town there still remained wide and well-marked belts of gardens, although they were soon to be devoured by the Victorian speculator (Wise, 1948; see Figure 1.1).

Birmingham's prosperity and growth rested largely upon the success of its four staple manufactures of guns, jewellery, buttons and brass products. The vigorous expansion of these trades in the period 1800 to 1860 cushioned the decline of the 'older' buckle and toy-making industries, which had made Birmingham the pre-eminent metal working centre for most of the eighteenth century (Timmins, 1866). The ways in which these 'newer' industries were organised and the timing of their emergence greatly influenced the urban form of Birmingham.

At first, in all cases, production was small-scale, carried out by 'small-masters' in workshops behind or within their own houses. Consequently, there was a close mix of industry and residence. As the trades began to prosper the subdivision of processes became pronounced, encouraging the strong localisation of trades. By 1800 the gun industry was already firmly established within the town. Its rise and expansion during the Napoleonic Wars coincided with the development of the New Hall estate

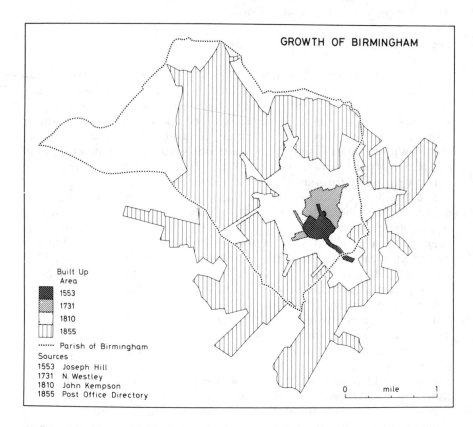

Figure 1.1 The growth of Birmingham

immediately to the north of the town, where a distinct gun-quarter became established. The jewellery trade was still in its infancy at this time, although its progress was to be rapid. As the trade progressed the small buildings at the centre of the town proved inadequate, and there was a widespread migration of jewellery firms to the new streets built on the edge of the New Hall estate. By 1845 its centre of gravity was located to the north-east limits of the town, in the Vyse Street and Warstone Lane area. The button and brass trades did not exhibit such high degrees of concentration. Instead they were found within broad axial belts to the north and north-west and the east of the central area, alongside other metaliferrous industries. The expansion of these trades coincided with the development of the Rea Valley, where many of the new large-scale premises were located.

In summary, by the mid-nineteenth century Birmingham's urban form had undergone considerable and largely recent expansion. However, there was much contrast between the new and old suburbs in terms of their housing style and quality, and between the quiet and comfortable homes of those residing to the south-west of the city and the clamour

Figure 1.2 An early nineteenth-century Birmgingham court prior to demolition

and often wretched conditions experienced by those living in the industrial districts to the north and east (Rawlinson, 1849).

The development of housing

During the nineteenth century the rapid growth of population was accompanied by a commensurate demand for housing. Some landowners sought to create and then preserve an exclusive suburb as occurred on the Calthorpe estate (Cannadine, 1980). On the other hand they might take a more *laissez-faire* attitude by not incorporating any restrictive covenants in the building leases they granted. Vance has suggested that in Birmingham the location of workers' housing was closely related to the establishment of craft quarters in areas where landowners were not unhappy for them to develop (Vance, 1967). These districts became not only the residences of workers engaged in a particular trade but also the abode of their relatives, creating working-class districts near the centre of the city. Chapman has described how such housing was developed. As early as 1731 gardens and orchards were being infilled with inferior housing, principally courts and 'the lining of yards with workmens' cottages', a process which continued into the nineteenth century producing '. . . proliferation of tiny courts of blind back houses that became so common in Birmingham' (Chapman, 1971. p.225). The *Morning Chronicle* gave a more graphic description: '. . . 50,000 supposed to be of the poorest class inhabit about 2,000 close, ill-built, ill-drained and unwholesome courts, for which Birmingham is as notorious as Liverpool' (*Morning Chronicle*, 7 October 1840).

In Birmingham the slum areas were not exclusively found in court dwellings; decayed housing which had become lodging-houses were described as the worst of the slums. Chadwick's report describes the location of the poorest lodging-houses which when mapped (Figure 1.3) provides an interesting comment upon the geography of poor housing. The areas of the city in which such lodging-houses were found were close to the commercial core and cheek-by-jowl with the housing of the 'more opulent inhabitants'.

Just to the east of fashionable St Philip's Square lay the notorious London Prentice Street, John and Thomas Street area. As early as 1751 Bradford's plan of this district shows small passageways leading from the front houses to courts built upon pre-existing gardens, the process of physical change associated with a modified socio-economic structure was beginning. By 1825, if not before, the area consisted largely of lodging-houses and there was a strong Irish presence. At this point in time slum conditions had been established and were to remain until the streets were cleared. These streets were the foci for diseases such as smallpox and periodic outbreaks of fever and of child diarrhoea, which drew attention to their continuing poor housing conditions (BPP 1842, XXVII, pp.197–8). The enduring slum nature of these streets to the end of the period under review is confirmed by the Medical Officer of Health who in 1860 described them as 'narrow, inhabited by labouring people, . . . very narrow and confined courts . . .', some of the privies are or were until recently underneath inhabited rooms (Birmingham Medical Officer of Health, second report, 1860).

The Chairman of the Improvement Committee described the area to be subject to Birmingham's Improvement Act of 1876 as follows: 'Narrow streets, houses without back doors or windows, situated both in and out of courts open at one end only, and this opening small and narrow; . . . houses and shopping so dilapidated as to be in imminent danger of

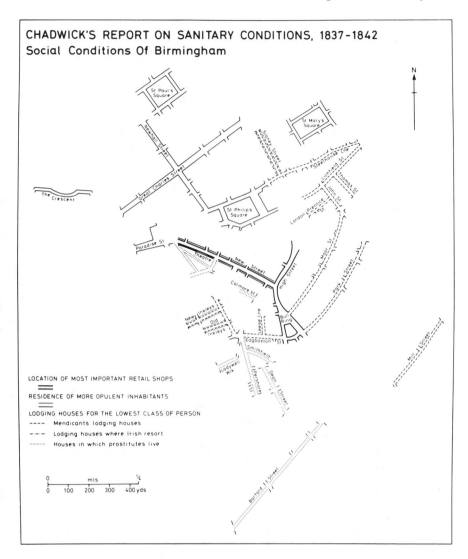

Figure 1.3 Edwin Chadwick's Report on Sanitary Conditions, 1837–42: social conditions of Birmingham

falling; . . . bowing roofs, tottering chimneys, tumble-down and often disused shopping, heaps of bricks, broken windows, and coarse, rough pavements'. He goes on to add: 'It is not easy to describe or imagine the dreary desolation which acre after acre of the very heart of the town presents to anyone who will take the trouble to visit it . . . damp and miserable, and lowering the health and spirits of the inmates'. He concludes that: 'One might say of the whole neighbourhood now under consideration that, if it were possible with safety to the lives of the inhabitants, the very best and cheapest thing to do would be to burn it right down'. (Townley et. al., 1988, p.6.)

A second area of notorious slums was the two streets known as New and Old Inkleys, identified by Chadwick in 1842 (Figure 1.3), as containing lodging-houses for the 'lowest class of person', principally mendicants or prostitutes. Just over a hundred years before this, Westley's plan of 1731 shows a scattering of houses in this area which at the time consisted mostly of gardens. By the time of Hanson's map of 1778 both streets were in existence but behind these frontages there is little evidence of the network of courts in existence in London Prentice Street area at this time, although they were there by 1825 and subsequently the district was densely built over (Townley et. al., 1988).

Such intensive development which was characteristic of the central areas of Birmingham succeeded in creating long-lasting slum properties. Ironically, the clearance of such districts often made matters worse. The removal of property in association with changing land-use took place as early as 1801 when the Bull Ring was redeveloped to build a new market-place (Gill, 1952). However, it was the railways and later slum-clearance schemes which made for large-scale problems. Gill described the railway demolitions as '. . . the first great work of slum clearance to be done in Birmingham'. (Gill, 1952, p.339.) At the time the Street Commissioners were concerned about the stopping or clearance of streets associated with the development of the railways, but their records made no mention of housing loss. The development of New Street was seen as a great benefit since it meant the demolition of Green's Village and the Inkleys, areas notorious for disease and crime. Thirty years later when the Improvement Act of 1876 was introduced, Briggs described the area affected as: '. . . forty-three and a half acres of land in the centre of the city, much of the area was a rookery of crime and wretchedness' (Briggs, 1952, p.19). Looking back at earlier efforts in slum clearance the Reverend Michael Hill commented in 1869:

The progress of improvement in the town was letting in light and air to quarters which had been hotbeds of disease and crime; but the classes were not improved—they were merely displaced to other localities which had hitherto enjoyed a more healthy reputation. To receive these persons long ranges and blocks of buildings had been put up in the south-west on the very boundary of the borough between two great thoroughfares dotted all along with villas and commodious shops and dwelling houses. Drainage, water supply and other sanitary works were unprovided for.

(Hill, 1869, p.624.)

Here then were the slums developed by design!

Slum clearance was seen as a useful by-product of transport development or as an end in itself. Henry Coleman, a Town Missionary looking at an area due for demolition in the wake of the 1876 Improvement Act, hints at a sequential movement of the slums when he noted that '. . . numbers of the people who had been driven out of London Prentice Street, The Gullett, etc. had gone into these houses which were in a tumble-down and filthy condition' (Report of the Birmingham Artisans' Dwellings Committee, 1884, p.94).

For Birmingham slum formation had two main elements which were different in time and space. During the main period of industrialisation in the eighteenth and early nineteenth century the tendency was to infill within the pre-existing urban frame. However, the later clearances of parts of the inner area produced a geographical shift eastwards in the location of the slums. Thus the improvement areas defined in the original proposals to the Town Council, subsequently modified and enlarged on the advice of the Medical Officer of Health, extended some way to the east of the town centre to include an area bounded by Aston Road, Coleshill Street and the Birmingham Canal.

The fundamental problems lay with the economic and social structures of the society within which Birmingham was set and are graphically illustrated by the case of a slum property described in 1884:

> The property is owned by two elderly ladies, its freehold was jerry-built in 1820 and the building needs wholesale repair or closure. The best tenant earned 14/2d a week and paid 2/3d a week. If the rent were raised he would have to find a house at the old rent or go to the workhouse. The total rent income for the property was 14/3d a week.
>
> (Birmingham Artisans' Dwellings Committee, 1884, p.63.)

Property ownership in the slums

Much furore was raised during the nineteenth century, primarily in relation to London, concerning the role of landlords and house-farmers in exacerbating, if not creating, slum conditions. From the rate books of 1851 however, it appears that the involvement of such individuals in Birmingham's slum housing was limited. Although later in the century one firm, Grimley and Son, managed 5,000 small houses in the city, at mid-century ownership and management of slum houses was far more diffuse. As Table 1.2 indicates, in poor streets such as the Inkleys and London Prentice Street, ownership was widely distributed, although in Sheep Street two owners, General Vyse and William Redfern, between them held 62 and 33 properties respectively.

This pattern also pertained with respect to house managers. In the eight enumeration districts with the highest number of outdoor paupers,

Table 1.2 Property Ownership in 1851 for Three Streets

Number of properties owned	Sheep Street	London Prentice Street	Inkleys	Total
		Number of owners		
0–5	3	7	0	10
6–9	6	5	1	12
10–19	5	2	8	15
20–39	1	1	1	3

Source: Birmingham Poor Rate Books, 1851

a total of thirty-one individuals acted as agents for property owners. Only rarely, however, were they responsible for more than twelve houses and in almost every case they operated within a single street. Exceptions to the rule occurred, such as Robert Potter who managed properties in thirteen different streets, but for the most part house agents confined their attention to housing within a single street. There is little evidence to suggest therefore that house owners or agents were instrumental in creating slum conditions on a wide scale, although in specific instances their activities may have contributed to the deterioration of individual houses.

Slum life in Birmingham

Within a mile of Birmingham's commercial centre lay areas which remained slums throughout most of the nineteenth century. These districts were added to by others as the city rapidly grew. The great Improvement Scheme initiated by Chamberlain in the 1870s did not solve the slum problem. At the turn of the century 'seedy' run down slum areas remained in abundance, revealed to a seemingly indignant middle class by J.C. Walters: 'But now the cry of hundreds of these distressed wretches driven by poverty to the purlieus is, "We have nowhere else to go". Is it not time a somewhere else was provided in what some King of humourists has called "the best governed city in the world"?' (Walters, 1901, p.11). In relation to these 'distressed wretches' one thing is clear—they were poor or close to poverty. The records of out-relief provide, especially for 1847, some insights into facets of life in the slums. During the 1840s the Birmingham Guardians attempted to apply the 1834 Poor Law Amendment Act with rigour, and there can be little doubt, therefore, that those who received outdoor relief were indeed in a state of poverty. Their geographical distribution demonstrates their concentration in known slum areas. Thus the majority of streets identified in 1847 as the principal locales for poverty were listed as slums in 1876 when the Town Council was putting forward its Improvement Scheme. In 1822 records of outdoor relief allow a limited view of poverty at a time when the city was much smaller. Although recipients were scattered throughout the central area (Figure 1.4), there were four main concentrations. Even at this time, when Birmingham was still surrounded by abundant land for development, the seeds had been sown and these areas were to remain the foci for poverty and slum living for the remainder of the century.

Taking the city as a whole it is clear that in 1847 (Figure 1.5), those in receipt of out-relief were not uniformly distributed; relatively few recipients were located at the western and south-western margins, whereas a pronounced crescent of paupers was found on the eastern side of the city. In detail there were pockets of poverty at the street and court level, and in some courts every household included at least one recipient of out-relief. Although there were districts with few or no recorded

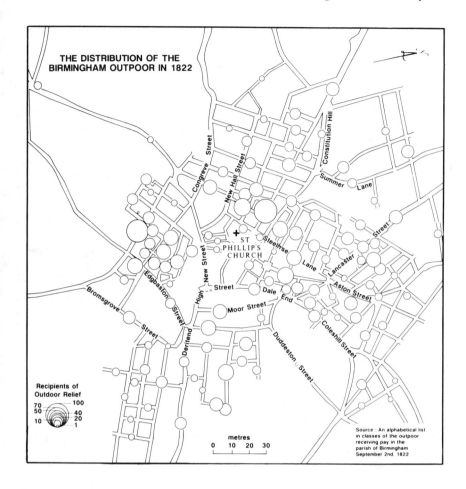

Figure 1.4 The distribution of the Birmingham outpoor in 1822

paupers adjacent to areas with large numbers, the pattern is complex
with several nuclei constituting cores from which fairly continuous
gradients were apparent. For example, in St George's Ward there were
two enumeration districts with twice the expected concentration of
paupers, sharply differentiated from contiguous districts with below-
average numbers. In contrast the wards of St Peter's and St Mary
exhibited islands of high values and transition through successively
descending concentrations. These core areas contained poor, slum
communities, the inhabitants of which were in and out of poverty and
near destitution. The housing in these areas, built before the Bye-Laws of
1876, was described by Councillor Middleman thus: 'The opinion which
anyone may form as to the housing of the poor in St Mary's or any other
ward will depend on the ideal he has in mind to test the houses by. If
his ideal is that of a pig-sty, a considerable part of this ward will give him

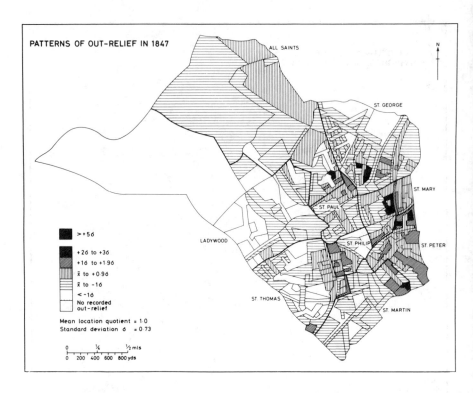

Figure 1.5 Patterns of out-relief in 1847

a great satisfaction'. (Report of the Birmingham Artisans' Dwellings Committee, 1884, p.48.)

These findings suggest that some attention must be given not only to the scale at which slum life was lived but also to the scale at which it is studied. Investigations of patterns of activity within working-class districts suggest that the spatial scale of life was relatively restricted. (Carter and Wheatley, 1980; Dennis, 1977, 1984; Lawton and Pooley, 1975; Pooley, 1977, 1979.) In Birmingham, for example, Bramwell discovered that over 75 per cent of offenders charged with drunkenness and brawling in pubs lived within half a mile of where the offence was committed (Bramwell, 1984). More significant perhaps, is the suggestion that emerges from these studies, that the experience of slum life as a subset of working-class existence needs to be studied at a finer scale than the enumeration district or ward, and that the street or the court may be a more apt unit of analysis. The location of the outdoor poor provides a case in point. Thus in Birmingham's St Philip's ward when individual paupers were located by address a large number of out-relief claimants were found in an area of poor housing around the Inkleys, some of which was subsequently cleared to build New Street Station (Figure 1.6).

One enumeration district consisting of the whole of Sheep Street was outstanding in terms of the concentration of paupers residing within its

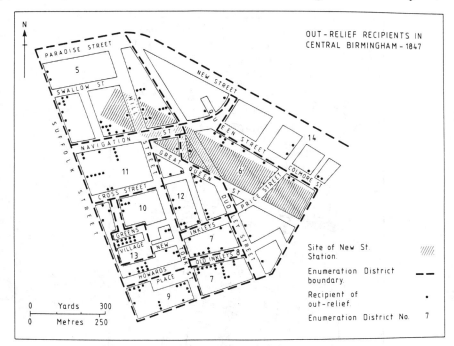

Figure 1.6 Out-relief recipients in central Birmingham 1847/OR

boundaries, and is the focus for more detailed investigation. Sheep Street lay in the eastern district of the city and was one of the older suburbs, having been originally built at the end of the eighteenth century. It was predominantly working class, the territory of the semi-skilled, with manufacturing accounting for 61 per cent of the occupations of all household heads. Twenty-four different trades were recorded, most demanding only rudimentary technical knowledge and it would seem, therefore, that the population of this area would be highly susceptible to the vagaries of the economic cycles. Although the inhabitants were poor, multiple occupation was not a feature of the household structure of Sheep Street, and no families were recorded as sharing the same house.

It is readily apparent from Figure 1.7 that this was a low-rated area with over 90 per cent of the property valued at less than £6.9 per annum. Some variation arises because of the incidence of business premises within the street, but overwhelmingly this is a district of working-class cottages and courts. It is within the courts and their front houses that the out-relief recipients lived (see Figure 1.6), although the 1851 Census shows that over two-thirds of the claimants had moved within the four-year period or had changed their social circumstance.

What then were the resources available to the inhabitants of such areas? The answer to this question is not straightforward; the complex industrial structure of Birmingham meant that there were a host of different jobs even within one industry, with a variety of wage rates.

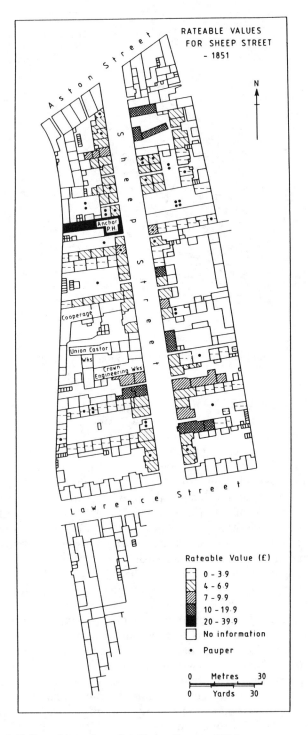

Figure 1.7 Rateable values for Sheep Street, 1851

Table 1.3 Occupations of those in receipt of Outdoor Relief, Birmingham 1847

	Males		Females	
	Number	Per cent	Number	Per cent
1.	147	49	219	27
2.	111	37	509	63
3.	42	14	79	10
Total	300	100	807	100

1. Artisans who make something
2. Labourers who do something
3. Hucksters who sell something

Source: A list of the out-poor chargeable upon the Parish of Birmingham, January 1, 1847

Thus an analysis of the occupations given in the Poor Law out-relief records of 1847 reveals that there were almost as many jobs as there were entries. Nevertheless an analysis of the types of work done by out-relief claimants is of some value in giving an insight into the likely income of poor families. A complex classification of occupations was rejected in favour of the simple but meaningful one given in the *Morning Chronicle* in 1849. Here the 'poor who will work' were divided into three categories:

1. Artisans who make something
2. Labourers who do something
3. Hucksters who sell something.

Table 1.3 suggests that amongst the poor there was a clear distinction between the sexes. In the first place more than twice as many women were recorded than men. Numerically the largest single group were female labourers; interestingly there were a significant number of female artisans reflecting the strong manufacturing base of the city. This gender division can be followed through into the differences pertaining in wage rates. Thus a large number of men were employed in the brass trade where they could earn 25s.0d. to 30s.0d. a week as a brass founder. At the other extreme, the female brass lacquerer, not an unusual job for women in the brass trade, would only earn at best 10s.0d. a week (Timmins, 1866). Although the dates are not co-incident the relativities undoubtedly still held good. Statistics presented in the Chadwick Inquiry reinforce the great gulf between male and female wage rates (Figure 1.8). In addition the differential between child and adult pay is highlighted together with a remarkable constancy of adult wages across the age range.

Undoubtedly the male experience of poverty, together with the often attendant and related bad housing, was partly shared with women. The

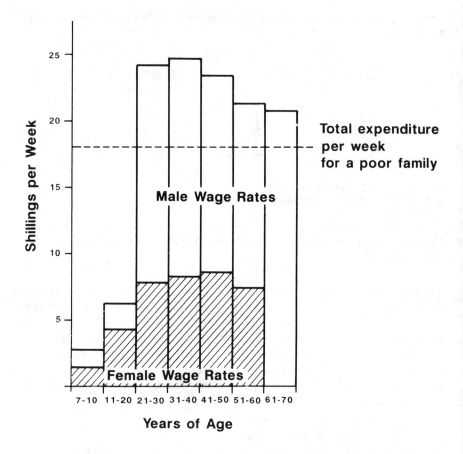

Source : Edwin Chadwick, <u>Report on the Sanitary Condition of the Labouring Population of Great Britain,</u> 1842

Figure 1.8 Wage rates in Birmingham, 1842

skilled artisan could earn up to 30s.0d. a week in 1845 (Timmins, 1866), which was quite a good wage. However, if he lost his job then he and his family would drop below the poverty line. Given the uncertainties of the *laissez-faire* economy, it is understandable that many Birmingham artisans erred on the side of caution in renting court houses at 2s.6d. a week, even though arguably they could have afforded more. With out-door relief at 2s.6d. to 5s.0d. a week there was at least the chance of keeping a roof over your head. Some indication of the gulf of experience separating the bourgeoisie from the proletariat is revealed by the comment of a member of the Birmingham Health Committee in 1875: '. . . we have got to teach the poor people that they must pay more for the rent of their houses than they have hitherto done'. (Minutes of Birmingham Health Committee, 1875.) This would have been small consolation to the labourer if his or her income fell below the level of subsistence but the plight of the female single parent or the widow was even worse. Their potential for finding employment was less than that of their male counterparts, and the work available to them was paid badly. Of the unskilled women receiving out-relief more than half were washerwomen or seamstresses, casual work which gave low returns. Yet others worked at humble, poorly paid tasks such as the fourteen women recorded as 'carding hooks and eyes', an occupation undertaken largely by women and children on a piece-work basis.

Robert Sherard provides an insight into slum life and labour which although written in 1905 could equally well be applied to earlier years:

There is a deep pathos in all these scenes, but the spectacle which, when I think back upon these heavy hours, will always haunt me with greatest sorrow, is one I saw in a kitchen, in a house off Jennens Row, in a courtyard under the lee of a common lodgings. Here, late one evening, I found three little children, busy at work at a table on which were heaped a pile of cards, and a vast mass of tangled hooks and eyes. The eldest girl was eleven, the next was nine, and a little boy of five completed the companionship. They were all working as fast as their little fingers could work. The girls sewed, the baby hooked. They were too busy to raise their eyes from their tasks—the clear eyes of youth under the flare of the lamp! Here were the energy, the interest, which in our youth we all bring to our several tasks in the happy ignorance of the weight and stress of the years of drudgery to come.

I looked at these bright eyes, these quick and flexible fingers, and I thought of the old woman of ninety whom I had seen in the morning in Unit Street. I remembered her eyes which had the glaze of approaching dissolution upon them; I remembered the knotted, labour-gnarled hands. Her eyes had been bright once. She, too, had brought interest and energy to the miserable tasks in which her life began. Years had followed years, decade had added itself to decade. There had been no change brought by chance or time.

The drudgery is eternal. There is no hope of relief.

(Keating, 1976, p.188.)

Amongst the hierarchy of the poor the 'hucksters who sell something' were at the lower levels of society in terms of both status and income. Amongst those receiving out-relief in 1847 there were 42 male and 79 female street dealers whose range of wares was considerable (see Table 1.4). The focus was upon food and household goods, the livelihood of such folk was undoubtedly precarious and would have yielded relatively little even on a good day.

Within the poorest districts certain subgroups, identifiable largely on ethnic grounds, were apparent. In 1842 Chadwick had reported that Italian street musicians congregated in Park Street and Lichfield Street, both of which he recorded as amongst the poorest in the city. (BPP 1842, XXVII, pp.197–8.) However, as in most British cities during this period, it was the Irish who formed the principal immigrant group who picked out with unerring accuracy the most impoverished areas of housing. In 1841 the census recorded 4,683 Irish in the city and by 1851 this had swelled to 9,341. They formed part of what can best be described as a residuum, taking unskilled, casual work as labourers, servants or

Table 1.4 Occupations of Hucksters in Receipt of Out-Relief 1847

	Male	Female
Food	2	29
Household Goods	8	10
Clothing	—	16
Picks Manure/Scavengers	9	1
Errands	11	14
Collectors — Rags, Glass, etc.	4	3
Miscellaneous	8	6
Total	42	79

Source: A list of the out-poor chargeable upon the Parish of Birmingham, January 1, 1847

Table 1.5 Irish Household Heads — Selected Streets 1851

	Irish Household Heads (per cent)
London Prentice Street	26.9
John Street	18.9
Old Inkleys	12.4
New Inkleys	45.0
Thomas Street	10.9

Source: Decennial Census 1851

hawkers. Poorly paid as they were, they were also poorly housed. The main concentration of Irish was found in the old, central area where they congregated in certain streets, such as New Inkleys and London Prentice Street (Table 1.5). At a finer scale, however, Irish households tended to share residences or live in contiguous housing, suggesting something of the cohesiveness associated with a community sharing a common origin.

Concern on the part of authorities regarding the Irish population focused largely on the threats they posed to public health and to the Poor Law. As Finnegan has noted for York, the Irish were labelled as dirty, riotous and as carriers of disease, particularly typhus, known collo-quially as 'the Irishman's Itch'. The fact that they settled in already existing slum areas made little difference in apportioning blame for their conditions of life. Outbreaks of fever were traced by the Poor Law Guardians directly to the Irish population: '. . . the majority of fever cases are Irish, for some time past the fever has been imported by the immigrant Irish and has spread to a fatal extent'. (Birmingham Poor Law Guardians' Minutes, June 1847.)

Irish lodging-houses, of which Chadwick's inquiry recorded 252 in the city, brought forth particular opprobrium. Of London Prentice Street it was said that:

The latter is now almost entirely occupied by the low Irish and is one of the filthiest streets in town. During the last summer the smallpox prevailed in this street . . . we find that the low Irish who reside in this town have a great repugnance to vaccination . . . The premises occupied by these persons are, for the most part, in a very neglected condition, and their furniture, bedding and clothes of a meagre and squalid description.

(BPP 1842, XXVII, p.198.)

Threats to public health, however, were not the only source of concern to authorities. Over and above the drain on public funds stemming from illness, the Irish represented a potentially heavy charge on the poor rates. Prior to 1847 paupers without a settlement could be removed, but following changes in the law which conferred rights to relief on those applicants who could prove five years' continuous residence in a union, it became clear that many who had hitherto been deterred from seeking relief for fear of removal might now apply (Rose, 1976). The Irish, whose conditions of life were such as to make their need for relief proportionately great, posed a particular problem. And the response on the part of the local Poor Law Guardians was immediate:

The Royal Assent, having been given on 21 June to a Bill facilitating the removal of the Irish . . . [the Guardians considered it their] duty to the ratepayers to lose no time in carrying its provisions into effect. The Clerk was instructed to go to Liverpool to make the necessary arrangements so that by 10 September the whole of the removals they were called upon to make were effected, the total number of which was 232.

(Birmingham Poor Law Guardians' Minutes, October 1847.)

London: slums and slum life

Urban change and slum formation

During the 1840s the problems of poverty and pauperism emerged with greater force in London than had hitherto been the case. So too did the problem of the slum or 'rookery', as witnessed by the growing usage of the terms themselves in contemporary works (Dyos, 1967, p.8). There were several reasons why this should have been the case. First, structural problems relating to the competitiveness of the metropolitan trades resulted in severe downward pressures on wages and working conditions in several occupations, notably clothing and shoemaking. Secondly, collapse of the house-building boom in 1825 resulted in higher rents and worsening housing conditions in inner areas throughout the 1830s and 1840s. Thirdly, these factors, coupled with deteriorating wages and conditions of work increased pressure on the Poor Law and in turn helped to fuel rate rises in central and eastern districts. Finally, worsening conditions and rising rates encouraged middle-class flight to the suburbs, leaving behind decaying housing and an increasingly impoverished population unable to support the mounting tide of pauperism (Green, 1984). At such times and under such conditions slum formation was both rapid and widespread.

London at mid-century was already a city with a distinctive geographical pattern of poverty. Differences in the fortunes of eastern and western districts were already evident by the time of John Stow's survey in 1598, and at the time of the Great Fire status distinctions between the areas were already engraved into the fabric of the city (Power, 1978, 1985). In the first half of the century, however, the bipolar distribution of wealth was disrupted somewhat by a growing distinction in social status between inner and outer zones radiating from the old commercial core (Green, 1985; Schwarz, 1982). In 1844 Joseph Fletcher described the city in terms of three contrasting geographical components. At the centre was the City of London, already 'one vast counting house and warehouse' with a declining population that consisted increasingly of poorer artisans, slop workers, labourers and street hawkers. The outer suburbs, in contrast, were growing rapidly as a result of the immigration of a wealthy population which had sought to escape the growing impoverishment of inner-city environments. Between the two came the inner industrial belt, stretching from St Giles in the west, eastwards to St George-in-the-East and southwards into Southwark, and here it was that the mass of poverty was concentrated (Fletcher, 1844).

According to a variety of social indicators this inner zone contained the most impoverished districts, particularly to the east and south of the City (Green, 1985). Districts such as Bethnal Green, Southwark and Bermondsey were characterised by a combination of factors indicative of poverty, including concentrations of sweated and unskilled occupations, high rates of illiteracy and mortality, large families with high dependency ratios, poor quality housing and high poor rates. Within such districts emerged some of the worst slums: the Church Lane rookery in St Giles; Whitecross Street near Smithfield in St Luke's, and Wentworth Street in Whitechapel. According to Fletcher, this inner zone was 'the great solicitude in a sanitary view', and medical topography confirmed his opinion (Fletcher, 1844, p.80). In 1842 Chadwick had drawn attention to the lower rates of mortality in the northern and western parishes compared to central, eastern and southern areas. Districts such as Bethnal Green and Whitechapel, investigated by the Poor Law Commission in 1837 and 1838 with a view to examining the relationship between ill health and pauperism, were noted as having extremely high rates of morbidity and mortality (Poor Law Commission, 1837, 1838). Mean female mortality in Whitechapel, for example, was twice as high as in St George, Hanover Square, or the suburban district of Hackney (BPP 1842, XXVI, p.165).

Important as the distinction was between western and eastern districts, insanitary courts and overcrowded dwellings could be found in all parts of the city and frequently close to the houses of the rich. 'Immediately behind some of the best constructed houses in the fashionable districts of London', wrote Chadwick, 'are some of the worst dwellings, into which the working classes are crowded' (BPP 1842, XXVI, p.166). Old decaying inner districts in the west, such as St Margaret's, Westminster and most notably St Giles, each contained slums as bad if not worse than anything to be found elsewhere in the city. Indeed, the close juxtaposition of poverty and wealth intensified fears of the spread of contagion and made the very existence of such rookeries the more shocking. During the 1840s surveys carried out by the Statistical Society of London showed that one-room living was the norm for working-class families, particularly in wealthier districts in which rents were high. In Marylebone an investigation of 205 houses found that 845 rooms were occupied by 859 families (Rawson, 1843, p.44). In the wealthy parish of St George's, Hanover Square, a survey of 1,465 families found that 929 lived in single rooms (Weld, 1843, p.17). Overcrowding was even greater in Church Lane, St Giles, where as a result of demolitions for New Oxford Street and an influx of Irish migrants, house occupancy rates had nearly doubled between 1841 and 1847 (Statistical Society of London, 1848, pp.16–17; Mann, 1848, pp.19–20). Nor was overcrowding confined to working-class housing in wealthy districts alone. In St George-in-the-East, where average rents were lower, rates of overcrowding were only slightly less with about one-third of families living in single rooms (Statistical Society of London, 1848, p.211). Hector Gavin's sanitary ramblings around Bethnal Green revealed a similar situation with four-roomed houses in the worst part of the district being occupied by up to thirty people (Gavin, 1848, pp.42–3). Overcrowding, therefore, was commonplace throughout London, though it was perhaps the more shocking to middle-class observers when it lay so close to wealthy areas, and slum formation proceeded rapidly under such intense pressures on space.

Overcrowding and slum formation in the inner areas of London was hastened during the 1830s and 1840s by demolition of housing arising from street clearances, warehouse construction and railway building (Dyos, 1950–56, 1957; Jones, 1971, pp.159–96). Most central districts lost housing from the 1830s and 1840s as Table 1.6 shows. The City itself lost over a quarter of its housing stock between 1831 and 1861 as it was transformed into a primarily commercial district. The displaced population crowded into the neighbouring localities, resulting in further increases in overcrowding, deteriorating sanitary conditions and higher levels of pauperism. Those who could afford to move to the suburbs did so, driven out by rising poor rates and a decaying urban fabric and leaving in their place an increasingly impoverished population living in worsening squalor and overcrowded conditions. In St George-in-the-East, George McGill ruefully remarked that 'as the better class go, the poor fill their place' (Association for Promoting the Relief of Destitution in the Metropolis, 1866, p.6), and in Clerkenwell in 1857 the Reverend Warwick Wroth noted that: 'The richer classes are continually moving to other localities and the poorer are taking their place. Houses which formerly were filled with tolerably well-to-do are now let out in lodgings, and the lodgers, instead of being able to aid others, sometimes need

Table 1.6 Districts which experienced housing loss, 1831–61

| | Number of Houses | | | | Decline (per cent) |
	1831	1841	1851	1861	1831–61
West London	3,724	3,010	2,657	2,580	30.7
City of London	8,707	7,951	7,297	6,362	26.9
St Olave, Southwark	2,883	2,523	2,360	2,209	23.4
St Saviour, Southwark	4,869	4,659	4,600	4,471	8.2
East London	4,817	4,796	4,739	4,489	6.8
St Giles	4,952	4,959	4,700	4,690	5.3
St Martin's	2,348	2,439	2,307	2,240	4.6
Strand	3,928	4,327	3,962	3,775	3.9
St James's, Westminster	3,461	3,590	3,390	3,333	3.7
St Luke's	6,451	6,385	6,349	6,356	1.5
St George-in-the-East	6,240	5,988	6,146	6,169	1.1

Source: Decennial Census 1831, 1841, 1851, 1861

aid themselves.' (Association for Promoting the Relief of Destitution in the Metropolis, 1858, p.6.)

The situation south of the river was no different. In Southwark in 1862 Edward Collinson, Chairman of the Board of Guardians, stated that: 'Unquestionably the improvements in the City at first tended very much to make poor persons' houses, which were formerly shops and dwelling houses, be let out in tenements and as lodging houses, and the consequence is that they are sometimes very closely packed with inhabitants.' (BPP 1862, X, q.7348.)

Closely packed the houses were. Between 1841 and 1861 substantial increases in the number of persons per house occurred in most districts surrounding the City, as shown in Figure 1.9, with the greatest increases in St Olave and Rotherhithe to the south, Strand to the west and Poplar to the east. In places such as St Giles, where housing was already grossly overcrowded, the increase as measured by the census was relatively small, though houses in the poorest streets continued to have a seemingly infinite capacity for taking in extra lodgers (Mann, 1848, pp.19–20; Cooper, 1850, pp.18–20). Elsewhere, however, conditions deteriorated noticeably during the 1840s and nascent slums matured quickly. In Southwark, housing vacated by the middle classes was soon taken up by house farmers and subdivided into weekly lodgings and by 1865 an estimated 4,800 houses out of a total stock of 7,700 were reckoned to be let out as rooms (BPP, 1862, X, pp.7037–8, 7372–4, 7399, 7570, 7770; BPP 1866, XXXIII, p.504). Bethnal Green, which in 1840 already had the dubious distinction of having a mean rateable value per house one quarter of that of the rest of London, experienced a similar pattern of abandonment and subdivision. In the inner parts of the parish, old houses were subdivided and in some cases over thirty people were crowded into no more than four rooms. Elsewhere in the parish pressure of numbers had resulted in garden summer houses, built partly of brick

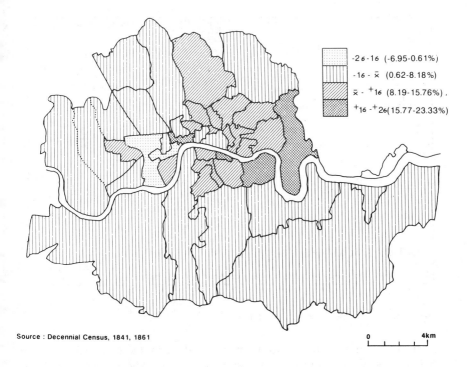

	-2₆-1₆ (-6.95-0.61%)
	-1₆ - x̄ (0.62-8.18%)
	x̄ - ⁺1₆ (8.19-15.76%) .
	⁺1₆ -⁺2₆(15.77-23.33%)

Source : Decennial Census, 1841, 1861

0   4km

Figure 1.9 London: change in persons per house 1841–61

and partly of wood and frequently without foundations, being taken into permanent occupation (Gavin, 1848, pp.12–18). The existence of such grossly inadequate living conditions, however, was in no sense unique to Bethnal Green, but instead mirrored the general pressures on housing throughout the inner zone of poverty. Given similar conditions elsewhere slums were not slow to form.

Whilst general processes relating to the timing and pattern of urban growth help to explain the broad geography of slum formation, local factors were important in transforming the pressures into shapes on the ground. Not all localities in these inner districts were slums and not all slums were located in these inner districts. Whilst known rookeries were mainly concentrated in districts bordering the City in which pressures on housing were most severe, as shown in Figure 1.10, there were exceptions to the rule, such as Agar Town to the north and the Potteries in Kensington to the west. Three aspects relating to the site and nature of housing were important in this respect. Firstly, low-lying and poorly drained districts, frequently physically isolated from neighbouring areas, were highly conducive to the creation of slums. In Bermondsey and Canning Town, both of which were so low-lying as to preclude the possibility of adequate drainage, cesspools and sewers ran into supplies of drinking-water. Nor surprisingly, perhaps, outbreaks of disease were

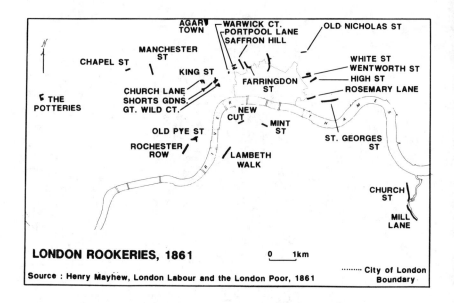

Figure 1.10 London rookeries, 1861

common as shown in the outbreak of cholera in 1849 at Jacob's Island in Bermondsey (Godwin, 1859, pp.57–8, 85–7). The Potteries in Kensington, formerly a brickfield but by 1850 better described as a swamp, housed an extremely poor community of Irish (BPP 1851, XXIII, pp. 12, 37; Malcolmson, 1976). At the centre of the district lay the 'Ocean', a putrid lake into which drained numerous pigsties and in which, Robert Grainger noted at the time of his visit, the dead animals were thrown (BPP 1851, XXIII, p.12).

Over and above the problems of drainage, the site of a slum was usually a nest of secluded streets or courts off the main street and without through traffic. Courts and alleys, frequently built up over what had formerly been back gardens or open space, rapidly deteriorated into slums (R. Williams, 1893). Often without through ventilation or drainage and lacking adequate light, such courts were little more than nurturing grounds for disease. Back Ball Alley in St Sepulchre, for example, no more than a yard wide and containing houses on the verge of collapse, was noted in 1840 as a fever spot by Samuel Millar, relieving officer of the district (BPP 1840, XI, pp.800–1). A similar picture emerged in Bethnal Green where back streets and courts inhabited by weavers and labourers had higher rates of mortality than did higher status housing fronting on the main streets (BPP 1842, XXVI, p.160). Though no overall estimate exists for the proportion of London's population housed in courts, a glance at Charles Booth's maps of poverty later in the century shows that the streets coloured dark blue and black, and therefore housing criminals, loafers and the chronically poor, were most frequently those which lay behind the main thoroughfares.

Finally, structural features relating to the construction and internal arrangements of housing itself also contributed to the creation of slums. In the older, central areas, decaying middle-class housing designed for single families but long since abandoned by their original class of occupants and subdivided to accommodate a poorer population, formed some of the worst slums (Beames, 1850, pp.60–72; Godwin, 1859, pp.9–10). Lacking adequate means of drainage or ventilation, the descent of such housing into slumdom was noticeably rapid. In London and elsewhere, however, slums were not confined to old, decaying structures, and in some cases relatively new buildings also beat a hasty path towards slumdom. Speculative jerry-built housing, constructed with a view to short-term profits, slipped easily and quickly towards slum status. Engels in Manchester commented how new working-class houses in Ancoats with walls only half a brick thick were old after ten years and ruined after forty (Engels, 1973, pp.88-9). In London houses built in Agar Town, St Pancras in the 1840s were little more than huts constructed from bricks and rubbish and within a decade had attained a justifiable reputation for squalor (BPP 1851, XXIII, p.7; Hollingshed, 1986, pp.70–2). But whether housing was newly constructed or was merely descending into slumdom as a result of abandonment by the middle class, the pressure to extort short-term profits had similar results. Construction was flimsy, materials were poor and repairs were ignored, with the general outcome that such housing decayed rapidly and slums were quick to form.

The role of landlords

The tremendous demand for cheap housing that occurred in the inner districts of London from the 1830s and 1840s provided high rates of return on property investment and from this period house farmers emerged as one of the principal agents of slum formation. The system of leasing and subleasing prevalent in the city provided ample opportunities for extorting profits from dilapidated houses. For ground landlords, letting blocks of housing towards the end of their lease represented a potent means of shifting responsibility for costly repairs whilst at the same time ensuring a moderate return on investment. In turn, house farmers who purchased the fag-end of leases themselves maximised short-term gains on housing through the evasion of repairs, subletting and rack rental. The result was a rapid deterioration in conditions wherever the system took hold.

Housing in the central areas abandoned by the middle class provided perhaps the worst examples of slum conditions but the most lucrative source of property speculation. Long since past its best, such housing was ripe for subdivision and subletting. The pattern was illustrated clearly in St Giles in the 1830s:

The way these houses are let out is this, the ground landlord lets out the whole estate, or two or three streets to one person, and he pays the rent by the year; and he again lets those houses to one person who pays him weekly; and that person gets in and lets in his turn every room separately, and when an inhabitant has got into a room he again lets off part of the room to anyone who comes in by the night.

(BPP 1836, XX, p.41.)

Where such a chain of tenancy arose, it proved difficult if not impossible to enforce repairs. In his report to the privy council on the state of common lodgings in the metropolis, Captain Hay of the Metropolitan Police commented: 'Such tenancy and occupation have rendered it extremely difficult to reach the person really responsible as "keeper" for the condition of the house; for there is, first, the owner; secondly his tenant for the whole house; thirdly, the subtenant for a room; and four-thly, five or six persons or families occupying one room as lodgers.' (BPP 1852-3, LXXVIII, q.2587.)

Speaking in 1866 of the worsening condition of housing in London, Dr Julian Hunter commented on this practice: 'There is a regular trade of dealing in fag-ends of leases, and the art of eluding covenants is well studied. Gentlemen in this business may be fairly expected to do as they do—get all they can from the tenants while they have them, and leave as little as they can for their successors.' (BPP 1866, XXXIII, p.573.)

Small tradesmen and shopkeepers, in particular, whose object was a quick return on capital as well as a continuous inflow of money, were most likely to enter this part of the property market and it was these local property owners that were frequently cited as the main cause for deteriorating housing conditions. Temptation was great; profits could be high, some claimed as high as 100 per cent if landlord expenditure was minimised (Cochrane, 1849). Evasion of repairs and opposition to sanitary reforms were understandable given the fact that any expenditure would either reduce profits or result in extra burdens on the rates. The reluctance of inferior landlords to cleanse cesspits on the grounds of expense had already drawn the ire of Chadwick but as housing condi-tions worsened in central areas, greater attention was paid to the inade-quacies of small property owners (BPP 1842, XXVI, p.45). In 1850 Hector Gavin had complained about the fact that owners of small house property were generally opposed to sanitary reform on the grounds of expense. His views were echoed elsewhere throughout the century (Gavin, 1850, pp.83-4). Thomas Tebaz, medical officer of health for Westminster, corroborated the fact that small owners— petty bricklayers and small shopkeepers—either would not or could not make necessary repairs to their properties for fear of losing their profit (BPP 1854, XXXV, p.125).

Though in reality their existence was merely a symptom of urban decay, slum landlords—known variously as house farmers, house knackers, land jobbers, property sweaters or rack-renters—were usually cast as villains of the piece and blamed for the slums' very existence. The attack by Thomas Beames on house farmers and middlemen—'whose heart is seared by the recollection of their own poverty and who learn to grind as he once was ground by others'—was repeated in several different quarters (Beames, 1850; *Builder*, 1854, p.25). The *Builder* was constantly sniping at the leasehold system that gave rise to house farming whilst the role of small property owners came under increasingly close and critical scrutiny as the housing problem worsened during the course of the century. (See: BPP 1882, VII, p.525; BPP 1884–85, XXX, qq.610, 615, 617, 626, 1141–46, 1265–72, 1277–8, 3404, 5760–63; Englander, 1983, pp.9, 50–76; Kemp, 1982a, 1982b.)

St Giles

Housing and slum formation

Of all the slums which existed in London during the period few, if any, surpassed in squalor or notoriety the Irish rookery in St Giles. Though the district as a whole contained pockets of decaying courts and houses inhabited by an impoverished population, none were so decayed or as deeply impoverished as the housing and population in the area centred around Church Lane. Bounded by Bainbridge Street, George Street and High Street, the St Giles rookery, known also as 'Little Ireland' and the 'Holy Land', housed an impoverished and largely Irish population in old decaying housing hidden within a maze of congested courts and alleys. Middle-class housing, long since abandoned by its original inhabitants and occupied now by a population of much lower social standing, had tumbled in status as a result of subdivision and neglect. Squalid courts existed where once there had been back gardens. The result was clear; nowhere in the district was the housing so poor and the poor so concentrated as in the Irish rookery. (See Figures 1.11 and 1.12.) And no other place in the city, perhaps, captured the imagination or came to symbolise more the depths of poverty in the capital than did St Giles (Flint, 1987, p.131).

In part, fascination with the district stemmed from the antiquity of the place. Decaying houses set amidst a honeycomb of courts and alleys reflected an earlier form of the city about to be swept away by the Victorian enthusiasm for clearances and street improvements (Gaspey, 1851–52; Saunders, 1844). One writer described the rookery as: 'One great maze of narrow crooked paths crossing and intersecting in labyrinthine convulsions, as if the houses had been originally one great block of stone eaten by slugs into innumerable small chambers and connecting passages.' (Weir, 1842, pp.226–7.)

Fascination also stemmed from the capital's social contrasts, none of which was greater than that between the poverty of St Giles and the wealth of the surrounding districts (Beames, 1850, p.37; Jerrold, 1851). Finally, the rookery represented a degree of filth, squalor and social disorder that was perhaps unmatched in the city at the time (Beames, 1850, pp.34–62; Cooper, 1850; Mann, 1848). So great was its reputation as the epitome of slumdom that for the more socially aware traveller, such as Frederick Engels and Flora Tristan, it became almost a tourist attraction. (*Builder*, 1853, p.129; Engels, 1973, pp.62–4; Tristan, 1982, pp.155–77.)

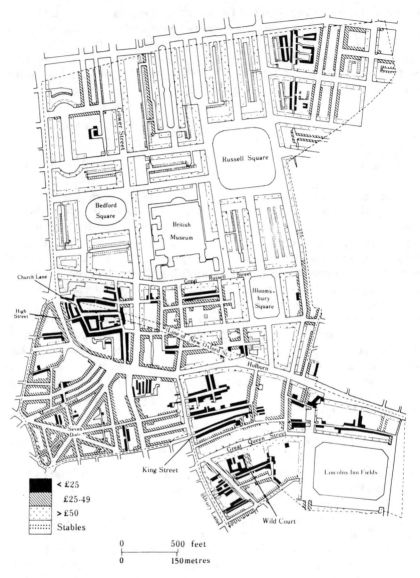

Source : St. Giles and St. George's Bloomsbury, Poor Rate Book, 1843

Figure 1.11 St Giles: rateable values 1843

The reputation for squalor so justly deserved by the rookery had a long ancestry. Even as a new seventeenth-century suburb, the district had stood out from the surrounding area by virtue of its higher proportion of poorer families and lower social status (Power, 1978). Its descent into squalor during the eighteenth century, however, was as rapid as it was spectacular and by mid-century its reputation for poverty and

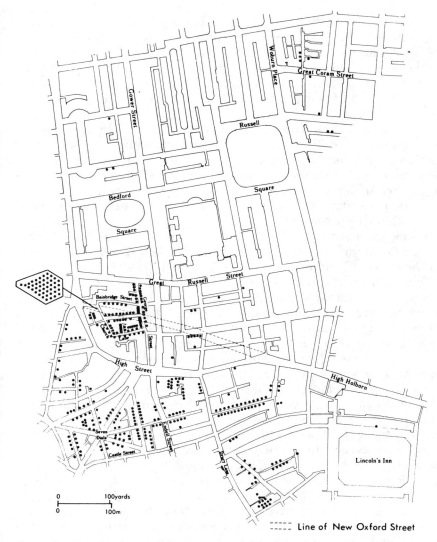

Source : St. Giles and St. George's Directors of the Poor, Settlement and Examination Books, 1840-49. (1 in 20 sample)

Figure 1.12 St Giles: applicants for poor relief, 1840–49

debauchery, as demonstrated by John Gay in *The Beggars' Opera* or by Hogarth in his drawing of Gin Lane, was well established. New aristocratic estates to the west had enticed those who could afford it to move away, leaving empty and decaying houses that were ripe for less salubrious uses. By 1750, it was estimated that one in four houses was a gin shop (George, 1966, p.54). Common lodging-houses abounded, attracting a transient population of beggars and thieves as well as a substantial number of Irish immigrants (George, 1966, pp.120–1; Lees, 1979). Its reputation at the start of the nineteenth century as the centre of beggary was well deserved since over one quarter of the beggars investigated by the Society for the Suppression of Mendicity came from the area (Society for the Suppression of Mendicity, 1819, p.4; see also 1830 and 1832). By the turn of the century, then, the district was long past its best and in the course of the following decades it became, in the eyes of many, the archetypal slum.

Once begun the downward spiral of impoverishment and physical deterioration was difficult to halt. St Giles, in common with other inner districts during the first half of the nineteenth century, was squeezed between an old, deteriorating housing stock and growing pressure of population. In the first decades of the century, rising population coupled with an almost static housing stock resulted in increased levels of over-crowding. In 1801 the number of persons per house stood at 9.8 but by 1831 this had risen to 12.7. Population continued to rise until 1851 but a sharp fall in the number of houses in the 1840s arising from clearances for New Oxford Street led to even higher average occupancy rates. Within the district, enormous variations in housing conditions existed. In Bloomsbury to the north, as shown in Figure 1.11, high status housing on the Bedford estate contrasted with concentrations of extremely poor housing in St Giles parish to the south. An investigation by the Statistical Society of London in 1847 revealed that in Church Lane houses frequently contained more than thirty people and that following the clearances for New Oxford Street in 1844 the same houses often accommodated forty or more people (Mann, 1848, pp.19–21). A further survey of Church Lane and its environs in 1849 revealed that in some houses with no more than four rooms between 50 and 90 inhabitants found nightly lodgings (Cooper, 1850; see also *The Times*, 11 November 1850). Even higher levels of overcrowding were recorded in the census. In 1841 the average number of inhabitants per house in Church Lane was 24—three times the average for London and nearly twice that of St Giles as a whole. By 1851, however, the situation had worsened dramatically with average occupancy having reached 46 per house. Even this enormous rise hid the fact that several houses in the street held over 100 persons and one house (number 21) contained 140 people (Census Enumerators Books, 1841, 1851; Beames, 1850, p.29).

Overcrowding was serious throughout the area but particularly in the numerous lodging-houses scattered throughout the district. In 1856, 69 houses were registered under the Common Lodging House Act, the majority of which were concentrated in the poorest streets, including Church Lane, Carrier Street and Queen Street (Board of Works, St Giles, 1856; *idem*, 1857). In reality, however, the number of lodging-houses was much greater, since to avoid the terms of the Act residents in the same rooms professed to be members of one family rather than lodgers (*idem*, 1859). Rooms contained anything from eight to forty people, depending on size, but all were universally crowded and equally filthy (Cooper, 1850). 'You would be startled', remarked Thomas Beames, 'to witness the crowding of inmates even in favoured localities' (Beames, 1850, p.137).

Figure 1.13 Carrier Street in the St Giles rookery, looking north. *Source: Illustrated London News*, 6 November 1858. Courtesy: Greater London Record Office, ref. no. Holborn F28787.

Rents were generally low, as befitted the quality of the accommodation, 1d a night bought space on the floor and 3d a share of a bed. The cost of a single room was between 3s.0d. and 4s.6d. a week, but this could be recouped by subletting corners or space on the floor (Bosanquet, 1841, pp.91–4; Cooper, 1850, pp.10, 20). A sample of 548 rents

Table 1.7 Weekly Rents in St Giles 1832–62

Rent	Number	Per cent
1d–11d	48	8.7
1s–1s 11d	144	26.3
2s–2s 11d	196	35.8
3s–3s 11d	105	19.7
4s–4s 11d	34	6.7
5s and above	21	3.8
Total	548	100.0

Source: St Giles and St George's Settlement and Examination Books

paid by applicants for poor relief, outlined in Table 1.7, shows that the majority of paupers paid between 1s.0d. and 3s.0d. a week, with the average cost being 2s.½d. Most were weekly tenants and the relatively low amounts suggest that it was usual for them to be sharing a room.

Low as the rents were, the returns on slum housing could be substantial. Profits were made at every stage in the chain, with houses let for £20 to £30 yielding profits of £70 after rates had been paid (Cochrane, 1849). 21 Church Lane, for example, in the heart of the Irish rookery, was rented from the owner for £25 per annum. The immediate tenant received £58.10s. in rent and his subtenants in turn let rooms to lodgers and received an estimated return of £120 (Cochrane, 1849). In turn these opportunities for profit attracted a host of house farmers and middlemen for whom slum housing represented a lucrative business and in common with the situation in other inner areas, subletting and subdivision of houses were frequent.

The outcome of such devolution of responsibility was clear to all: houses were neglected; repairs were avoided and regulations evaded. Local slum landlords were primarily responsible for some of the very worst property in the district. 7 Church Lane, for instance, which was owned by Charles Innis but leased to Thomas Fitzgerald, was described in 1849 thus:

The privy had been taken away and the cesspool covered with boards and earth. The soil underneath oozed up through the boards, saturating the earth with foetid matter . . . In one of the back rooms several Irish families lived . . . The room opposite was occupied by only three families during the day, but as many as could be got into it at night. The price ranged from 'anything they could give me' to 1d and 2d per night. This room fetched 2s.0d. per week. Two cases of fever had been taken away from it. The window slid back only eight inches—that was the only means of ventilation. Although this room was not more than nine feet square, daylight did not reach the back of it. It was scarcely high enough for an ordinary man to stand upright in. The person who took the rents came to the door for them every Monday morning.

(Cooper, 1850, p.20.)

Table 1.8 Property Ownership in the Church Lane Rookery 1843

| | Number of Houses | | | | |
	1–2	3–9	10–19	20+	Total
Owners	2	7	6	3	18
Number of houses	2	35	68	102	207
Percentage	1.0	16.9	32.8	49.3	100.0

Source: St Giles Poor Rate Book 1843

Table 1.9 House Ownership in St Giles (Houses less than £25)

Owner	Owned	Owner-Occupied	Sub-let	Occupied	Total
C. Innis	60	20	40	3	63
T. Parker	20	19	1	10	30
J. Corwan	25	25	—	—	25
T. Fitzgerald	13	12	1	11	24
R. Hughes	15	—	15	—	15
T. Grout	13	5	8	2	15
G. McCabe	15	14	1	—	15
D. McLaren	13	13	—	—	13
J. McLaren	12	12	—	—	12

Source: St Giles Poor Rate Book 1843

In 1864 George Buchanan, the local medical officer of health, complained that: 'Much of the poor house property in the district is owned by some few landlords who wanted incessant looking after, and had come to regard the lenient measures of warning as adopted by the Board as a cheap way of keeping them informed about the state of their premises.' (Board of Works, St Giles, 1864.) When attempts were made by the local Board of Works to enforce bye-laws relating to overcrowding, cleansing and general repairs, as permitted under the 1866 Sanitary Act, Section 35, a deputation of house owners and agents proved powerful enough to ensure that the notices of repair were withdrawn (Board of Works, St Giles, 1866–67; Board of Works Minutes, 23 April, 14 May, 8 October 1867). The only matter to be dealt with promptly and regularly, it seems, was the collection of rent.

Reconstruction of the pattern of property ownership in the area for 1843, based on the ratebooks, reveals the existence of an intricate chain of ownership and tenancy. In the Church Lane rookery, ownership was concentrated in relatively few hands. As Table 1.8 shows, prior to demolitions for New Oxford Street, nine owners held over 82 per cent of the total house property in the rookery with the three largest owners holding nearly half the building stock between them. When the ownership and tenancy structure of this group as a whole is examined for all properties in St Giles, as shown in Table 1.9, it becomes clear that they

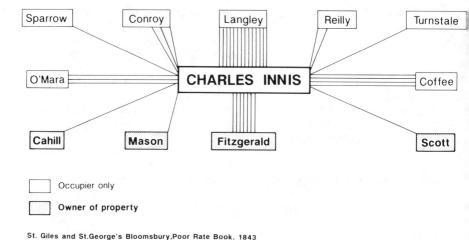

Occupier only

Owner of property

St. Giles and St.George's Bloomsbury,Poor Rate Book, 1843

Figure 1.14 Ownership structure of Charles Innis

were not only recorded as owners of housing but also as occupiers, suggesting that they took an active role in managing their concerns. Moreover, their interests were highly localised, with properties usually concentrated in one or a few neighbouring streets. Robert Hughes's properties, for example, were found in three streets, whilst the 25 houses belonging to John Corwan were located in six streets in the rookery.

By far the largest house owner was Charles Innis, a local solicitor who held a total of 60 houses in St Giles, all but five of which were in the rookery. Innis himself was a house farmer. In addition to owning property he was also recorded as the occupier of three houses in the area. Whilst he took an active role in managing some of his housing, as witnessed by the fact that he was recorded as the owner-occupier of 20 properties, it was more usual for him to sub-let the house to a secondary tenant. His property linkages shown in Figure 1.14 reveal a systematic pattern of letting to a small number of sub-tenants, several of which were local house owners in their own right. Thomas Fitzgerald, himself a 'slumlord' with 13 houses, also sub-let at least seven of Innis's houses. Others, such as Richard Langley, merely underlet houses without actually becoming involved in ownership. The pattern that emerges is complex but nevertheless provides a clear indication of the central role of subletting in the rookery, with the implication that similar patterns were to be found elsewhere in the inner districts.

Income and employment

If the Church Lane rookery represented the archetypal slum, then its inhabitants were similarly representative of the residuum that peopled the courts and alleys of the London slums. Though the area had its own 'aristocracy of labour' of regularly employed workers, including lodging-house keepers, shopkeepers and pawnbrokers, nevertheless the majority of its inhabitants followed more precarious and poorly rewarded livelihoods, such as street trading, service, begging and theft. However, although poverty and insecurity provided the unifying context of slum life, experiences were filtered through differences in occupations, ethnicity, age and gender, resulting in a highly variegated and complex internal ordering of slum life. Just as 'the microscope shows the subdivision of the atom', so too 'a minute enquiry into the various classes subdivides society into unimaginable grades' (Miles, 1839, p.88). The social order of the slum was no exception.

Inhabitants of the Church Lane rookery and other slums in the area derived a precarious livelihood predominantly from unskilled occupations. The demand for labourers, porters, costermongers and street sellers arising from proximity to Covent Garden meant that such groups dominated the occupational structure. In 1851 in St Giles as a whole 9.9 per cent of men were recorded as labourers but in the poorest streets and courts, such as Church Lane and Wild Court, the proportion rose to 54.7 and 41.6 per cent respectively. Hawkers, costermongers and street traders were similarly over-represented. Whilst it is impossible to judge the numbers of street traders from the census abstracts, the enumerators' books show that in Church Lane in 1851 20.6 per cent of men and 61.6 per cent of women were engaged in hawking. In Wild Court the figures were 15.0 and 39.3 per cent respectively. In these two streets alone, labourers and street traders accounted for over 68 per cent of the occupied population with the remainder involved in various manufacturing and construction activities or in different forms of service (Table 1.10).

Occupations of those squeezed out of the labour market and forced onto the poor law reflected the general tendency in the slums for an over-representation of unskilled labour. As shown in Table 1.11, general labouring and manufacturing activities accounted for over half the total number of adult male applicants for poor relief, followed by street trading, construction and services. Female applicants were relatively equally divided between service, manufacturing, charring and hawking, with prostitution also accounting for a significant if somewhat smaller proportion of women. Compared to the overall occupational distribution in St Giles, the occupations of paupers reveal an over-representation of unskilled work compared to an under-representation of more skilled manufacturing employment. Those employed in manufacturing, moreover, were primarily engaged in the cheap, dishonourable sector of slop work in clothing or shoemaking, both of which were characterised by extremely low rates of pay and notoriously bad conditions of work (Alexander, 1983; Bythell, 1978). Needlework, second only to domestic service as the major female trade, was particularly poorly rewarded and many of those employed, as Mayhew claimed, resorted to prostitution to supplement insufficient wages (*Morning Chronicle*, 13 November 1849).

Low wages and insecure employment characterised the host of

Table 1.10 Occupational Structure — St Giles 1851

Occupation	Male		Female		Total	
	Number	Per cent	Number	Per cent	Number	Per cent
Manufacturing	6,992	47.3	2,750	31.7	9,742	41.5
Professional	1,957	13.3	285	3.3	2,242	9.6
General labour	1,463	9.9	72	0.8	1,535	6.5
Food	1,298	8.8	412	4.7	1,710	7.3
Transport	1,120	7.6	66	0.8	1,186	5.1
Domestic service	899	6.1	4,768	55.0	5,667	24.2
Commercial and retail	562	3.8	277	3.2	839	3.6
Agriculture	477	3.2	40	0.5	517	2.2
Total	14,768	100.0	8,670	100.0	23,438	100.0

Source: Census Abstracts 1851

Table 1.11 Occupations of Applicants for Poor Relief 1832–62

Occupations	Male		Female		Total	
	Number	Per cent	Number	Per cent	Number	Per cent
Labour	156	28.2	—	—	156	14.2
Manufacturing	156	28.2	118	21.6	274	24.9
Hawking	56	10.1	97	17.7	153	13.9
Construction	42	7.6	—	—	42	3.8
Service	40	7.2	127	23.2	167	15.2
Charring & Washing	—	—	103	18.8	103	9.4
Prostitution	—	—	45	8.2	45	4.1
Others	103	18.6	57	10.4	160	14.5
Total	553	99.9	547	99.9	1,100	100.0

Source: St Giles and St George's Bloomsbury, Settlement and Examination Books, 1832–62 (1 in 20 sample)

unskilled occupations into which many slum dwellers drifted. Apart from those gatekeepers in the rookery, such as lodging-keepers, pawnbrokers and shopkeepers, few could rely on a regular and sufficient income. Although fluctuations in household earnings associated with the family life-cycle meant that at times individuals and families could rise above the poverty line, escape was usually only temporary. For female-headed households, moreover, such escape was well nigh impossible. Some indication of the particular difficulties faced by women can be gained from Table 1.12 showing average weekly incomes of applicants for relief in St Giles. Although average household incomes were 12s.2d., the experiences of men and women diverged sharply. Whilst less than 28 per

Table 1.12 Household Incomes for Paupers in St Giles 1832–62

Income	Male		Female		Total	
	Number	Per cent	Number	Per cent	Number	Per cent
1s–4s 11d	22	9.6	50	29.6	72	18.1
5s–9s 11d	41	17.8	78	46.2	119	29.8
10s–14s 11d	26	11.3	20	11.8	46	11.5
15s–19s 11d	64	27.8	13	7.7	77	19.3
20s and above	77	33.5	8	4.7	85	21.3
Total	230	100.0	169	100.0	399	100.0

Source: St Giles and St Georges' Bloomsbury Settlement and Examination Books 1832–62 (1 in 20 sample)

cent of male-headed households earned below 10s.0d., this figure rose to nearly 76 per cent for female-headed households. Some of the difference may be accounted for by male-headed households also including the earnings of wives, but a more potent factor was the extremely low earning capacity of women in the Victorian city. The difficulties faced by women as a result of such low wages were in part alleviated by networks of support which developed in slum communities (Ross, 1983). Many, however, turned elsewhere for support, to prostitution as well as the poor law.

Rhythms of poverty

Life in the slum was circumscribed by the uncertainties brought about by powerlessness and inadequate resources. Always liable to live in housing that could be condemned as unfit for human habitation, or to dwell in areas that were ripe for street clearance and demolition, the poor inhabited a physical world over which they had relatively little control. Streets ploughed through the heart of the slums and demolition of poor housing constantly threatened the stability of slum communities during this period. Uncertainty stemming from external factors was compounded by the exigencies arising from the many critical life situations, such as illness, accident or childbirth, that punctuated the lives of the poor. But though seemingly chaotic, slum life was also structured by the rhythms of poverty resulting from weekly, seasonal and cyclical fluctuations in income and employment. The casual nature of much work meant that weekly incomes were rarely adequate and never predictable. Seasonal fluctuations in employment and the cost of living etched out a perennial theme in the lives of the poor, whilst cyclical pressures in the economy provided a deeper context to slum life. Few families escaped these pressures and the shared experience of poverty helped to create a framework within which slum life operated.

At its most general level, the rhythm of poverty was influenced by

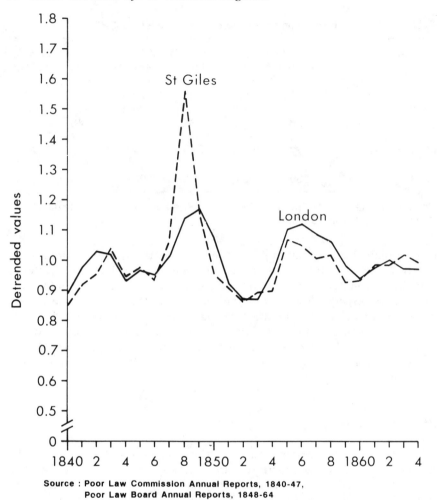

Source : Poor Law Commission Annual Reports, 1840-47,
Poor Law Board Annual Reports, 1848-64

Figure 1.15 Poor law expenditure in St Giles and London 1840-64

cyclical fluctuations in the economy. Though the diversity of the metropolitan economy meant that fluctuations were not as extreme as elsewhere, nevertheless cyclical swings were a marked feature of London's economy and they reverberated to a greater or lesser extent throughout the districts comprising the capital. Expenditure on poor relief, which showed an inverse relationship with economic indicators such as bankruptcies and construction, provides an accurate estimate of the fluctuations in poverty within the city (Green, 1984). During the period from 1840 to 1864 three clear cycles of expenditure occurred in London with peaks in 1841-42, 1848-49 and 1855-56 representing the heights of distress (see Figure 1.15). The pattern in St Giles mirrored the situation elsewhere. The depression of the late 1840s, in particular, appears to have been exceptionally severe, although the rise in expenditure was in part due to the cost of workhouse construction rather than simple pressure of numbers. Local factors also exacerbated the crisis, notably an influx of poverty-stricken Irish immigrants fleeing the famine and a higher level of overcrowding arising from clearances for New Oxford Street. Nevertheless, despite these local factors, St Giles experienced periods of crisis in common with most other districts in the city and these deeper rhythms provided the general context of slum life within the locality.

Superimposed on the deeper rhythms of the economic cycle were the shorter term fluctuations associated with the seasonal nature of London's economy (Jones, 1971; Webb and Freeman, 1912). Though to a limited extent dovetailing of employments could mitigate the worst pressures of seasonality, for many of the poor such opportunities were strictly limited. Operating in already overstocked labour markets, unskilled casual workers had to contend with seasonal influxes of other workers, thereby exacerbating the worst pressures and reducing the likelihood of earning a sufficient income to make ends meet. For most workers, but particularly for those employed in casual occupations, winter was a harsh period. Shorter hours of daylight and interruptions from the weather meant that for a whole host of outdoor trades slack work prevailed: inclement weather and shorter hours interrupted construction and street trading alike, both of which provided a large proportion of casual employment for slum-dwellers. Other casual trades also experienced slack demand during the winter, notably clothing manufacture and shoemaking. Lower earnings, however, were not matched by reduced costs. Indeed, precisely the opposite was the case since the cost of living rose with the need to provide extra light and heat.

In London as a whole the pressures of winter were reflected in higher rates of pauperism. The combination of slack work and higher costs meant that for many slum-dwellers already living close to the margin of poverty, if not beneath it, there was little choice but to seek assistance from friends and relatives, or relief from more formal institutions, notably the Poor Law. During the 1850s the number of paupers in receipt of relief on 1 January usually exceeded the total on 1 July by between 10 and 30 per cent (see Annual Reports of the Poor Law Board). St Giles was no exception and the seasonal rhythm of poverty was well illustrated by the pattern of applications shown in Figure 1.16. The pronounced winter peak is clear, particularly in relation to able-bodied applicants seeking relief on account of want of work or destitution.

The seasonal rhythm of poverty was punctuated by the exigencies of coping with critical life situations, such as birth, death, illness or unemployment, each of which appeared with greater regularity in poorer districts of the city. Higher fertility rates occurred in poorer localities, reflecting the fact both that women in such areas tended to bear larger numbers of children and also that large families were themselves a cause of poverty (Green, 1985, pp.116–18). In every slum, bouts of illness were common and mortality rates high, particularly that of infants. Chadwick's *Sanitary Report* of 1842 had highlighted the extent

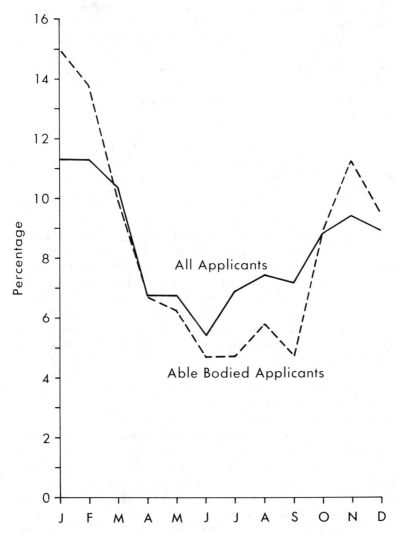

Source : St. Giles and St. George's Bloomsbury, Settlement and Examination Book
(1 in 20 sample)

Figure 1.16 St Giles: seasonal pattern of applications for relief

to which death rates varied according to class and locality, with the highest rates occurring in slum districts such as Bethnal Green and Whitechapel compared to more salubrious parts of the city (BPP 1842, XXVI, pp.159–65). Generalisations, moreover, were borne out by more detailed investigations of specific neighbourhoods. In Church Lane the Statistical Society of London recorded that infant mortality was twice as high as in the suburban district of Islington, and that the rate for children

Table 1.13 Causes of Pauperism in St Giles 1832–62

Cause	Male Number	Per cent	Female Number	Per cent	Total Number	Per cent
Illness, accident, death in family	419	65.1	360	47.6	779	55.6
Childbirth	—	—	160	21.1	160	11.4
Unemployment	76	11.8	48	6.3	124	8.9
Destitution, distress	70	10.9	86	11.4	156	11.1
Main wage-earner absent	24	3.7	33	4.3	57	4.1
Old age, infirmity	20	3.1	22	2.9	42	3.0
Insanity	11	1.7	8	1.1	19	1.4
Others	24	3.7	40	5.3	64	4.5
Total	644	100.0	757	100.0	1,401	100.0

Source: St Giles and St George's Bloomsbury Settlement and Examination Books, 1832–62 (1 in 20 sample)

aged between one and two years old was more than six times as high (Mann, 1848, p.22–4). Mortality, however, was merely a superficial manifestation of a far larger amount of morbidity which struck with monotonous regularity the population of slum districts. In St Giles between 1 July 1847 and 27 January 1848, only 2 out of 88 persons who received medical treatment in the workhouse on account of typhus died (ibid, p.24). A similar ratio was recorded for Bethnal Green for approximately the same period (Gavin, 1848, pp.94–5).

The regularity with which illness and death, not to mention unemployment and underemployment, struck slum communities is evident from the figures shown in Table 1.13. If childbirth is included together with illness, accident or death of the main wage earner, nearly two-thirds of pauperism was attributable to reasons of morbidity or mortality. For women the workhouse provided an alternative to the lying-in hospital and over one in five of those admitted gave birth there. For the remainder of applicants, the majority of which were able-bodied, unemployment or destitution were cited as the main reasons for poverty and although this probably underestimates their true extent within slum communities, the situation is consistent with the avowed antipathy of the Poor Law towards able-bodied paupers and the reluctance of such a group to apply for relief.

Without reserves to tide over such crises, the poor were forced to seek assistance either from informal contacts, such as friends, relatives and neighbours, or from more formal channels of credit such as local pawnbrokers or shopkeepers. When these avenues of aid were closed there was, finally, private philanthropy and the Poor Law.

Neighbourhood and community

As befitted the precariousness of working-class life, residential shifts were a common feature in poor communities. The need to tailor the costs of accommodation to uncertain incomes necessitated frequent moves, albeit often within the immediate locality. Credit with landlords may have sufficed to tide over temporary shortfalls in rent but often even this reprieve was shortlived and families were soon forced to vacate lodgings for cheaper accommodation elsewhere. Moonlight flits, often as much to avoid arrears of rent as to safeguard furniture from the bailiffs, were all too common. But despite the restless mobility which pervaded working-class communities, there was nevertheless a degree of stability founded upon the restricted spatial scale of movement. (Booth, 1902, First Series, Poverty, I, p.81; Lawton and Pooley, 1975; Pooley, 1979.) Overall population turnover in working-class districts was slow, and people remained if not in the same house, then at least in the same street or locality for lengthy periods of time, allowing the formation of close social ties born from spatial propinquity. In such a context of residential stability, communities bound together by links of reciprocity, kinship and ethnicity flourished.

Slum-dwellers in St Giles reflected both the fears of contemporaries and the underlying reality of working-class communities. The Church Lane rookery and the poorer streets had a dubious reputation for housing a shifting population of tramps and thieves (Miles, 1839, pp.155-6). In Monmouth Court during the winter of 1861, Joseph Oppenheimer, the London City Missionary for the area, recorded that more than half the population changed each month, 'so that I seldom meet the same people again.' (Oppenheimer, 6 February 1862.) In the rest of the rookery, it was claimed, transient lodgers were at least as numerous as the regulars (Beames, 1850, p.48). Against this image of transiency and shiftlessness, however, needs to be set an alternative view, borne out by the pattern of applications to the Poor Law, which hints at a more settled community of the poor, characterised by common bonds of ethnicity, kinship and propinquity and linked together by networks of aid and credit.

In their investigations of the Church Lane rookery in 1848, the Statistical Society noted how despite the poverty of the Irish population the majority were long-term residents of London (Statistical Society of London, 1848a, p.16). Even in the lodging-houses, although a good proportion of the inhabitants were merely passing through, half the residents were thought to have been regulars (Miles, 1839, p.95). The suggestion that despite poverty and transiency a relatively permanent community persisted in the rookery is borne out with reference to the Poor Law, applicants to which had to provide details of previous residence in order to satisfy requirements for the receipt of relief. Until 1847 rights to relief depended on obtaining a settlement in an area, determined usually by birth, marriage or service. After that date, however, it became possible to establish a claim for relief based on continuous residence in an area for five years, later reduced to one year.

Table 1.14 Length of Residence in St Giles by Birthplace in Ireland or Great Britain (adults aged over 15)

	Less than 1 year		1-2 years		2-5 years		5-10 years		Over 10 years	
	Number	Per cent	Number	Per cent	Number	Per cent	Number	Per cent	Number	Per cent
Great Britain	53	18.2	17	5.8	40	13.7	60	20.5	122	41.8
Ireland	65	30.9	21	10.0	23	11.0	23	11.0	78	37.1
Total	118	23.5	38	7.6	63	12.6	83	16.5	200	39.8

Source: St Giles and and St George's Bloomsbury, Settlement and Examination Books, 1832–62 (1 in 20 sample)

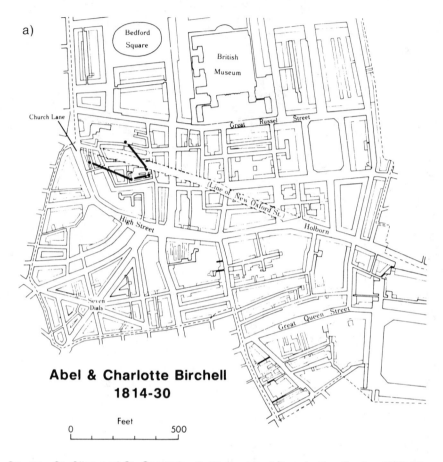

Abel & Charlotte Birchell
1814-30

Source : St. Giles and St. George's, Settlement and Examination Books, 1832-62

Figure 1.17 St Giles: residential mobility of the poor (a–d)

The need to satisfy residency requirements meant that the local Poor Law undertook detailed investigations of the pattern of residential mobility of applicants for relief. It becomes clear from this data that although residential mobility was relatively frequent, the majority of the poor maintained a long term residence in the area.

As shown in Table 1.14, despite the fact that nearly a quarter of the applicants for poor relief had been in St Giles for less than one year, representing primarily a shiftless substrata of tramps, vagrants and in the 1840s recent Irish immigrants, over half the total applicants had resided in the district for longer than five years, representing a much more stable

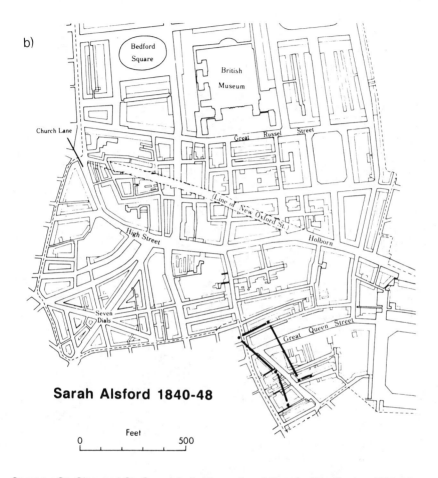

Sarah Alsford 1840-48

Feet
0   500

Source : St. Gies and St. George's,Settlement and Examination Books, 1832-62

Figure 1.17(b)

group amongst the poor. Though English-born paupers formed the larger proportion of this settled group, nevertheless nearly half the Irish who sought relief had also been in the area for over five years. Long-term residence, however, did not preclude rapid residential mobility and shifts of accommodation were relatively frequent within working-class communities, even though most moves were for short distances (Statistical Society of London, 1840, 1848a). High rates of residential turnover, however, did not necessarily imply an impermanent community. The neighbourhood provided a frame-work and the main context of life for slum-dwellers. Tied to localities by social networks revolving around

c)

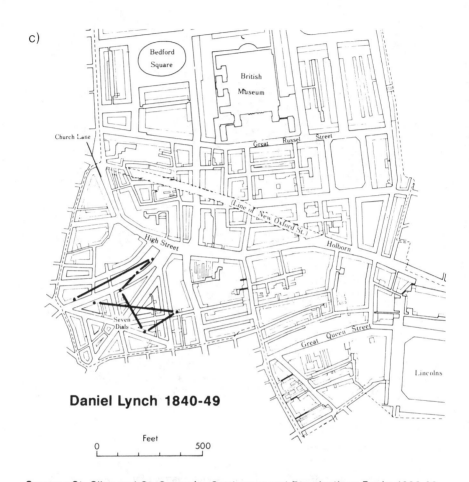

Daniel Lynch 1840-49

Feet
0   500

Source : St. Giles and St. George's, Settlement and Examinations Books,1832-62

Figure 1.17(c)

employment, credit and the poor law, working-class households frequently remained in the same area for lengthy periods of time despite the frequency of residential shifts.

At a more detailed level of analysis, however, the distinction between the district as a whole and individual neighbourhoods becomes apparent. The physical context of court and back street living provided an enclosed spatial world within which much of the daily activity associated with slum life occurred (Carter and Wheatley, 1980). The neighbourhood in this case consisted of no more than a handful of streets within which social relationships were formed and residential mobility took place. As

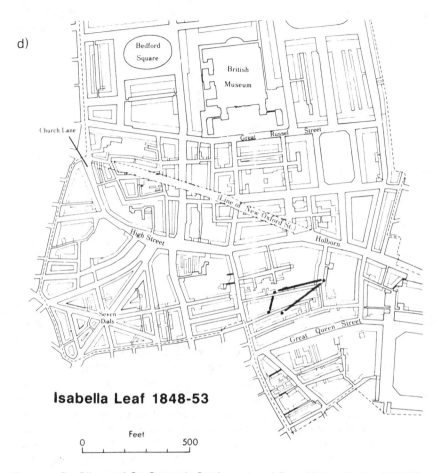

Isabella Leaf 1848-53

Feet

0 ⊢⊣⊢⊣⊢⊣⊢⊣⊣ 500

Source : St. Giles and St. George's,Settlement and Examination Books,1832-62

Figure 1.17(d)

shown in Figures 1.17 (a–d) paupers tended to remain within their immediate locality, often returning after several moves close to their original starting point.

Proximity, moreover, fostered kinship links and social relations and as a result dense social networks were built up between neighbours, kin and friends within such small enclosed worlds. That social networks were established within the slum was apparent from the pattern of contacts maintained by the poor. Applicants for relief were asked to give a reference to vouch for the veracity of their situation and in approximately half the cases this information was provided. In the minority of

Table 1.15 Social Contacts in St Giles 1832–62

Address of Contact	Kin*		Others**		Total	
	Number	Per cent	Number	Per cent	Number	Per cent
Same or previous address	92	10.5	76	8.7	168	19.2
St Giles	94	10.7	103	11.8	197	22.5
London	140	16.0	63	7.2	203	23.2
Elsewhere/ unspecified	115	13.1	43	4.9	158	18.0
Total	441	50.3	285	32.6	726	82.9
(Unknown to anyone					150	17.1)

 * Excluding husbands or wives
** Including employers, landlords and others of no stated relationship

Source: St Giles and St George's Bloomsbury Settlement and Examination Book 1832–1862 (1 in 20 sample)

cases the applicant was unknown within the area and the situation was recorded as such. Although not necessarily evidence of an active relationship, nevertheless the name of a reference was indicative of some form of social contact and therefore can be used to assess the existence of neighbourhood and kinship links. The pattern of contacts, shown in Table 1.15, reveals that kinship was central to the social networks with over half the applicants maintaining some form of kinship links, the majority of which were either within St Giles or elsewhere in London. Within the district, over one in five paupers were either living with kin or had lived with them at a previous address in the district. Nor was kinship the only form of local contact; employers, landlords and other persons were also called upon to act as references for applicants and again the majority of these were located either at the same address or elsewhere in the district. Treated in conjunction with the other evidence, the pattern of contacts suggests that far from being a place of transiency and anonymity, where a person might sink into the crevices of the city, for many inhabitants the slum was the location of a close and spatially bounded social network dominated by kinship linkages and focused primarily on the immediate residence and local neighbourhood.

Conclusion

Viewed from the outside, the world of the urban poor was shrouded in uniform shades of grey. Those who commented on the slums at mid-century saw the poor as an undifferentiated mass leading lives of drab uniformity in conditions which almost belied the possibility of maintaining a decent existence. The coarseness and vulgarity of slum life was reflected in the characteristics of those forced to endure the conditions. This opinion was shared not only by radical thinkers, such as Marx and Engels, but also by those of a more conservative bent, such as Disraeli and Carlyle. Indeed, all were in agreement that the brutishness of slum life dominated and indeed overwhelmed all other aspects of existence.

In part this view was the outcome of the physical realities of the nineteenth-century city in which decaying inner-city environments were complemented by social polarisation and spatial segregation. The slums themselves—often ill-drained quagmires pervaded by the stench of sewage and decaying matter, overfilled with a seemingly innumerable and largely unwashed population, rooms which housed both people and vermin and sometimes also animals—these places of the lower depths were hardly conducive to detailed investigations by anyone save relieving officers, police or city missionaries. Social polarisation and spatial segregation, resulting in increasingly privatised and secluded spheres of activity, effectively created a situation in which contact with, and knowledge of, the urban poor on the part of the middle class was both fleeting and partial. Under such circumstances accounts of the slums were rarely able to do more than paint a picture of poverty in the mass in which the colour of slum life was transformed to a monochrome representation of a much richer and varied fabric.

Viewed from the inside, however, the lumpenproletariat were anything but 'lumpen'. Although inhabitants of the lower depths shared a common bond of poverty, nevertheless individuals participated to varying degrees in communities based on age, ethnicity, gender, occupation and place. Experiences of slum life were filtered through this complex and interrelated pattern of internal stratification. It was all too simple for the urban bourgeoisie to ignore these distinctions in the face of what appeared to be a crushing uniformity born of poverty. But as we have indicated here, such internal stratification was indeed a significant facet of slum life. Minute differentials in income related to age, gender and occupation were critical when life was conducted as a hand-to-mouth existence. Ethnicity, too, not only structured opportunities for employment but also represented a set of cultural and social resources from which individuals drew support. Finally, the encapsulated world of the urban poor, reflected in the tightly constrained spatial scale of life focused on the court and street, provided a basis upon which reciprocity could function.

All this adds substance to form, transforming our understanding of the slums from that of a mere container of the poor to the stage for a varied and complex set of economic, social and cultural relationships. Unravelling the threads which comprised slum life requires a keen attention to detail and an ear for the muted tones of the urban poor as they went about their daily lives. Only whispers of their existence remain in the historical record but we have only to listen to the silence in order to learn the lessons so crucial for the present.

References

Primary sources

a) National

Census enumerators' books, St Giles and St George's Bloomsbury, 1851 (HO 107)
Census enumerators' books, Birmingham, 1851 (HO 107)
Poor Law Commission, Annual reports 1837, 1838, 1842, 1843
Poor Law Board, Annual reports 1848

b) London

Association for Promoting the Relief of Destitution in the Metropolis, Annual reports, 1858, 1866
Diary of Joseph Oppenheimer, London City Missionary 1861–62 (St Giles parish church)
St Giles and St George's Bloomsbury, Board of Guardians, Settlement and Examination Books, 1832–62
St Giles and St George's Bloomsbury, Board of works, Annual Reports, 1856–69
St Giles and St George's Bloomsbury, Board of works, Minutes, 1867
St Giles and St George's Bloomsbury, Poor Rate Books, 1843
Society for the Suppression of Mendicity, Annual Reports, 1819, 1830, 1832, 1841

c) Birmingham

A list of the out-poor chargeable upon the parish of Birmingham, 1 January 1847
An alphabetical list of the out-poor receiving pay in the parish of Birmingham, 6 September 1822
Birmingham Coal and Coke Society, Rules, 1850
Board of Guardians' Minutes, 1846, 1847
Good Intent Friendly Society (Birmingham), rules and regulations, 1841, 1856
Guardians of the poor, rules and regulations, 1841
Medical Officer of Health, Second Annual Report, 1860
Poor Rate Books, 1847, 1851
Report of the artisans' dwellings committee of Birmingham Corporation, 1884
Street Commissioners' Minutes, 1847

Newspapers

Builder, 1853, 1854
Morning Chronicle, 1840, 1849
Poor Man's Guardian
The Times

British Parliamentary Papers

BPP 1833 VI *Select committee on manufactures, commerce and shipping*
BPP 1836 XX *Select committee on metropolis improvements*
BPP 1840 XI *Select committee on the health of large towns*
BPP 1842 XXVI *Report to her majesty's principal secretary of state for the Home Department on an inquiry into the sanitary condition of the labouring population of Great Britain (House of Lords)*
BPP 1842 XXVII *Local reports on the sanitary condition of the labouring population of Great Britain (House of Lords)*

BPP 1844 XVII *Royal commission for inquiring into the state of large towns and populous districts*

BPP 1845 XVII *Appendix part II to the second report of the commission of inquiry into the state of large towns and populous districts*

BPP 1845 XVIII *Royal commission for inquiring into the state of large towns and populous districts*

BPP 1851 XXIII *Report made to the Board of Health in reference to the sanitary condition of Agar Town, St Pancras*

BPP 1852-3 LXXVIII *Copy of supplemental report on common lodging houses by Captain Hay, commissioner of police, made to the secretary of state*

BPP 1854 XXXV *Second report made to the secretary of state for the Home department by Captain William Hay on the operation of the Common Lodging Houses Act*

BPP 1854-5 XLV *Report on the common and model lodging houses of the metropolis (with reference to epidemic cholera in 1854) by George Glover*

BPP 1862 X *Select committee on poor relief: third report*

BPP 1866 XXXIII *Eighth report of the medical officer of the Privy Council (report by Dr Julian Hunter on the housing of the poorer parts of the population in towns)*

BPP 1882 VII *Select committee on artisans' and labourers' dwellings improvement*

BPP 1884-5 XXX *Royal commission on the housing of the working classes*

Contemporary books and articles

Adshead, J., 1842, *Distress in Manchester: evidence of the state of the labouring classes*, Hooper, London

Beames, T., 1850, *The rookeries of London: past, present and prospective*, Bosworth, London

Bigland, J., 1813, *A Topographical and historical description of Yorkshire*, Sherwood, Neeley & Jones, London

Black, C., 1915, *Married women's work*, Bell, London (reprinted Virago, London, 1983)

Booth, C., 1902, *Life and labour of the people of London*, Macmillan, London

Bosanquet, S.R., 1841, *The rights of the poor and Christian almsgiving vindicated*, Burns, London

Carlyle, T., 1840, *Chartism*, Fraser, London

Carpenter, M., 1851, *Reformatory schools for the children of the perishing and dangerous classes and for juvenile offenders*, Gilpin, London

Cochrane, C., 1849, *How to improve the homes of the people*, published by the author, London

Cooper, C.P., 1850, *Papers respecting the sanitary state of the part of the parish of St Giles in the Fields, London*, Newman, London

Cowan, R., 1840, 'Vital statistics of Glasgow illustrating the sanitary conditions of the population', *Journal of the Royal Statistical Society*, 3: 257-92

Dickens, C., 1854, *Hard times*, (Penguin, Harmondsworth, reprinted 1952)

Disraeli, B., 1845, *Sybil*, (Oxford University Press, London, reprinted 1926)

Edgell, E.W., 1838, 'Moral statistics of the parishes of St James, St George and St Anne, Soho, in the City of Westminster', *Journal of the Royal Statistical Society of London*, 1: 478-92

Fallows, J.A., 1899, *Facts for Birmingham—the housing of the poor*, Midland Socialist Pamphlets 1, Birmingham

Fallows, J.A. and F. Hughes, 1905, *The housing question in Birmingham*, Birmingham

Faucher, L., 1844, *Manchester in 1844: its present condition and future prospects*, (Cass, London, reprinted 1969)

Felkin, W., 1837, *Remarks upon the importance of an inquiry into the amount and appropriation of wages by the working classes*, British Association, London

Felkin, W., 1838, 'Moral statistics of a district near Gray's Inn, London, in 1836', *Journal of the Royal Statistical Society*, 1: 541–2

Fletcher, J., 1844, 'The metropolis: its boundaries, extent and divisions for local government', *Journal of the Royal Statistical Society*, 7: 69–85, 103–43

Garwood, J., 1853, *The million peopled city—or one half of the people of London made known to the other half*, Wertheim & Macintosh, London

Gaskell, E., 1854, *North and south*, (Dent, London, reprinted 1914)

Gaspey, W., 1851–52, *Tallis's illustrated London*, J. Tallis & Co., London

Gavin, H., 1848, *Sanitary ramblings, being sketches and illustrations of Bethnal Green*, Churchill, London

Gavin, H., 1850, *The habitations of the industrial classes*, Society for Improving the Condition of the Labouring Classes, London

Godwin, G., 1859, *Town swamps and social bridges*, Routledge, Warnes & Routledge, London (reprinted Leicester University Press, Leicester, 1972)

Grant, J., 1842, *Lights and shadows of London life*, Saunders & Otley, London

Hill, M., 1869, 'On the dwellings of the labouring poor in Birmingham', *Transactions of the National Association for the Promotion of Social Science*

Jaffray, J., 1857, *Hints for a history of Birmingham, cuttings from the Birmingham Journal 1855–56*, Birmingham

Jerrold, D., 1851, *The Writings of Douglas Jerrold*, vol. 1, Bradbury & Evans, London

Kay, J.P., 1832, *The moral and physical condition of the working classes employed in the cotton manufacture in Manchester*, J. Ridgeway, London

Langford, J., 1847, *The advantages of co-operation*, address to the members of the Birmingham Co-operative League, Birmingham

Lhotky, J., 1844, *On cases of death by starvation and extreme distress among the humbler classes*, Oliver, London

Mann, H., 1848, 'Statement of mortality prevailing in Church Lane during the last ten years with the sickness of the last seven months', *Journal of the Royal Statistical Society*, 11: 19–24

Mayhew, H., 1861, *London labour and the London poor*, 4 volumes, Griffin Bohn, London (reprinted Constable, London, 1968)

Miles, W.A., 1839, *Poverty, mendicity and crime*, Shaw & sons, London

Nettlefold, J.S., 1905, *A housing policy*, Cornish Brothers Ltd., Birmingham

Nunns, T., 1842, *A letter to the right honourable Lord Ashley on the condition of the working classes in Birmingham*, Langbridge, Birmingham

Parker, J., 1853, 'On the literature of the working classes', in *Meliora*, edited by Talbot, C.J.C., 181–97

Pember Reeves, M., 1912, *Round about a pound a week*, Bell & sons, London (reprinted Virago, London, 1979)

Rawson, R., 1843, 'Results of some inquiries into the condition and education of the poorer classes in the parish of Marylebone in 1838', *Journal of the Royal Statistical Society*, 6: 44–8

Saunders, J., 1844, 'A parting glimpse of St Giles', *Illuminated Magazine*, 3: 79–84

Statistical Society of London, 1837-38, 'Report on 4,102 working families of men in certain districts of the town of Manchester', *Proceedings of the Statistical Society of London*, 1: 1-2

Statistical Society of London, 1840, 'Report of the committee of the council of the Statistical Society of London on the state of the working classes in the parishes of St Margaret and St John Westminster', *Journal of the Royal Statistical Society*, 3: 14-24

Statistical Society of London, 1848a, 'Report of the committee of the council of the Statistical Society of London to investigate the state of the inhabitants and their dwellings in Church Lane, St Giles', *Journal of the Royal Statistical Society*, 11: 1-18

Statistical Society of London, 1848b, 'Investigation into the state of the poorer classes in St George's-in-the-East', *Journal of the Royal Statistical Society*, 11: 193-249

Symmons, J.C., 1849, *Tactics for the times as regards the condition and treatment of the dangerous classes*, Oliver, London

Timmins, S., 1866, *The resources, products and the industrial history of Birmingham and the Midland hardware district*, Robert Harwicke, London

Vaughan, R., 1843, *The age of great cities*, Jackson & Walford, London

Wakefield, E.G., 1831, *Households in danger of the populace*, Wilson, London

Walters, J.C., 1901, *Scenes in slumland*, reprinted from *Birmingham Daily Gazette*, Daily Gazette Co. Ltd., Birmingham

Webb, S. and A. Freeman (eds), 1912, *The seasonal trades*, Constable, London

Weir, W., 1842, 'St Giles, past and present', in *London*, vol. 3, edited by Knight, C., 266-7

Weld, C.R., 1843, 'On the condition of the working classes in the inner ward of St George's parish, Hanover Square', *Journal of the Royal Statistical Society*, 6: 17-27

Williams, R., 1893, *London rookeries and colliers' slums: a plea for more breathing room*, Reeves, London

Secondary works

Alexander, S., 1983, *Women's work in nineteenth-century London: a study of the years 1820-50*, Journeyman Press, London

Allen, G.C., 1929, *The industrial development of Birmingham and the Black Country, 1860-1927*, George Allen & Unwin, London

Anderson, M., 1971, *Family structure in nineteenth-century Lancashire*, Cambridge University Press, Cambridge

Beresford, M., 1967, *Leeds and its region*, Edward Arnold, London

Beresford, M., 1971, 'The back-to-back house in Leeds 1787-1937', in *The history of working-class housing*, edited by Chapman, S.D., 93-132

Bramwell, W., 1984, 'Pubs and localised communities in mid-Victorian Birmingham', *Queen Mary College, Department of Geography*, occasional paper, 22

Briggs, A., 1952, *History of Birmingham*, vol. 2, Oxford University Press, London

Burnett, J., 1986, *A social history of housing 1815-1985*, Methuen, London

Bythell, D., 1978, *The sweated trades: outwork in nineteenth-century Britain*, Batsford, London

Cairncross, A.K. and B. Weber, 1956-57, 'Fluctuations in building in Great Britain', *Economic History Review*, second series, 9: 283-97

Cannadine, D., 1980, *Lords and Landlords: the aristocracy and the towns 1774–1967*, Leicester University Press, Leicester

Carter, H. and S. Wheatley, 1979, 'Fixation lines and fringe belts, land uses and social areas: nineteenth-century change in the small town', *Transactions of the Institute of British Geographers*, New series, 4(2): 214–38

Carter, H. and S. Wheatley, 1980, 'Residential segregation in nineteenth-century cities', *Area*, 12: 57–62

Chapman, S.D. (ed.), 1971, *The history of working-class housing*, David & Charles, Newton Abbott

Chilton, C., 1965, *Victorian folk songs*, Essex Music, London

Cullen, M.J., 1975, *The statistical movement in early Victorian Britain*, Harvester Press, Hassocks

Dennis, R.J., 1977, 'Intercensal mobility in a Victorian city', *Transactions of the Institute of British Geographers*, New series, 2(3): 349–63

Dennis, R.J., 1979, 'The Victorian city', *Transactions of the Institute of British Geographers*, New series, 4(2): 125–7

Dennis, R.J., 1984, *English industrial cities of the nineteenth century*, Cambridge University Press, Cambridge

Dennis, R.J. and S. Daniels, 1981, '"Community" and the social geography of Victorian cities', *Urban History Yearbook*, 7–23

Dyos, H.J., 1955–56, 'Railways and housing in Victorian London', *Journal of Transport History*, 2: 11–21

Dyos, H.J., 1957, 'Urban transformation: a note on the objects of street improvement in Regency and early Victorian London', *International Review of Social History*, 2: 259–65

Dyos, H.J., 1967, 'The slums of Victorian London', *Victorian Studies*, 11: 5–40

Dyos, H.J. and D. Reeder, 1973, 'Slums and suburbs', in *The Victorian city: images and realities* edited by Dyos, H.J. and M. Wolff, Routledge & Kegan Paul, London, 359–86

Engels, F., 1973, *The condition of the working class in England*, Lawrence & Wishart, London

Englander, D., 1983, *Landlord and tenant in urban Britain 1838–1918*, Clarendon Press, Oxford

Finnegan, F., 1982, *Poverty and prejudice: a study of Irish immigrants in York 1840–1875*, Cork University Press, Cork

Flinn, M., 1974, 'Trends in real wages 1750–1850', *Economic History Review*, second series, 27: 395–413

Flint, K. (ed.), 1987, *The Victorian novelist: social problems and social change*, Croom Helm, London

Forster, C.A., 1972, 'Court housing in Kingston-upon-Hull', *University of Hull*, occasional papers in geography, 19

Fraser, D., 1980, *A history of modern Leeds*, Manchester University Press, Manchester

Gauldie, E., 1974, *Cruel habitations*, George Allen & Unwin, London

Gayer, A., W. Rostow and A. Schwarz, 1953, *Growth and fluctuation of the British economy 1790–1850*, Clarendon Press, Oxford

George, M.D., 1966, *London life in the eighteenth century*, Penguin, Harmondsworth

Gill, C., 1952, *History of Birmingham*, vol. 1, Oxford University Press, London

Gilley, S.W., 1973, 'The Garibaldi riots of 1862', *Historical Journal*, 16(4): 697–732

Green, D.R., 1982, 'Street trading in London: a case study of casual labour

1830–60', *The structure of nineteenth-century cities*, edited by Johnson, J. and C. Pooley, Croom Helm, London, 129–52

Green, D.R., 1985, 'A map for Mayhew's London: the geography of poverty in the mid-nineteenth century', *London Journal*, 11(2): 115–26

Harrison, B., 1965, 'The Sunday trading riots of 1855', *Historical Journal*, 8(2): 219–45

Himmelfarb, G., 1971, 'Mayhew's poor: a problem of identity', *Victorian Studies*, 14(3): 307–20

Himmelfarb, G., 1973, 'The culture of poverty', in *The Victorian city* edited by Dyos, H.J. and M. Wolff, Routledge & Kegan Paul, London, 707–38

Himmelfarb, G., 1984, *The idea of poverty*, Faber & Faber, London

Hollingshed, J., 1986, *Ragged London in 1861*, Dent, London (first edition 1861)

Holloway, J. and J. Black, 1979, *Later English broadside ballads*, Routledge & Kegan Paul, London

Humphreys, A., 1977, *Travels into the poor man's country*, Caliban, Firle

Johnson, P., 1985, *Saving and spending: the working-class economy in Britain 1870–1939*, Clarendon Press, Oxford

Jones, G.S., 1971, *Outcast London: a study in the relationships between classes in Victorian society*, Oxford University Press, Oxford

Keating, P.J., 1976, *Into unknown England 1866–1913: selections from the social explorers*, Fontana, Glasgow

Kemp, P., 1982a, 'Housing landlordism in nineteenth-century Britain', *Environment and Planning A*, 14: 1437–47

Kemp, P., 1982b, 'House property as capital: private rental housing in the late Victorian city', *University of Sussex, Department of Urban and Regional Studies*, working paper, 29

Kondratieff, N., 1935, 'The long waves in economic life', *Review of Economics and Statistics*, 17: 105–50

Lawton, R., 1978, 'Population and society 1730–1900', in *An historical geography of England and Wales*, edited by Dodgshon, R. and R. Butlin, Academic Press, London, 313–66

Lawton, R. and C. Pooley, 1975, 'David Brindley's Liverpool: an aspect of urban society in the 1880s', *Transactions of the Historical Society of Lancashire and Cheshire*, 125: 149–68

Lees, L., 1985, *Cities perceived: urban society in European and American thought*, Manchester University Press, Manchester

Lees, L., 1969, 'Patterns of lower class life in Irish slum communities in nineteenth-century London', in *Nineteenth century cities* edited by Thernstrom, S. and R. Sennett, Yale University Press, New Haven: 359–85

Lees, L., 1976, 'Mid-Victorian migration and the Irish family economy', *Victorian Studies*, 20(1): 25–43

Lees, L., 1979, *Exiles of Erin: Irish immigrants in Victorian London*, Manchester University Press, Manchester

Lewis, O., 1965, *La Vida: a Puerto Rican family in the culture of poverty—San Juan and New York*, Random House, New York

Lewis, O., 1970, *Anthropological Essays*, Random House, New York

Ley, D., 1974, 'The black inner City as frontier outpost: images and behaviour of a Philadelphia neighbourhood', *Association of American Geographers*, monograph series, no. 7, Washington, D.C.

Liebow, E., 1967, *Tally's corner*, Little, Brown & Co., Boston

Malcomson, P., 1976, 'Getting a living in the slums of Victorian Kensington', *London Journal*, 2(1): 28–55

Mandel, E., 1980, *Long waves of capitalist development*, Cambridge University Press, Cambridge

Marx, K. and F. Engels, 1968, *Selected Works*, Lawrence & Wishart, London

O'Brien, P.K. and S. Engerman, 1981, 'Changes in income and its distribution during the industrial revolution', in *The Economic history of Britain since 1700*, volume 1, edited by Floud, R. and D. McCloskey, Cambridge University Press, Cambridge, 164–81

Pooley, C., 1979, 'Residential mobility in the Victorian city', *Transactions of the Institute of British Geographers*, new series, 4(2): 258–78

Power, M.J., 1978, 'East and West in early-modern London', in *Wealth and power in Tudor England*, edited by Ives, E.W., R. Knecht and J. Scarisbrick, Athlone Press, London, 167–85

Power, M.J., 1985, 'The social topography of Restoration London', in *The Making of the Metropolis*, edited by Beier, A.L. and R. Finlay, Longmans, London, 199–223

Richardson, C., 1968, 'Irish settlement in mid-nineteenth century Bradford', *Yorkshire Bulletin of Economic and Social Research*, 20(1): 40–57

Robb, J.G., 1983, 'Suburb and slum in Gorbals: social and residential change 1800–1900', in *Scottish urban history*, edited by Gordon, G. and B. Dicks, Aberdeen University Press, Aberdeen, 130–67

Roberts, R., 1971, *The Classic Slum*, Penguin, Harmondsworth

Rose, M., 1976, 'Settlement, removal and the New Poor Law', in *The New Poor Law in the nineteenth century*, edited by Fraser, D., Macmillan, London

Ross, E., 1982, '"Fierce questions and taunts": married life in working-class London 1870–1914', *Feminist Studies*, 3: 575–602

Ross, E., 1983, 'Survival networks: women's neighbourhood sharing in London before world war one', *History Workshop Journal*, 15: 4–27

Samuel, R., 1973, 'Comers and goers', in *The Victorian City* edited by Dyos, H.J. and M. Wolff, Routledge & Kegan Paul, London, 126–60

Schwarz, L.D., 1982, 'Social class and social geography: the middle classes in London at the end of the eighteenth century', *Social History*, 7(2): 166–85

Shannon, H.A., 1934, 'Bricks—a trade index 1785–1849', *Economica*, new series, 1: 300–18

Sheppard, F., V. Belcher and P. Cottrell, 1979, 'The Middlesex and Yorkshire deeds registries and the study of building fluctuations', *London Journal*, 5(2): 176–212

Sponza, L., 1988, *Italians in nineteenth-century Britain: realities and images*, Leicester University Press, Leicester

Suttles, G., 1968, *The Social Order of the Slum*, University of Chicago Press, London

Taylor, I.C., 1974, 'The insanitary housing question and tenement dwellings in nineteenth-century Liverpool', in *Multi-storey living*, edited by Sutcliffe, A., Croom Helm, London, 41–87

Tebbutt, M., 1983, *Making ends meet: pawnbroking and working-class credit*, Leicester University Press, Leicester

Thompson, E.P., 1967, 'The political education of Henry Mayhew', *Victorian Studies*, 11(1): 41–62

Thompson, E.P., 1973, 'Mayhew and the Morning Chronicle', in *The Unknown Mayhew* edited by Thompson, E.P. and E. Yeo, Penguin, Harmondsworth, 9–55

Townley, J.F. et al., 1988, 'Death and disease in early modern Birmingham', *University of Birmingham*, Department of Extra-Mural studies

Tristan, F., 1982, *The London diary of Flora Tristan*, Virago, London (first edition 1842)

Tucker, R., 1936, 'Real wages of artisans in London 1729–1935', *Journal of the American Statistical Association*, 31: 73–84

Valentine, C., 1968, *Culture and poverty: critique and counter proposals*, Chicago University Press, Chicago

Vance, J.E., 1967, 'Housing the worker: determinant and contingent ties in nineteenth-century Birmingham', *Economic Geography*, 43: 95–127

White, J., 1980, *Rothschild Buildings: life in an East End tenement block 1887–1920*, Routledge & Kegan Paul, London

White, J., 1986, *The worst street in north London: Campbell Bunk, Islington, between the wars*, Routledge & Kegan Paul, London

Williams, K., 1981, *From pauperism to poverty*, Routledge & Kegan Paul, London

Wise, M.J., 1948, *Birmingham and its regional setting*, Buckler & Webb, Birmingham

Wohl, A.S., 1971, 'The housing of the working classes in London 1815–1914', in *The History of working-class housing* edited by Chapman, S.D., 13–54

Wohl, A.S., 1977, *The eternal slum: housing and social policy in Victorian London*, Edward Arnold, London

Yelling, J., 1986, *Slums and slum clearance in Victorian London*, George Allen & Unwin, London

Yeo, E., 1973, 'Mayhew as social investigator', in *The unknown Mayhew*, edited by Thompson, E.P. and E. Yeo, Penguin, Harmondsworth, 56–109

Young, M. and P. Willmott, 1957, *Family and kinship in East London*, Penguin, Harmondsworth

Unpublished theses and reports

Green, D.R., 1984, 'From artisans to paupers: the manufacture of poverty in mid-nineteenth century London', Ph.D dissertation, University of Cambridge

Matthews, M.H. and A.G. Parton, 1982, 'The geography of poverty in mid-nineteenth century Birmingham: a pilot survey', Report to the Social Studies Research Council

Acknowledgement

The authors would like to thank the Central Research Fund of the University of London for their grant towards the cost of completing this research.

2 The rural slum

Gordon Mingay

I

The term 'slum' is usually construed in a strictly urban sense, and indeed a standard dictionary definition reads: 'Dirty back street or court or alley in city'. Nonetheless, there were in many country towns of the past dirty backstreets, courts and alleys, and even in small villages groups of cottages which in terms of defective construction, dilapidated condition, inadequacy of water supply and sanitation, overcrowding, polluted atmosphere and general unhealthiness would rank equal to city slums in everything but extent. As Seebohm Rowntree was to remark in 1913, the cottages 'might very often have been transplanted, singly or in rows, from some cheerless little street in a sordid city area'.[1]

As in the cities, or even more so, the housing of the countryside exhibited great variety. Partly this arose from differences in the age of dwellings, but more from the regional differences in building materials and building styles. When Rowntree was investigating rural conditions just before the Great War, the cottages ranged in age from survivals of the seventeenth and even earlier centuries down to numbers of quite modern construction, some of them boasting three or four bedrooms and modern conveniences of piped water supply, drainage and sewage disposal. The regional variations reflected the local distribution of building materials, with limestone and sandstone common in the north, limestone over large parts of the midlands, sandstone and timber in the west country and the south-west, scattered flint, chalk, clay and sandstone over East Anglia and the central south, and timber in the weald of Kent and Sussex. Bricks had come to be used in the sixteenth century, though at first largely to provide only footing walls and to strengthen or conceal a timber framework or decayed joists. Bricks were more widely used in the eighteenth century where stone was not available and suitable deposits of clay for brick-making were at hand. Welsh slate also came into use for roofing, supplanting the older materials of stone, tile and thatch.

At the end of the eighteenth century many old types of house existed alongside the new. There still survived a few late medieval cruck cottages, usually ones that had been improved by incorporating upright walls and a broader roof. The original design was based on pairs of tree trunks or crucks, tied together at the top and linked horizontally by a ridge pole, rather like a simple tent. In time brick nogging (brickwork in a timber frame) replaced some of the infilling of clay-daubed wattle, and glazed windows superseded the primitive apertures closed by shutters. A much more common survival was the box-framed or balloon-framed timber house, which dated mainly from the hundred years after 1550, but may have begun to be built as much as a century earlier. Commonly known as 'half-timbered', these houses consisted of raftered roofs supported by a framework of vertical posts known as studs, tied together by horizontal beams. This timber framework rested on low footing walls of rubble or brick, the spaces between the timbers filled in by wattle and daub or laths and plaster. A brick or masonry chimney stack was attached to the exterior gable end.[2]

Houses of this construction suffered from a variety of drawbacks. With age the decay of the sleeper beam laid on the footings on which the wall rested caused the upright members to sag and the walls to lean, while the effects of seasonal cold and heat gave rise to movement of the external timbers and the opening of gaps between the beams and the infilling, allowing rain and cold draughts to penetrate to the interior. It is not surprising, then, that substantial frame houses, originally built for small farmers, tradesmen and craftsmen, might well have come to be used for labourers' dwellings as the buildings deteriorated and their owners found more modern and comfortable houses of stone or brick nearby.

In the north and west of England, and also in Wales, the longhouse was frequently found. The name derives from the single-storey living room and shelter for the livestock being placed side by side under a single extended roof line. The more ancient types, such as the Cornish long-house, built of unhewn granite with mud pressed into the gaps between the stone to make it weather-tight, might well go back to the fifteenth century or earlier. The roofs were made from flat stones or from thatch.[3] The longhouse, in various materials, persisted in the poorer parts of the west, Wales, and the north well into the nineteenth century, and in 1850 James Caird described how in some parts of Northumberland the cottagers' cow and pigs were still lodged under the same roof, divided from the single human living room by only a 'slight partition'. Elsewhere in Northumberland Caird saw half-timbered cottages, some with thatched roofs, others covered by turf; 'one little pane of glass admitted a meagre portion of light, and a simple hearthstone on the ground served for the fire of peat or turf'.[4]

In the districts where stone was readily available for building the cottages might be solid but were generally very small. Indeed, many cottages in a variety of areas were tiny. Frequently they consisted of only two rooms; a second room downstairs was often merely a scullery or dairy; a second bedroom, if it existed, was so confined that, as one villager told Rowntree, 'You fit into it as you will one day in your coffin'.[5] Good enduring buildings of stone could be seen in the north, in the Cotswolds, and in the west country from Somerset south to Dorset. The humbler type of small stone cottage was built of stone rubble with a few small and irregular windows. Originally the loft was used for storage for grain or cheese, but later it might be converted into a sleeping loft, still reached by a ladder from below rather than by a staircase.

Mud cottages could be found everywhere, but were especially widespread in the south-west, notably in Devon. Though constructed only of mud or 'cob', clay and chalk mixed with straw, these houses would last for centuries if the outside were protected by a plaster skin or was frequently whitewashed, and the thatched roof was made large enough to keep the rain water off the walls. They were quickly and cheaply built, the dough of cob, trodden firm by the feet of men and women, thrown by pitchforks on to a stone base, trodden again down to a thickness of some three feet. When the walls had risen to about three feet high they were left to settle and dry for a day or two, and then were built up again to the required height, usually about six feet.[6] It was reported from Devonshire in 1808 that a substantial cob cottage having a principal room, with fireplace and oven, about 14 feet square, with two smaller rooms behind for storing fuel and provisions, and two rooms above, could be built for about £60. This might be compared with £30–£40 to build a two-room cottage of mud and stud in Lincolnshire and £60 for a two-room one of brick and tile.[7]

Generally, cottages were newer, larger and better built in the south and east, and became older, smaller and more primitive towards the north and west. Changes in building styles, accommodation, and materials spread slowly from the south-east to the north-west, taking perhaps half a century or more to become adopted in more remote areas. Many of the northern cottages, of stone, with thatched or more recent slate roofs, might contain only one large room, 16 feet by 15 feet, though others had two rooms, the 'kitchen' in which the family lived, cooked and ate, and the 'parlour', sometimes used as a dairy, where they slept.[8] In the south-east, old seventeenth-century framed houses were in the eighteenth century frequently modernized by a covering, at least on the front elevation, of brick or clapboarding with hung tiles to give an up-to-date Georgian appearance. The existence of the older basis can often be detected from the unusual width of the walls and the irregular placing of the windows, as also the huddle within of small rooms and the presence, perhaps, of an ingle-nook fireplace.

In the later eighteenth century the upsurge of population placed greater pressure on housing. The better houses were still built of stone, when available, but brick became more common, especially in the south and the midlands. Thatch was still employed for roofing, but more frequently stone, tile or slate. New departures were the appearance of semi-detached cottages and rows of terraced ones, with both having additional rooms in the roof space. The growing pressure on housing led to more of the older farmhouses and craftsmen's homes being converted to the use of labourers, while very simple single-storey cottages in a variety of cheap materials were thrown up, often by their occupiers, on any odd piece of waste ground or road verge. There was a tradition that a structure erected in the space of a single night—a 'Mushroom Hall' or 'now-or-never'—acquired a permanent site and could not be removed, and whether this was really so or not, many crude timber or turf huts of squatters—the huts known to the eighteenth century as 'hovels'—sprang up on the margins of commons and waste lands, and were still to be seen in some places as late as the 1870s. It was reported in 1869, for instance, that more than 800 cottagers had acquired land by the roadside on the Duke of Beaufort's estate in Monmouthshire, some paying as little rent as 6d a year.

The character of the housing reflected in some degree the structure of landownership and the nature of the farming. On large estates 'model' villages and model cottages were built, especially by those landowners who wished to impress visitors; (and so they were more likely, as at Holkham, to be found on the approach to the house itself). Newly-built villages of well-constructed and pleasantly designed houses appeared where a landowner had removed an old settlement to make way for his park, as in the well-known examples of Blaise, near Bath, laid out by John Nash, Nuneham Courtney near Oxford, and Milton Abbas in Dorset. The great era for model villages, however, was to be the nineteenth century rather than the eighteenth.

Arable farming, when carried on on a large scale as in parts of eastern England and Wiltshire, required considerable numbers of hands. The villages thus tended to be populous, and where there was no squire to interest himself in the conditions in the neighbourhood, the district swelled with cheap homes thrown up cheek by jowl on tiny pieces of ground by speculative builders and local tradesmen who saw the opportunity for a profitable investment. The more solidly built cottages, standing singly or in twos and threes, were more likely to have been built by a landlord or a large farmer, and were often situated across the lane from the farmhouse. Scattered cottages in ones and twos were a common feature of upland and pastoral and forested districts, particularly in the north and west. And it was here that the old practice of the worker living in with his master, eating at the same table and sleeping in a loft or outhouse, persisted longest. Where it survived it helped reduce the demand for separate cottages. By contrast, in areas of great arable farms the youths and young men were lodged and fed in large outhouses by the farmyard, and sometimes they and older men with families were housed in long sheds or 'barracks' as Cobbett called them in 1833, having 'neither gardens, nor privies, nor back doors. . . no upstairs; one little window and one doorway to each dwelling in the shed or barrack'.[9]

It is often supposed that the period of heavy enclosure of commons and waste in the later eighteenth and early nineteenth centuries caused a deterioration in the supply of homes for the rural poor. Certainly we know from estate documents that in the later decades of the eighteenth century squatters on the waste were becoming so evident as to merit recording their numbers in rentals; and it must be likely that where waste lands were enclosed it was less easy for the poor to find a patch of ground on which to build themselves a simple shelter. It should be remembered, however, that the squatters of pre-enclosure days, even if growing in numbers, formed only a small proportion of the labouring population, and that long after the enclosure movement was over squatting continued to be widespread. Moreover, in the midlands the enclosures were primarily concerned with the common fields, and the available commons and pieces of waste were often so limited as to be carefully regulated by the villagers prior to enclosure; in such villages it was unlikely that any large-scale appropriation of land for squatting would have been permitted by landowners and farmers anxious to keep the common-field farming system operating as efficiently as possible.

The enclosures of large areas of waste were concentrated in districts of poor soils and exposed hills, woodlands, and in the rough grazings of moors and fells. In such districts the population tended to be small and scattered, and the pressure on housing was perhaps less great than in regions of better soil. Indeed, where former waste lands were brought into cultivation after enclosure it was often necessary to build cottages for the labour force now required, or to hire hands from a distance. Furthermore, much waste land was never enclosed because it was not considered worth the cost, and even where an enclosure Act was obtained it did not necessarily follow that the actual fencing or walling-in would be undertaken if circumstances indicated that the expenditure would be uneconomic.

In any event, the parliamentary enclosures of the period affected only a quarter of the total acreage of the country, including common fields as well as commons and wastes. Large parts of the country were very little affected since they had been enclosed long before, if indeed they had ever been open, and in the heavily-affected midlands a shortage of free land for cottage building was a frequent situation before the days of parliamentary enclosures. Even in southern England there were numerous commons on very poor soils or steep hillsides which had survived through the centuries, and indeed not a few of them are still in existence today, such as Ashdown Forest in Sussex, the Devil's Punchbowl in Surrey, the New Forest in Hampshire, and Dartmoor and Exmoor, to name but the best-known. Squatters making homesteads for themselves were remarked on by Richard Heath when he described the Surrey commons in 1893,[10] and indeed this practice of making homes on unclaimed land has continued in the present century.

Much more important than enclosure for housing in the countryside at large was the growth of the population, which began its most rapid phase in the later part of the eighteenth century. The highest rate of increase occurred in the early decades of the following century, and although the population growth was associated with rapid urbanisation, even those counties which remained predominantly farming ones recorded substantial increases in numbers. There the increase over the fifty years after 1801 was generally of the order of 50–60 per cent or more, and this despite some outward migration to industrial areas. More extreme examples were Lincolnshire, whose inhabitants nearly doubled, and Devon, which experienced a rise as high as 108 per cent. Since the supply of cottages failed to keep pace with the increased population, a greater degree of overcrowding was inevitable. Families, with two, three or even four adults and several children, had to live in cottages which

possessed only two bedrooms, many only one. It has long been the practice for children to leave home between eight and twelve or in their early
'teens to go into service, as farm or domestic servants, or as apprentices,
and this was in part a means of relieving intolerable pressure on living
space. This reason for youngsters leaving home was still influential in the
later nineteenth century with the majority of the rural poor still housed
in dwellings that were simply too small for them.

As the population grew, so pools of surplus labour began to accumulate in some farming areas, notably in East Anglia and southern counties.
Parishes which lacked alternative outlets for employment had numbers of
able-bodied men who, in winter time at least, were in excess of the
labour force required for the farms and the local trades and crafts.
Reliance on the relief offered by the Poor Law thus increased, and this,
together with the settlement system of relief entitlement, made it difficult
(though not impossible) for the under-employed to migrate to districts
where more work was available. Hence, there was often little movement
in those parishes where relief demands were heavy, and with the growth
in population the expanding number of young people seeking homes
must have intensified the effects of any shortage of cottages. Plans for
organised migration mounted by the Poor Law authorities to transfer
surplus families to the industrial north, or to encourage emigration to
North America, were not pursued sufficiently long or on a sufficient scale
to affect the general situation much. Then, and later in the nineteenth
century, there were private charitable schemes to assist both migration
and emigration, and some labourers themselves formed clubs to raise
funds for the purpose. Again, however, when compared with the consequences of the mounting population the effects were small, although it
is true that in the later nineteenth century farmers were often heard to
complain of a shortage of skilled men, the better hands having moved
away to the towns or gone abroad.

A development which is often attributed to the Poor Law was the creation of 'close villages', where landowners and farmers deliberately
cooperated to keep down the numbers of the resident workers, additional hands being hired when required from outside the parish. It is
uncertain, however, how far the burden of poor rates and the parish-
based settlement system were influential in this development. Landlord-
controlled parishes had existed earlier, before the poor rates had become
oppressive, and the motives of those controlling close parishes were
often concerned with creating model communities living in houses of
uniform and attractive designs which might embellish the estate and the
owner's name. More widely, there was a concern to keep out of the
village families of bad reputation, poachers, thieves, drunkards, and
other undesirables. There is, in fact, little evidence of any deliberate pulling down of cottages merely to keep down the numbers who might claim
a settlement; rather, the destruction of old cottages was often a prelude
to rebuilding with improved dwellings, or perhaps in order to move the
whole village a mile or two away to a different site, so as to clear the
way for a park or unobstructed views from the mansion. In general, it

Figure 2.1 Improved farm cottages built in 1848, with a sample of those they replaced

is probable that close villages, where all or most of the property was in one owner's hands, were marked by housing standards superior to those of 'open' villages where no kind of control was desired or was possible. In the nineteenth century some landowners saw the building of improved cottages in their own villages as a social duty, a reform which it was believed would have beneficial implications for the morals of the labouring families, for the class of men attracted to the district, and for the reputation of the estate. Among the many owners who accepted this responsibility may be mentioned the 10th Duke of Bedford, the Duke of Northumberland, Lord Kenlis, the Earl of Chesterfield, the Dukes of Newcastle and Westminster, the Earl of Derby and Lord Crewe, and later in the century the Duke of Manchester, Lord Leconfield and Lord Wantage, who were particularly noted for building sound, roomy houses at rents within the pockets of their inhabitants.

II

The various forces which have been discussed as bearing on rural housing thus included the structure of landownership and landowners' personal interest in the matter, the nature of the soil and the type of farming, with consequent effects on the demand for labour, the decline of the former practice of boarding workers in or near the farmhouse, enclosure and the reduced supply of waste land for occupation by squatters, and the effects of the Poor Law. All worked to produce a highly varied situation where housing needs and supply differed greatly from one district to another, and even in neighbouring villages. The extent of rural out-migration, for example, tended to reduce with increasing distance from large cities and industrial areas. Thus even in a county so close to London as Kent, there were substantial differences between north-west Kent, that part of the county closest to London, and east and central Kent which remained for long little influenced by the labour demands of the capital. Again, there were areas of former rural industries which had declined or disappeared, such as, for example, the old iron industry of the Kent-Sussex weald, and the Forest of Dean, or the old cloth-making trades which had once flourished widely in East Anglia, the West Country and over much of southern England. Those country towns and villages which had once been centres of such trades inevitably declined, people moved away, and houses fell into disrepair for lack of inhabitants.

The housing situation, in detail, in any one place, might thus be the result of a whole variety of influences. Even the structure of the cottages themselves, and how they were looked after, could be potent factors. Those built of cob and lacking sound foundations and good thatch soon disintegrated, and in Devon so many were badly built and poorly maintained as to be unsafe. A midsummer rainstorm was said to have demolished twenty, and the rain was heavy enough to make the walls collapse within hours, one old lady being drowned in her bed.[11] Even with houses of stone or brick, the landlord's failure over a protracted

period to carry out repairs led to ruinous conditions. The very farmhouses on the estate of the absentee Sir Marmaduke Constable had their
sagging walls and roofs supported by beams, and some houses became so
dangerous that the tenants evacuated them in fear of their lives.[12]

When Charles Vancouver carried out his survey of Devon for the Board
of Agriculture in 1808, he found an extremely diverse state of affairs. It
was said in one district that the scarcity of cottages was due to the unwill-
ingness of the farmers to let out land to the poor, thus obliging families
to quit the neighbourhood, while numbers of existing homes were 'daily
going to ruin, and have fallen down within a few years'. Former
farmhouses were now 'often inhabited by three or four peasant families'.
However, Lord Clifford had built some 'very neat' new cottages, each
with a small piece of ground for potatoes and a small orchard sufficient
to produce one or two hogsheads of cider, the last in lieu of the grazing
for a cow which the inhabitants had previously enjoyed.

In another part of Devon there was 'a general want' of cottages, and
at Chilworthy the position was so bad that 'three mud walls and a hedge-
bank' formed the homes of many of the inhabitants. But in the Dartmoor
village of Bridstowe the parson, Mr Luxmore had recently pulled down
two old ruinous cottages, 'scarcely sufficient to afford a single night's
shelter for a gang of gypsies', and replaced them by a row of twelve new
ones, and the parson proposed doing the same with three other
uninhabitable houses. His first new cottages had a single large room,
16 ft square, on the ground floor, with a fireplace and oven, a lean-to for
fuel, tools and a pig, a small backyard and a garden. A pantry was fitted
under the stairs, and the single bedroom was the same size as the large
downstairs room: it was assumed that the children would be apprenticed
away from home as young as eight or nine. In the parson's later cottages
two bedrooms were provided, it being appreciated that not all the
families needed to apprentice their children so young. The cottages were
built with stone walls to the height of eight feet, a superstructure of cob
and a slate roof, and were erected for some £38–£40 apiece. The rent
charged was 1s a week, and disorderly families were liable to instant
removal, the parson expecting his tenants to attend church and behave
soberly and in a neighbourly fashion. Elsewhere in the county many of
the cottages were grouped together in the villages and lacked the amenity
of gardens, while at Woodbury, near Exmouth, Lord Rolle had encouraged the poor to leave the village with the moral dangers of its alehouse
and settle on the borders of the commons and wastes. Those doing so
were permitted to enclose an acre of land for their own use, and if this
met his lordship's approval a further three, four or five acres were
granted. In some cases the cottager was allowed to enclose even more
and was given a long lease of the whole at 'a very moderate' rent.[13]

In 1813 Arthur Young found in Suffolk that although some gentlemen
had provided the poor with comfortable homes, the low rents that could
be charged, between £2 and £3 a year, discouraged others from imitating
them. The return on the investment was only between two and four per
cent, and moreover was considerably reduced by outlays on repairs,

especially if the houses were of lath and plaster or wattle and clay. Generally the homes were deficient in warmth and convenience, 'the door very generally opening immediately from the external air into the keeping-room, and sometimes directly to the fireside; the state of reparation bad, and the deficiency of gardens too general'. The cottagers themselves sometimes made bad worse by neglecting their gardens, where they had any, or even letting them to a neighbouring farmer. It would, Young considered, have been advantageous to the poor if their cottages had been let to them immediately by the landlord and not annexed to the farms, since the farmers often let them as high as they could in order to offset their own rents.[14]

Young's report on Lincolnshire of the same date noted that in the low rich parts of the county the homes were generally of stud and mud, a type of construction favoured for its cheapness. Cottages of this kind could be put up for a third less than similar ones of brick, though some proprietors, such as a Mr Cartwright at Brothertoft, had gone to the expense of the latter. He had erected 29 cottages of brick and slate with rooms varying from 12 ft square to as much as 12 ft by 18 ft, each with a pantry, a pigsty, a small backyard for coal and wood, and a small garden at front. The average cost of building was some £88 each. At Revesby, near Horncastle, a brick cottage for two families could be put up for £84, a smaller kind for one family for £50. In the newly-enclosed fenlands many new cottages had been built, and around Folkingham, east of Grantham, the enclosures had been followed by the provision of cow-pastures of at least three acres assigned to every cottage.[15]

In Northumberland in 1805 it was reported that building styles had changed: the older homes were of stone and clay covered with thatch, the newer ones of stone and lime, covered with tiles, and with a floor of lime and sand. The cottages had only one large room, 15 ft by 16 ft for living in, with a small one at the entrance for a cow, coal, and tools, 9 ft by 16 ft. They had only one storey and no separate bedroom, but few lacked a garden. Some use was made of brick, but stone was more common, with roofs of tiles or slate, the small dark blue variety of slate from Scotland being preferred as more durable than tiles.[16]

The brief discussions included in the county reports to the Board of Agriculture bring out many of the factors which were to influence the supply and condition of cottages throughout the nineteenth century and much of the present one. As regards supply, the low wages paid to many country workers put a restrictive ceiling on the rents they could afford. Accordingly at the low level of rents that could be charged the building of sound cottages in durable materials was uneconomic: hence the persistence of old ruinous one-room dwellings and the very limited accommodation and amenities provided in new ones. The physical conditions of the homes depended on additional factors: defects in the original design and construction, inferior materials, the willingness or otherwise of the owners to pay for repairs, and the ability and readiness of the tenants to look after their houses and make the best of what room and garden space they had.

III

Although wages varied considerably from region to region, and even from village to village, it was generally supposed that ordinary farm-workers could not be expected to pay more than 1s 6d or 2s a week in rent. These figures represented (in the early decades of the nineteenth century) about 15 to 20 per cent of average cash wages, but a lower proportion of total earnings (which were increased by high harvest wages, piecework payments, and various non-cash perquisites). At this period cottages could be built for sums varying between about £30 and £90, depending on size and materials used, but for the better homes at the upper end of the range a rent of 2s a week represented a gross return of less than 6 per cent, without making any allowance for interest and repairs. It seems, too, that the figures quoted by contemporaries usually made no allowance for the value of the land and did not always include all the costs of construction since some materials and their carriage were provided from the resources of the estate.

Farmworkers were among the lowest paid of country dwellers, and most craftsmen and tradesmen earned substantially more and could afford a superior standard of housing. Some farmworkers did own their own homes, they or their parents having been able to find the sum necessary to acquire a freehold or long leasehold; others had built a home on the waste, claiming a right to possession which had not been disallowed. However, we do not know how large a proportion of families were in this position, although it has been suggested from Sir Frederic Eden's work of 1797 that those who owned their own homes, or had them rent-free, may have amounted to only about 10 per cent of the whole. Certainly the majority of low-paid country workers could not have hoped to raise the money to buy a cottage, although it is true that some farm servants were able to save part of their wages and accumulated moderate sums in savings banks. The great majority expected to be always tenants, either renting a cottage from the farmer or his landlord, or taking a house in a village owned by a local tradesman, dealer, builder or publican who had invested spare funds in cheap cottages. Some farmworkers, especially the more skilled perma-nent hands, and also estate workers received a free cottage as part of their hiring bargain, though this might be reflected in a lower level of cash wages. The prevalence of tied cottages, dwellings that went with the job, made it easy for workers to change masters every year or so, and equally for masters to replace them. There was a high turnover of labour in many parts of the country, with new hands hired at the regular hiring fairs or more casually—some farmers taking the sons of neighbours or men met by chance on the road or who called at the farmhouse on the off-chance. The permanent worker who served one master over a long period of years was generally untypical, except perhaps in the more remote and thinly-populated pastoral districts of the country.

The great variety of hiring terms and rents makes generalisation extremely hazardous. In parts of north Lincolnshire, for example, the better farm servants were relatively well off. They were paid £18-20 a year and did not live in the farmhouse, being provided with a rent-free cottage, the keep of a cow, a fat hog and three or four bushels of malt for brewing their own beer. In Hertfordshire it was reported that on the estates of gentlemen the cottages had lower rents than those owned by lesser proprietors. The first rented at between £2 and £4 a year, the second at £4-6, when cash wages averaged only 7s in winter and 8s in summer. Most of the cottages, however, had good gardens, some as large as a quarter of an acre. In Northamptonshire the cottages attached to farms rented at £2-3 with a garden; but generally there was a great lack of cottages, and consequently the poor were driven into the towns and large villages where they had to pay as much as £4-5. This was a large sum when compared with farm day wages for ordinary labourers ranging from 9s to 11s a week in the 1840s, though horse-keepers earned 2s more and shepherds 2s 6d more. The wages were doubled in harvest time, and piece-workers on mowing, threshing, hedging, ditching and draining earned 2s-3s a week more than those paid by the day. Similar wages were paid in Norfolk, where the rent of a cottage with little or no land was £3-4 a year. Those having gardens of a fair size fetched from £3.5s to £5.5s. And in south Wiltshire, the arable region of the county, a cottage with a good garden rented at between 30s and 50s a year, while in the northern dairying part 40s to 70s was common. The difference reflected the lower wages paid in the southern district, though the total earnings there were increased by piecework payments, higher harvest pay, and the provision of free land for potatoes, ploughed and manured by the farmers free of charge.[17]

By the middle decades of the nineteenth century rents in general were substantially higher than they had been before the inflation of the Napoleonic Wars, and they still varied greatly from place to place. A figure as low as £1 or £1.15s a year could still be found in counties as far apart as Yorkshire and Wiltshire, though rents as low as these usually related to one- or two-room dwellings of an extremely poor description. For better homes of three rooms £3 to £5 was more common, and proportionately more for additional rooms and amenities, a house with two living rooms and three bedrooms costing as much as £7.10s in Yorkshire.[18]

The general level of rents was forced up, no doubt, by the pressure of the rapid increase in population. Farm wages varied greatly as we have seen, but experienced no large or widespread improvement over the first half of the nineteenth century. Increased numbers meant larger families which needed larger homes (if they could afford them), and rents were commonly related to the extent of the accommodation. There was undoubtedly a growth of overcrowding, made worse in many cases by young families living with parents, and the taking in of a lodger to help with the rent, even in the smaller houses. An inquiry relating to conditions in 1851, which surveyed 821 parishes scattered over England, showed that 69,225 cottages housed 305,567 persons, an average of 4.4 persons per cottage. This moderate figure, however, conceals the real

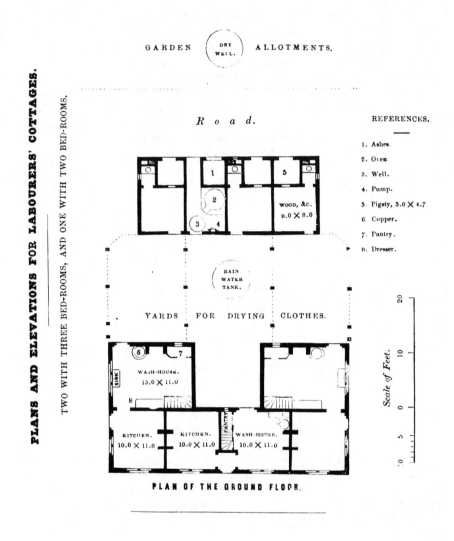

Figure 2.2(a) Plans of cottages erected on the Duke of Bedford's estates in the 1840s

situation. A large proportion of the cottages, 40 per cent in fact, had only one bedroom and averaged as many as four persons to the sole bedroom. Two-bedroom cottages averaged 2.5 persons to each bedroom, while less than five per cent of the cottages had more than two bedrooms. The overcrowding is seen to be even worse when the small size of most bedrooms is taken into account.[19] Some, indeed, were mere shallow lofts or lean-to additions, so low as to make it impossible to stand upright or use a normal bed, and the makeshift cots had to be laid on the floor.

ELEVATION OF THE FRONT.

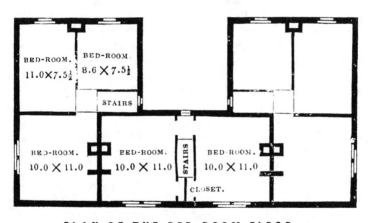

PLAN OF THE BED-ROOM FLOOR.

Figure 2.2(b)

The growth of overcrowding and sharing of bedrooms had obvious implications of a moral kind where labouring families had teenage boys and girls still at home, and these greatly concerned some of the landlords of the mid-century period. It was in 1849 that the 10th Duke of Bedford sent to the Royal Agricultural Society for publication in its *Journal* the plans and quantities of the new cottages he had recently built on his estate (often replacing old ones pulled down), in the hope that other proprietors might benefit from his experience. The demand for cottages, he pointed out, had been increased by the various labour-intensive improvements in farming, notably drainage and the conversion of inferior pastures and woodlands to tillage, which were going on in all parts of the country. But what concerned him more was the lack of separate bedrooms for the sexes, a defect made worse by the taking in of lodgers. Cottage building, he accepted, was 'a bad investment of money', except to speculators who charged excessive rents for badly-built homes. Landlords who were engaged in improving their farmhouses and cattle sheds should also accept the need for cottage improvement.

To improve the dwellings of the labouring classes, and afford them the means of greater cleanliness, health, and comfort, in their own homes, to extend education, and thus raise the social and moral habits of those most valuable members of the community, are among the first duties, and ought to be amongst the truest pleasures, of every landlord.[20]

The subject was one which aroused a certain amount of interest among the members of the Royal Agricultural Society, and about mid-century a number of articles appeared in its *Journal* offering advice, plans and detailed costings of improved cottages. George Nicholls, a member of the Poor Law Commission, declared that new cottages should have at least four rooms, one with a fireplace for use in the case of sickness, and that the ground floor, of brick, tile or stone, should be raised a foot or eighteen inches above the level of the surrounding earth to obviate dampness. Henry Goddard, an architect, produced plans for a pair of cottages, each with a living room 13 ft by 12 ft 6 ins and a scullery 8 ft 6 ins by 7 ft. The three bedrooms measured 11 ft by 10 ft, 11 ft by 7 ft, and 8 ft by 7 ft; they were all to be 8 ft high to give air spaces of 860, 645 and 419 cubic ft respectively. (The air space laid down for workhouses and prisons was 500 cubic ft per person.) Ventilation was to be ensured by installing air bricks in the walls of the scullery and pantry, and perforated wood blocks in the ceilings. The cost of building came to £201 for the pair. At the same date, 1849, J. Young MacVicar published his plans for a somewhat larger pair of cottages, with a living room 14 ft by 13 ft, a scullery 9 ft 6 ins by 9 ft, and a pantry 8 ft by 6 ft. The three bedrooms measured 14 ft by 10 ft, 9 ft by 8 ft, and 9 ft 6 ins by 9 ft, and included in the plans were a substantial coalhouse and pigsty. The cost worked out in this case at £296 for the pair.[21]

More elaborate plans and recommendations were published in the Society's *Journal* a few years later. T.W.P. Isaac was concerned to show how cottages could be built for only £85 each. He arrived at this figure by assuming that no labourer could pay a rent of more than £5 a year, and that the investment should produce a gross return of 6 per cent for the landlord. The living room measured 12 ft by 12 ft, with a washhouse of 12 ft by 8 ft, and a pantry of 8 ft by 6 ft. The three bedrooms, to be 8 ft high, were one of 12 ft by 12 ft, and two smaller ones of 9 ft by 8 ft. The large bedroom had an air space of 1152 cubic ft, the two smaller ones 576 cubic ft. The flooring of the ground floor should—unusually—be of wood, raised at least 6 ins above the surrounding earth. Damp was to be prevented from rising by incorporating a damp course in the walls—perhaps the first occasion on which this important advance had been recommended for labourers' dwellings. One of a number of recommended manufactured kitchen ranges should be installed, and the water supply was to consist of rainwater which drained into a well or tank under the kitchen floor, and was raised for use by a pump. The disposal of waste water was to be so arranged as to serve for flushing the privy, and this was to empty into a cesspool via a trapped pipe, again an innovation in humble houses.[22] It would be interesting to know to what extent these novel recommendations were adopted, and how so relatively well-appointed a cottage could be built so cheaply. As was usual, the cost of the land and the expenses of cartage of materials were not included in these estimates.

It was also about this time that the modern concern with public health first appeared, marked by the publication in 1842 of Edwin Chadwick's famous *Report on the Sanitary Condition of the Labouring Population*. Chadwick was primarily concerned with conditions in the slum areas of towns but his material included a number of examples of the appalling state of affairs in some country towns and villages. An extreme case of overcrowding was reported by the Medical Officer of the Cerne Poor Law Union in Dorset. There fever had broken out in a former poorhouse, now occupied by nearly fifty persons who paid no rent for their accommodation. The rooms were neither boarded nor paved and were generally damp, and some housed two families. The upstairs rooms were small and low and separated from each other only by boards. Eleven persons were sleeping in one room. A gutter running two feet from the front of the house contained 'an accumulation of filth of every description', and a large cesspool was situated only a few feet behind the building. The dirty state and badly-fed condition of the inhabitants contributed to the diseases prevalent among them. In another village there were cottages with beds standing directly on the damp ground floor. Scarcely one had a fireplace in the bedroom, and one had a single pane of glass stuck in the mud wall as its only window, with a large pile of wet and dirty potatoes in one corner.

Elsewhere, also in the south-west, dampness was held to be a cause of disease. In and near Tiverton many of the cottages had been built directly on the ground without flooring, or erected against a damp hill. Windows and doors were inadequate for protection against the elements, or for ventilation, and the thatch roof was frequently 'saturated with wet, rotten and in a state of decay . . .'. In some parts of Tiverton open drains ran immediately before the doors, and some houses were surrounded by open drains full of refuse. In Truro, similarly, the ill-constructed homes had 'decomposing refuse close upon their doors and windows, open drains bringing the oozings of pigsties and other filth to stagnate . . .'. The existence of a central sewer in the street was no guarantee of adequate drainage when the connecting house drains were mere gutters running into pits and only slightly covered over, 'a concentrated solution of all sorts of decomposing refuse being allowed to soak through and thoroughly impregnate the walls and ground adjoining'.

In Toddington, Bedfordshire, most of the cottages lacked privies, and by every door was heaped a dunghill intended for eventual use in the allotments or to be sold as manure. At Witham in Essex the nuisance was compounded by the refuse of the slaughterhouses situated in the midst of the populated area; the refuse was allowed to accumulate for weeks, and there was also the waste of the innumerable pigs kept at the back of a great number of the houses. The Medical Officer of the Epping Union recalled that he had often to attend a woman in labour 'where the wet has been running down the walls, and light to be distinguished through the roof, and this in the winter season, with no fireplace in the room'. And again, in the Bromley district of north-west Kent, the presence of disease was ascribed to the total lack of drainage around the cottages, while their inhabitants made matters worse by heaping refuse near the dwellings. The heaps were sometimes not removed for long periods, and there were always 'decomposing matters' surrounding the pigsties kept near the homes.[23]

It has to be borne in mind that the picture drawn by the Poor Law Medical Officers consulted by Chadwick emphasised the blackest spots in their districts. They were employed to treat the indigent poor, those receiving relief, and their work necessarily took them into the worst slum streets and most poverty-stricken homes. Some of them, indeed, pointed out that better conditions obtained in other parts of the very towns and villages they cited, the report on Truro, for instance, noting that only rarely were families found occupying less than two rooms, while the more recent cottages mostly contained four rooms with a garden, and were occupied by single families. It is clear that the Medical Officers drew a distinction between the very poor, those who lived in the crude, dilapidated and insanitary homes described, and a superior class of regularly employed labourers housed in two-bedroom cottages who kept themselves and their homes cleaner, were less inclined to frequent the beer-shops or to indulge in poaching, and often sent their children daily to school.[24] It is indeed very easy for the casual reader of Chadwick's work to come away with an overriding impression of universal squalor, neglect and misery, not appreciating that the localities examined were limited in extent and generally untypical of labouring dwellings taken as a whole.

In some country towns the rapid mushrooming of new working-class districts, with streets of small houses thrown up at the lowest possible cost, resulted in the creation of instant slums. The population of Banbury, Oxfordshire, climbed from 5,906 in 1831 to 8,793 twenty years later, an increase of nearly 50 per cent. It is not surprising to learn that it was a town of small landowners and speculators—a larger version of an open village—and many of its cottages were built in short terraces and courts named after the local tradesmen who built them. In the 1840s a rapid expansion of working-class housing consisted in part of cottages costing a mere £35 to build, inclusive of land, yielding £6.10s a year in rent. The better types cost £70 and produced between £8 and £10 a year. The whole cost of erecting them could be recovered in twelve years or less, the profits fuelling the throwing up of further houses as cheaply as possible. The results were predictable: an outbreak of a severe disease, 'Banbury Fever', in 1831, typhus in 1832 and 1833, smallpox in 1848. In 1849 the Board of Health's inspector found alarming defects in sanitation with one privy to 43 people in Crown Yard, and one to 47 in Mill Lane. The privy facilities presented 'perhaps as extreme cases of the kind as are to be found in the filthiest and most crowded towns in England'. In the recently-built working class streets new houses had been built on ill-drained land and were subject to fever; the contents of cesspits were often left in the street for several days.[25]

The campaign for sanitary reform launched by Chadwick was slow to make itself felt in the large towns; even slower in country towns and villages. Indeed, questions of rural water supply, drainage and sanitation were still being raised in the 1930s, when it was pointed out that some cottages still drew their water from streams, ponds or wells infiltrated by sewage and other dangerous waste materials. The problem in the countryside had many facets: that many of the worst houses were old or so badly built and ill-maintained as to need complete replacement by new improved houses; that in rural areas piped water supplies and systems of pipe drainage were expensive to install—indeed there are, in 1990, numerous villages that still lack main drainage for this reason; that, as in the towns, many of the poor had no understanding of hygiene and the need for it, and continued with habits that positively endangered their own health. Above all the question of cost loomed large. To improve, rebuild, or provide entirely new and adequate dwellings cost money and, at rents that labouring families could afford to pay, there was no profit to be made from them. As the Duke of Bedford had remarked, everyone knew that housing was a bad investment.

Many of the inhabitants of defective cottages could do little or nothing to help themselves. It was difficult to persuade housewives to keep the home cleaner when every drop of water had to be drawn at a distance and carried into the cottage, when floors were of earth or cracked paving or old broken and crumbling bricks, when the means of heating water were absent or expensive, and when the husband and children tramped into the house from the lane or garden with boots caked with mud. Some labourers were afraid to ask the owner for repairs to be made because they feared the response would be a notice to quit. Dampness could not be cured when gutters were absent or broken, the walls porous, the thatch ruinous and the floor laid direct on the earth. Fuel, often only turf or bracken and branches of trees picked up in the lane, was scarce or expensive, and had to be reserved for cooking and for heating in depth of winter. Often, in any case, only the living-room possessed a fireplace, which not infrequently smoked abominably unless the outside door was kept open. The well or pond might have sewage or animal dung oozing into it, the cottage roof might be leaking and the ground round the house puddled with rainwater—but how was the labourer on ten shillings a week and working six days out of the seven from early to late, how was he to remedy such matters?

Sometimes, indeed, cottagers contrived to overcome at least some of the difficulties. The menfolk of neighbouring houses agreed to sleep together so that their grown-up daughters could enjoy the privacy of a separate bedroom. They dug trenches to that the surplus night-soil from the privies could be shovelled into buckets and then buried. Similarly they buried household refuse and kept the pigsty at the bottom of the garden rather than against the back of the house. Sometimes, indeed, they moved the privy from a hole too near the water supply to another site more distant. There was little they could do, however, where there was a cesspool and it was located by the well. As an observer wrote in 1860, 'It is almost incredible to see the universal contiguity of the pump and the cesspool or of the well and the cesspool. This is a mistake often fatal and always injurious to the health . . .'. Those men with a little skill at carpentry and possessing a few tools repaired sagging gutters, mended broken windows and patched up rotting doors. But, equally, there were many who neglected everything and settled fatalistically amongst ever-increasing dirt and squalor. Heaps of rubbish accumulated by the back door where it was carelessly thrown and the slops flung over it, privies were allowed to become unusable rather than take the trouble of shovelling out the night-soil or moving the structure to a new hole, and the overflowing wastes of the privy, pigsty and rubbish heap were allowed to wash down into an open drain where it remained to fester, or to flow away in a stream to pollute the cottages further down. When, near the end of the nineteenth century, earth closets were advocated as the best solution for isolated dwellings, it was often impossible to get the cottagers to go to the trouble of drying and sifting the earth which was supposed to be thrown into the pail after each use, or to persuade them that the pail's contents needed to be emptied regularly and buried below the top soil in the garden.

The fundamental difficulty in improving the public health conditions in the countryside lay in the question of cost. The relevance to health of adequate living and sleeping space, a supply of pure water, drainage and rubbish disposal, and an efficient system of sanitation were already well recognised when the eminent agricultural engineer, J. Bailey Denton, discussed the problem in 1870. He pointed out that although the average death rate in the countryside was one-sixth lower than in the cities (in the ten years ending in 1866 20.10 per 1,000 compared with 24.59), there were remarkable variations. Some villages, indeed, had death rates higher than those in nearby towns. That of Hoo in north Kent, for example, was 2 per 1,000 higher than in neighbouring Gravesend and Chatham; Hemel Hempstead and Berkhamsted in Hertfordshire, similarly, had rates 2 per 1,000 higher than in St Albans. These exceptions to the general rule of lower rural death rates, Bailey Denton believed, arose from unhealthy locations and insanitary living conditions. It was not a question of inability to establish a public health authority, although it was true that the existing legislation was complex, and was also permissive, which meant that responsibility for making improvements was easily evaded. The real problem was the low income of most villagers which made it impossible, or at least very difficult, for cottage-owners to recover the cost of improvements in higher rents.

The implication of Bailey Denton's figures for air space was that the great majority of existing homes were simply too small for a sufficient circulation of pure air. The living room, for instance, would have to be 15 ft by 12 ft and at least 6 ft 6 ins. high; the main bedroom 12 ft by 12 ft by 6 ft 6 ins. high; and the children's bedroom 10 ft by 10 ft by 6 ft high. Few cottages, anywhere, could boast these dimensions. A pure water supply, similarly, was rarely possible where cottagers relied on shallow wells, ponds or a stream. An adequate supply of rainwater to meet the needs of a family would require the roof to be of slate (rather than tiles or thatch) and the provision of large storage tanks. A better alternative was a wind-driven pump which could draw up subterranean supplies (as was used by settlers on the Great Plains of America): a large central pump could be used to supply and distribute water through pipes to the whole village. Disposal of sewage was best achieved by water closets and underground sewers, leading to a treatment works; the disposal of household slops was also best arranged in this way, instead of saturating and polluting the ground immediately round the cottage. But progress in all these advances—adequate room sizes, piped water from a subter-ranean source, sewers for human excreta and household waste—foundered on the twin obstacles of cost and how it was to be met.[26]

By the 1870s and 1880s, in fact, some larger villages already had water drainage installed. Installation depended on the village or town being compact—it was impossible to introduce sewers to scattered villages—and there being suitable land available. The pipes drained down to a deeply-drained plot of land which was surrounded by a clay bank to prevent overflow. There the sewage drained through filter beds, which were often planted with osiers or ash-poles, plants which were gross feeders of sewage. The effluent water percolated through the subsoil and escaped through deep under-drains, the water being sufficiently pure to be allowed to flow away in a convenient stream. The sewer pipes themselves were periodically flushed with water, farmers, using water carts, being sometimes employed for the purpose. In the Brixworth Poor Law Union it was claimed that the introduction of a sewer system carried out in the years 1874–86 had been effective in reducing substantially the former high death rate of the area. The cost of installing sewers varied enormously according to the size of population to be served, the situa-tion of the village, and the cost of the land needed. It could be as low as £120, as at Kibworth Beauchamp, or £280 at Castle Acre, Norfolk, to as much as £495 at Ashwell, Rutland, and £1,000 at Whissendine, Rutland. The small town of East Dereham, Norfolk, with a population of 6,000 was sewered for £4,911.[27]

The results, however, were not always satisfactory, as seen in the case of Brixworth in Northamptonshire. There the drain pipes leaked, and either the filtration beds became clogged through lack of sufficient water to clear them, or an excess of water flushed the effluent into nearby brooks, which perhaps were used for drinking water by cottagers a mile or two distant. And where the authorities had installed a main drain, not all the proprietors wanted to go to the expense of making the connections to their property; where they did, and pan closets were installed, the connecting pipes became completely choked because the cottagers would not trouble to fetch the water needed to flush the pan. It was argued, in fact, that contrary to what was claimed, villages still using the time-honoured hole in the ground enjoyed better health than those which had been sewered.[28]

IV

The connections between overcrowding in damp and dilapidated cottages, defective water supplies and improper sanitation, emphasised by the public health reformers, were reinforced by other motives for making improvements, not least the adverse publicity which antiquated and unhealthy homes on landowners' estates began to receive from mid-century. There were, as has been noticed, numerous examples of enlightened owners, such as the Earl of Winchelsea, the Marquess of Buckingham, the Earls of Stradbroke and Leicester, the Dukes of Newcastle, Northumberland and Rutland, Earl Grey and Lords Dacre and Wenlock, to cite only the most prominent.[29] But although conscientious owners such as these did much to raise standards on their own estates (though not always everywhere there), many others, for want of funds or lack of interest, allowed the workers' homes to remain miserably and unhealthily inadequate.

Evidence of activity in house building in rural areas shows a rise to have occurred in the three decades beginning in 1841, a trend encouraged, no doubt, by more prosperous conditions and new developments in farming. The 1850s and 1860s formed a period when progressive landlords, aroused by the loss of agricultural protection and the threat of increased overseas competition, took advantage of cheap government loans to make their farms more efficient. They drained heavy clay lands and rebuilt farmhouses, farmsteads and barns and cattle sheds. 'High farming' was in vogue, and the new manures, improved breeds of cattle, and extended use of steam power required large new investment. Sometimes the cottages were rebuilt along with the farms; this step was encouraged in due course by the 1865 reform of the Poor Law, which spread the burden of poor rates equally across the whole union of twelve or fifteen parishes rather than falling unequally on individual parishes as formerly. Those proprietors who failed to move with the times found themselves the subject of caustic lampoons in *Punch*. In the *Punch Almanac* of 1861 a landowner was shown taking Mr Punch over his new stables: '"Yes, Mr Punch", says he, "handsome, clean stall, well aired, plenty of light, drainage, perfect ventilation, the best water and the best feed possible, and good treatment, that's my plan."' They move on to

The Cottage

Mr. Punch (to Landlord). "Your stable arrangements are excellent!
Suppose you try something of the sort here! Eh?"
(Punch Almanac, 1861)

Figure 2.3 The Cottage (1861)

a squalid cottage where a family of seven are trying to sleep and warm
themselves in a single room. Mr Punch is moved to remark: 'Your stable
arrangements are excellent! Suppose you try something of the sort here!
Eh?' The *Punch* issue of September 19, 1863, included another attack on
the same theme. A drawn and bent labourer in a ragged smock frock
leans over the wall of a well-constructed pigsty, observing the pigs
happily wallowing in their straw: 'Ah!', he says to himself, 'I'd like to be
cared for half as well as thee be!'[30]

Influenced by contemporary architects' liking for the Romantic and the
Picturesque, some proprietors built entire villages or hamlets which consciously sought to achieve a uniform effect. An early example was Blaise
Hamlet, built in 1810, which soon became 'a port of call on Picturesque
tours of the West Country', and influenced subsequent developments
such as Somerleyton, Ilam, Old Warden and Harlaxton.[31] Unfortunately,
artistic objectives often over-rode practical considerations. Overhanging

The Pig and The Peasant
Peasant. "Ah! I'd like to be cared vor half as well as thee be!"
(Punch, September 19, 1863)

Figure 2.4 The Pig and the Peasant. (1863)

thatch, obtrusive gables and windows consisting of tiny criss-cross panes kept interiors dark and gloomy, and Gothic designs often meant steep, narrow and twisting staircases, with bedrooms much restricted and inconvenienced by the steeply-sloped roofs. Fortunately, in the cottages of the later nineteenth century the Gothic features were moderated, the bargeboards, finials and porches used more sparingly. Estate cottages were substantial and well-finished but plainer and more adapted to the needs of the people who were to live in them. The change was assisted not only by revised ideas of style but also by some loss of interest by landowners in small-scale domestic buildings in favour of churches and country houses.[32]

Estate cottages came to be readily recognisable, as the great owners, with widely scattered estates, adopted plans of standard size built in a more or less uniform estate style, and their achievements were discussed in architectural and agricultural journals. The Duke of Bedford's cottages, for example, all contained two ground-floor rooms, with the kitchen having a cooking range and the scullery a copper. There were either two or three bedrooms, one of them fitted with a fireplace, while the outbuildings included a WC and an oven common to each block of cottages. The cottages were built of nine-inch brick walls and cost in mid-century £90–100 each, the expense being kept down by mass-production methods, with a hundred workmen constantly employed to make windows, doors, staircases and fittings to standard patterns. Originally, let at 1s or 1s 6d a week the cottages were said to produce a profit of 3 per cent. By 1885, however, somewhat higher standards and increased building costs had raised the price to £500 a pair and lowered the profit to ½ per cent.[33]

Landowners' model villages, of course, contained only a tiny proportion of the total of rural housing, and that at the upper end of the market. The picturesque environment, artificially created, bore little relation to the squalid, ugly and higgledy-piggledy reality of the great majority. And in 1864 the true nature of this reality was revealed by a survey carried out by Dr H.J. Hunter at the behest of the Medical Officer of the Privy Council, Dr John Simon. Dr Hunter's investigation covered 821 country parishes and fully justified the claims of those who argued the need for urgent improvement. In the parishes examined by Dr Hunter the population had risen by almost 16,500 over the ten years following the census of 1851, while the number of cottages available had actually fallen, by as many as 3,116, or 4.5 per cent. As a result, the average number of persons per house had risen from 4.41 to 4.87. Again, this average conveyed little of the real situation. The overcrowding, for example, was better indicated by the average number of persons per bedroom, which worked out at almost three. Moreover, 40.8 per cent of the cottages surveyed had only one bedroom, and 54.5 per cent only two; under 5 per cent had more than two. Those cottages with only one bedroom held an average of four persons to that room, and over the whole sample of 5,375 cottages examined in this respect, the average air space was only 165 cubic feet per person—a figure which again may be compared with the statutory requirement of 250 cubic feet in common lodging-houses, and 500 cubic feet in workhouses.[34] The comparison with Bailey Denton's figures are even more damning: 624 cubic feet as against the 900 cubic feet which he estimated as necessary for the main bedroom.

In Bedfordshire, to take examples of the detailed material collected by Dr Hunter, a number of cottages had deteriorated to such an extent that 'their condition is often a mere precarious holding together of rotten materials . . . there are hundreds on which no repairs can now be bestowed with advantage'. At Wrestlingworth near Biggleswade, some homes had two bedrooms made out of one by erecting a board partition, but this was a questionable improvement when the total outside measurements were only about 15 ft by 11 ft. Sometimes, again, the situation was eased by placing a bed in the tiny kitchen, and a large family might occupy the two bedrooms of a pair of cottages, leaving the kitchen for an old couple next door. One house had a total measurement of only 11 ft by 7 ft 6 ins. Privies were scarce, and the tenants had to build their own over a ditch or hole provided by the landlord. But as soon as one was built, all the neighbours used it.

Dr Hunter emphasised the contrast between 'close' villages, like Cockayne Hatley, where the few residents had large houses with good gardens, wells, privies and allotments at a low rent, and others like Wrestlingworth and Dunton, open villages which had to supply the extra labour required in the neighbouring close village of Eythorn. At Dunton the high rents of the new cottages could be met only by families combining together to share the accommodation, and by supplementing their income with the wives' and children's earnings from straw plaiting. A one-bedroom house, let at £3.10s a year, was occupied by six adults and four children. A little outside the village stood what was in Dr Hunter's experience 'the worst inhabited house in England'. Three adults and five children paid 25s a year for it: there was no privy and the tenants 'dunged against the house side'; a piece of matting hung inside the door to cover the bottom nine inches which had rotted away; a full half of one window was missing, both frame and glass. At Houghton Regis, near Dunstable, the one privy which served eight houses was 'always occupied' since straw plaiting kept all the families at home, the men doing the housework while the women were earning a living by plaiting. In Beech Street in Biggleswade, 'a half-drained street, full of stinking gullies', 2s a week was paid for the houses, some having no back openings and a mere closet for the second bedroom. The privy and cesspool of one cottage were actually within the house. Also very bad, at Eggington, was a newly-built row of eight cottages, placed back to back, without gardens, and with built-up uncovered cesspools. In the eight single bedrooms slept 22 adults and 12 children.[35]

An agent's survey made in 1864 of the cottages on a newly-purchased estate in the close village of Eythorn offers an interesting supplement to Dr Hunter's report. In particular, it brings out the extent to which labourers' housing consisted of old buildings converted from an earlier use. Of the 24 dwellings on the estate eight were deemed by the agent to be 'nearly new, and good Cottages in every respect'. Seven, however, had been made out of two former farmhouses, and nine were 'old mud Cottages, that may be kept in repair for many years to come'. Six of the eight nearly new cottages had two bedrooms, and two had three; all but one of the converted cottages had two bedrooms, as did four of the nine mud ones, the remainder having only one. One of the old farmhouses was divided into three tenements, with one tenant, Mr Tilcock's wagoner, occupying the old brewhouse. The second old farmhouse was divided into four tenements, with one of the tenants having the old brewhouse there as his kitchen and pantry, and two bedrooms, one on the ground floor and the other over the kitchen.[36]

Further evidence of the varied local conditions, the contrast between superior new housing and the old persisting slums, was provided in the reports, published between 1867 and 1870, of the Royal Commission on the Employment of Children, Young Persons and Women in Agriculture. There was renewed horror at the physical, moral and intellectual degradation, the lack of modesty and decency, the wretchedness and acute hardship. In Norfolk the petty speculators in open villages like Docking were found to charge the highest rents for the worst housing. Overcrowding was such that a Building Act to limit the number of occupants to cubic capacity was advocated as the only remedy. The large landowners of the county, such as Lord Leicester, charged less than half as much, £3.3s a year, for model cottages let direct to the labourer. In Northumberland and Durham also the great proprietors had built numbers of model dwellings, but elsewhere was still to be found the traditional type of home consisting of only one large room, about 18 ft square, with a floor of earth, no ceiling or upper storey, the byre for a cow placed at one end. In such rooms as many as eleven persons slept in box-beds, 'coffins for the living', finding comfort in the ever-burning fire and the heat gradually built up during the winter. Yorkshire, Lancashire and Derbyshire emerged as the best counties, Leicestershire, Shropshire, Gloucestershire and Worcestershire as bad, and the south-west generally as a region of 'whole-sale neglect', with Dorset, Wiltshire and Somerset vying for the title of worst. In Dorset the mud cottage with its thatch roof was still commonplace, the house filled with the acrid smoke of the peat fire, homes where one could not stand upright, and the smoke, dirt and filth such as to make them unsuitable shelters for animals let alone human beings.[37]

Very soon the Public Health Act of 1875 created rural sanitary authorities, which came to form the nucleus of the later Rural District Councils. Over the years their medical officers drew attention to conditions now familiar, some of them affecting even the new cottages. Thus, as a medical officer noted in April 1889, the water from a well of a new cottage, one of two, at Kempston West End, very near Bedford, was said to be brackish and in any case was situated too near a cesspit. Fever had broken out there and he found that the inhabitants of the two cottages were in the habit of using the pond rather than the well for their drinking water. The pond was liable to 'pollution by soakages from the privy and ash hole; the outbreak of fever is attributed to these sanitary defects . . .'. Two weeks later two new cases of enteric fever were removed from these cottages to a fever hospital. It was reported that people in other houses in the same village were also using ponds because their wells were out of order. At Boot Yard in Riseley, north of Bedford, there was an example of severe overcrowding: 'a house occupied by Jesse Gammons his wife and six children, sons aged 16, 12 and 6, daughters 23, 20 and 18 consists of only two rooms, a living room 13 ft x 10 ft and a sleeping room over it in which there is next to nothing in the way of furniture; this house requires cleansing and is so overcrowded as to be a nuisance and injurious to health'.[38]

Under the Public Health Act of 1875 the sanitary authorities' medical officers had powers to inspect properties and to condemn as nuisances any which were so insanitary or overcrowded as to form a serious danger to health. Houses shown to be unfit for human habitation could be compulsorily closed and their further occupation forbidden. Occasionally, where there was a strong local initiative, the Act was used to compel the farmers or other employers to provide new dwellings in place of those condemned, but generally the effects were small.[39] One difficulty was that the cottage owners—landlords, farmers, tradesmen, builders, publicans, retired professional men, widows—were among the most important ratepayers in the district and might be prominent local figures with seats on Boards of Guardians, School Boards, Watch Committees, and even the sanitary authority itself. It was a bold medical officer—bearing in mind his low status and derisory salary—who would be willing to embroil himself in disputes with such persons of influence. Another difficulty, one more cogent perhaps, was the lack of alternative accommodation. The medical officer faced a frightful dilemma. Was it worse to allow a family to continue to live in conditions which he knew to form a real and imminent danger to health, or to close the house and force a family with children, perhaps babies, out on the street with nowhere to go?

Compromise seemed often the only solution. Pressure, formal and informal, might be applied by issuing reports containing the unvarnished facts and by talking privately to the owners of the worst slums, pointing out the health hazards of defective and neglected houses. Some might thus be inclined to make improvements voluntarily, even if the outlays could not be recouped in higher rents. But though in some instances the worst dangers of defective water supplies and sanitation might be overcome, a new well or an earth closet did not expand the size of rooms, prevent over-crowding, nor make a filthy home clean. As yet the untrammelled rights of property owners remained almost intact; and as for the tenants of cottage property a long process of education and creation of self-respect had hardly begun.

V

In the 1880s and after, the state of rural housing achieved greater publicity, partly through new Royal Commissions, and partly through a wider growth of interest in the subject fuelled by a flow of new investigations and writing. Just as depressed conditions in farming reduced the incomes of those connected with agriculture and led to a decline in the rate of rural housebuilding, so the political and economic position of the landowning class was now brought under renewed attack: a potent weapon to hand in this struggle was the 'flight from the land' and the plight of those workers who remained in the countryside. One arm of the assault was concerned with the landlords' alleged failure to see that country labourers were properly housed. A number of specialised works appeared, such as those by Richard Heath and William G. Savage,[40] which however dealt mainly in isolated and often anonymous examples. More concrete and detailed were the discussions which formed part of the debate arising before the First World War between the (Liberal) Land Enquiry Committee and the (Conservative) Land Agents' Society.[41]

The first major official inquiry of the late nineteenth-century period was that of the Royal Commission on the Housing of the Working Classes of 1884, the year when the franchise was extended to the rural workers. Their housing was now a matter of some political importance, even if many country people lacked the necessary property qualification and still did not have the right to vote, while others among the newly-enfranchised did not care to exercise it. Cases of over-crowding as disgraceful as any in the past were brought to the attention of the Royal Commission—from Wiltshire seven and nine persons sharing one small bedroom, numerous one-bedroom houses in Essex and elsewhere—and there were references to bare thatch, wattle and daub, earth floors and ladders serving as staircases (the last not entirely outmoded in the middle of the following century). The farm labourers' unions, however, protested most strongly about insecurity of tenure, the tied cottage from which a family could be evicted on notice of only one week, even one day. When cottages went with the job the labourer was afraid to complain of disrepair, bad water or evil sanitation, and he dared not move to some better-paid or more attractive employment.[42]

The nature of the situation near the end of the century was made evident in the reports of the Royal Commission on Labour of 1892–94. Owing to the decline in the rural population and the large numbers of cottages built in the past by landowners and others there was no general shortage of housing, though the distribution of housing was irregular and cottages were often situated in places very inconvenient for their inhabitants. There was indeed some evidence of vacant cottages lacking tenants, though it may be that these were generally homes of the worst kind, or even derelict. Although the supply was generally adequate, there were still widespread deficiencies in the number, size and comfort of the rooms, and in the water supply and sanitation. There was as ever a marked contrast between the good and the bad, and evidence that the labourers themselves were beginning to expect something better than one-bedroom shacks, clay walls, brick or earth floors perpetually damp, meagre windows and a dearth of ovens, coppers and sinks. A desire for higher standards, along with the increased life-span of labourers and a growing demand by townspeople for country homes, contributed to the shortage of housing still found in some areas. And there was evidence, too, that not all country people valued improved amenities when they were provided. A third bedroom was used for housing a lodger, storing grain and potatoes or for lumber, and a ladder was preferred to a stair-case as taking up less space. Better ventilation was not valued by people who had been brought up to like a fug, and some did not find much advantage in a w.c. or earth closet over the old familiar privy. Rents, which varied greatly but could be said to be usually about 1s 6d a week, often bore no relation to the size of the cottage, its cost and accommodation, its condition and amenities, or the earnings of the tenant.[43]

Some evidence taken from the Census of 1901 may be drawn on to bring out the extent of regional and local variations in both the size and the occupation of cottage housing at that time. Hertfordshire appears as a relatively good county in these respects. There, of all the cottages in 13 Rural Districts having less than five rooms, only 21.6 per cent had less than four rooms; and the great majority of the 116 single-room homes were occupied by only one person. Nevertheless, there were some black spots where overcrowding existed. In Hatfield Rural District, for instance, six of the two-room cottages held six persons each, and another two-room home held as many as eight. In Hitchin Rural District 14 of the three-room cottages were occupied by eight or more persons, and 16 of the four-room ones held ten or more. Watford Rural District, too, had three three-room cottages with nine inhabitants each, five four-room cottages which had the same number, and one with as many as 11 people.

The Rural Districts of Leicestershire showed a marked deterioration in cottage accommodation as compared with those of Hertfordshire. In Leicestershire over 32 per cent of all cottages with less than five rooms in 13 Rural Districts had less than four rooms, nearly 11 per cent of them having only one or two rooms. Again, however, the bulk of the one-room homes had only one occupant, and the majority of two-room ones had three occupants or fewer. Hallaton Rural District was exceptional in its high proportion of two-room and three-room cottages, a total of 81 out of the 181 cottages having fewer than four rooms (45 per cent), but only four of the two-room tenements and 21 of the three-room ones held three or more persons. The majority of the four-room cottages, too, 66 out of 100, had four or fewer persons living in them. Clearly, a high proportion of small cottages was no indication of the extent of over-crowding, at least in terms of persons to rooms. There were certainly worse districts. Market Bosworth RD, for example, had one two-room tenement occupied by as many as nine persons, 12 of its three-room homes held eight persons or more, and 27 four-room homes were filled by ten or more persons.

Warwickshire's Rural Districts showed an even higher proportion of cottages with fewer than four rooms, 50.5 per cent compared with 32.2 per cent in Leicestershire and 21.6 per cent in Hertfordshire. The tenements with only one or two rooms accounted for over 11 per cent, a very slightly higher figure than that for Leicestershire, and considerably worse than the 8.7 per cent for Hertfordshire. Again, in Warwickshire the majority of one-room homes held only one person, although in Foleshill Rural District 25 of the two-room cottages housed five persons, 11 held six, and four as many as seven; and in Atherstone RD 44 of the two-room cottages held more than five persons, two having as many as eight, and one having nine. Once again a high proportion of smaller cottages was no indication of the extent of overcrowding. Of the 197 cottages with fewer than five rooms in Farnborough RD as many as 134 had only two or three rooms; nevertheless, none of the two-room homes held more than five persons, and only 17 of the 112 three-room ones did so. Atherstone RD, on the other hand, had 60 three-room cottages holding eight persons or more, ten of them with ten persons or over, while 34 of the four-room cottages held ten persons or over.

The figures for 11 Rural Districts in Northumberland appear horrifying, though one must remember the tradition in that county of families living and sleeping together in only one or two large rooms. In fact, by 1901 just under 8 per cent of all cottages with less than five rooms consisted of a single room, though not a few of them held five or more persons, some as many as eight, nine, or even ten. A very high proportion of the homes, 42.2 per cent, had only two rooms. Altogether, over 80 per cent of Northumberland's rural cottages of less than five rooms had fewer than four rooms. Averages are always liable to mislead, of course, and there were some Rural Districts in the county where the figures were much higher than those just given. Alnwick RD, for example, had a total of 2,134 cottages of less than five rooms, but only 325 of these (15 per cent) had as many as four rooms; in Norham and Islandshires RD almost two-thirds of such cottages had only one or two rooms; and the figures for Belford and Glendale Rural Districts, at 59 per cent and 55 per cent respectively, were little better. In Alnwick RD 36 of the two-room tenements and 82 of the three-room ones held eight or more persons, and the corresponding figures for Norham were 44 and 43, for Glendale 56 and 62. Belford RD was considerably better than these districts in this respect, having 42 two-room homes and only 29 three-room ones housing eight or more persons. Tynemouth RD, however, had a far worse housing situation with its figures of 107 and 159 respectively.[44]

In the absence of information on the size of rooms, the figures given above form only a very rough and ready guide to the extent of inadequate cottage housing, though they do at least serve to bring out the very wide variations that existed both regionally and locally, and provide a comparison with the figures produced by Dr Hunter in 1864. The numbers of rooms, of course, might well be much less significant than their size or the situation and state of repair of the cottage as a whole, as also the presence or absence of vital basic amenities such as a convenient supply of pure water, adequate facilities for heating and cooking, and proper provision for disposal of sewage and rubbish. The reality of cottage life depended on these factors, and the number of rooms available to a family might be only a minor element in whether or not it enjoyed a sufficient and wholesome home.

New legislation, the Housing of the Working Classes Act of 1890, and the Housing and Town Planning Act of 1909, made little impact on the rural situation. The legislation was permissive, relied on local initiative, and hence very largely a dead letter. Even the extended powers and encouragement offered by the later Act failed to bring about any substantial building of new houses by local authorities. Economy was the watchword, and councillors were more concerned to keep down the rates than to accept an expensive responsibility for replacing notorious slums with new council houses.

Almost nothing was done in the way of new building under the 1890

Act: in twenty years a mere ten loans were sanctioned totalling only £34,800 (of which £23,300 was sanctioned in the one year 1908), enough to build no more than 180 houses. The 1909 Act produced a little more enthusiasm, though by 1912 only 29 out of a total of 655 Rural District Councils had applied for loans, to build between them 398 dwellings.

There was considerably more activity in issuing orders for improvement. To March 1912 16,900 orders had been issued by 303 Councils, though 352 Councils had issued none. The nearly 17,000 improvement orders, and the 3,270 orders for closure or demolition, would no doubt have been many more but for the considerable pressures against making use of the 1909 Act. In the first place it took a bold and determined councillor to go so far as to force his Parish Council to send a complaint to the Rural District Council. Secondly, there was the difficulty of getting the tenants of unfit houses to put their names to a complaint, or to speak up at a public meeting, often with good reason. Some landlords, knowing who had dared to indict them, were not above using intimidation, moving tenants from one house to another, threatening eviction, and sometimes going so far as to carry it out.

Of the 16,900 orders for improvement, in only 90 cases was the authority obliged to act through default of the landlord. Over 11,000 cases were successfully dealt with, and in 377 cases the owner chose voluntarily to close the house rather than carry out improvements required. Under a different section of the Act a total of 3,270 orders for closure or demolition were issued by 364 Rural District Councils. Many owners did not wait for a closing order to be issued: over 12,000 houses were made fit by the landlords without an order being issued, and over 2,000 were closed or demolished voluntarily. Altogether a total of nearly 5,800 cottages were closed or demolished in a little over three years following the passing of the 1909 Act. Against this substantial figure a mere 398 new houses were built by local authorities. There is no doubt, therefore, that the Act of 1909 added to the shortage of working-class housing in the countryside, even though over 12,000 homes were improved to avoid their being subject to closing orders, and a further 11,268 had been made fit as the result of orders for improvement.[45]

Such figures pale into insignificance when placed against the total of rural working-class dwellings. Unfortunately, we have no statistics which enable us to tell precisely what this figure was. We do know that for the rural districts of England and Wales taken as a whole, 1,753 million inhabited houses existed in 1911 for a population of 7.9 million. Roughly a third of the population was classed as agricultural, and allowing for four or five persons per house, the number of agricultural cottages required to house this poorest section of the rural population would have been about 600,000. If the estimate of the Land Enquiry Committee that a 10 per cent shortage of agricultural cottages existed is near the truth, then this implies a figure of 540,000 and a shortage of 60,000. The total number of agricultural workers in 1911 (excluding farmers and their relations but including bailiffs or foremen) was about 680,000. Allowing for a proportion of about a third of the homes having more than one agricultural worker in the family, this implies a need for about 525,000 houses. To this figure has to be added, however, houses occupied by farmworkers' widows and the elderly past work, so that perhaps the 600,000 figure suggested by the Land Agents' Society is a reasonable one. (It was estimated in the 1920s that rural dwellings occupied by the working classes probably totalled about one million, and that some 60–70 per cent of the homes were those of persons employed in agriculture, which fits in well with the Land Agents' Society's figure.)

Another estimate, also derived from the investigations of the Land Agents' Society in 1913, unfortunately does not tally very closely. The Society's enquiries showed that on 265 landed estates covering nearly 1.5 million acres there was a total of 22,727 cottages suitable for agricultural workers.[46] It is probable that since many labourers lived in small towns and open villages, the estate cottages housed only a part of the labour employed on estates and their farms. The figure of 22,727 cottages is probably not, therefore, a suitable one for estimating on an acreage basis the total number of cottages in the countryside. If the calculation were made, however, it would produce a figure of only about 370,000.

There is the considerable complication that substantial numbers of estate cottages were in fact occupied not by farmworkers but by other, somewhat better-paid, types of workers. The Land Agents' investigation revealed that only 13,200 of the 22,727 estate cottages were actually occupied by farmworkers, the remainder being in the occupation of other workers (including the employees of rural industries, and local government employees, accounting for 6,390 cottages), and pensioners and widows (3,137 cottages). Only 58 per cent of cottages suitable for agricultural workers, therefore, were actually occupied by them. The conclusion of the Land Agents' Society was that the housing situation for the farmworker would be much improved if all employers, including the government and local authorities, accepted their responsibility for 'housing their labour in the same manner as the agricultural landowner had done'.[47]

Whatever the true number of farmworkers' homes may have been, it is clear that the 470 cottages built by local authorities between 1909 and 1913 was a minuscule proportion of the total of cottages, almost certainly under 0.1 per cent of the total. Similarly the 15,000 houses improved and the 5,000 compulsorily closed together represented almost certainly well under five per cent. Of course, some non-agricultural employers had accepted responsibility in some degree for housing their labour. Country railway stations often had a house attached for the station-master, if not for his signalman, booking clerk and porters, just as village schools had a house for the headteacher and his wife, though not for the assistants and pupil-teachers. Country factories and works commonly had accommodation for the manager, though the workforce, usually recruited locally, had to shift for themselves. Where housing was scarce, non-agricultural workers competed with farm people for available cottages, and so estate houses came to be occupied by the employees of rural works and trades (taking up 22 per cent of the cottages according to the Land Agents' figures), by council roadmen (2 per cent), railway and canal workers (1.6 per cent), post office employees (1.2 per cent), and police and other government employees (together 1.6 per cent). A similar situation occurred no doubt in country towns and large open villages, where the low-paid agricultural labourer tended to be priced out of the better housing. It is probable that the occupants of the rural slums were primarily agricultural workers, together with the elderly and the lowest paid of other occupations. Certainly the investigators of rural housing appear to have associated slums with farmworkers.

Meanwhile, if local authorities were doing little to help the housing situation, there were nevertheless some general advances in the village environment. The new parish councils which were established from 1894, though sometimes lethargic to the point of total ineffectiveness, might in the more active cases involve themselves in such matters as allotments, encroachments on public land, preservation of greens and commons, provision of recreation grounds, and removal of obstructions to rights of way and the barbed wire fencing which festooned roads and footpaths. Landowners and farmers were badgered into erecting stiles and taking down dangerous barbed wire. Allotments, or the lack of them, were a sore subject in many villages, but where they were available under suitable conditions they could provide an important supplement to a family's income and diet. Recreation spaces for the children were valued, too, but of more direct concern to most villagers, perhaps, were developments in public water supplies to replace wells and springs, improvements to the roads, and the introduction of street lighting.[48] The provision of metalled road surfaces and their tar-painting were especially appreciated as reducing the clouds of dust which flew in at cottage doors and windows in dry summers, and the mud which was tramped inside during winter.

Parochial sanitary committees, appointed under the Public Health Act of 1875, had already done useful work in dealing with nuisances, though sometimes the measures adopted were palliatives rather than solutions. In Batheaston, near Bath in Somerset, there were, for example, drains which gave rise to offensive effluvia, including a 'foul and dilapidated slop drain to a foul open privy with cesspool underneath the floor at two cottages at North End'. New sewers proved eventually to be the only adequate solution for old drains and privies which discharged through an open ditch into a brook, causing periodical blockages and highly unpleasant odours. There was even the offence caused by a horse kept in a back kitchen. In Batheaston the collection of house refuse was begun in 1884 but only on the modest basis of three collections a year. Responsibility for this service was taken over by the Rural District Council in 1903. The church and entrance to the churchyard were lit by gas in 1868, but the introduction of street lighting had to wait until 1881, and then depended on a public subscription being taken up to relieve the burden on the rates of installing 25 lamps. Even so, the lighting season extended only from early September to May, and the lamps were not lit at all on moonlit nights.[49]

How far these environmental improvements went in stemming the outflow of country people to towns and overseas is doubtful. The losses by migration were considerable, as shown by the example of the six rural counties, Cumberland, Herefordshire, Huntingdonshire, Rutland, Somerset and Westmorland, which showed together an actual *decrease* in numbers of 25,597 over the twenty years following the census of 1891, and this in a period when the total population of England and Wales rose by over 24 per cent. In general the outflow of labour from the countryside had already become large by the 1850s, and from then down to the 1870s the greatest movement was from the southern and eastern counties. Subsequently, the outflow from these regions continued to be substantial, but in the 1880s and 1890s Wales and the north of England also experienced substantial losses. There was, however, little fall in total numbers, and therefore no serious degree of depopulation. The birth rate remained high despite the movement of young men and women, and in effect, the natural increase made good the losses through migration, so that, overall, the numbers in the rural districts of the country marked time while the urban population increased rapidly.

Contemporary observers were generally of the opinion that the bad conditions in which people often lived were a major influential factor causing out-migration, although it was remarked that the state of cottages varied considerably in every district. There were, of course, many other factors: the lowness of wages and lack of prospects in agriculture; the greater variety of town occupations and their somewhat better wages; the attraction to country youths of donning a uniform and having housing provided, and receiving a pension at the end of the day, as in the army, the police and the railways, occupations of particular interest to country men. There were also; the dullness of country life as compared with the imagined liveliness of the towns; the greater ease and cheapness of travel which made once distant places much more accessible; the newspapers, leaflets, magazines and public meetings which advertised the advantages of America, Australia or New Zealand; and, not least, the infectious example set by those who had already moved away, and the letter from a friend or relation recounting his experience of the better life elsewhere and offering help in taking the crucial step. And, according to the farmers, the education received compulsorily by all country children from the 1870s exerted a pernicious influence in making them unfitted for farm work and discontented with their lot.

With so many influences involved in migration, it was clearly impossible to determine the role played by bad housing, or in some places, indeed, the complete lack of any dwelling that a young couple would care to call home. That these played some part was self-evident to some well-informed observers, such as the Norfolk farming squire and novelist, Ridger Haggard. His extensive tours of the countryside, published at the turn of the century as *Rural England*, gave a number of examples of disgraceful slums, notably some cottages at Eltisley, near St Neots in

Cambridgeshire, which had an open sewer running close to the houses, and were known locally as 'Eltisley death trap'.[50] Another contemporary who took this view was the distinguished Royal Commission investigator and authority on labourers' conditions, A. Wilson Fox. Writing in 1903, he remarked as 'extraordinary' the contrast between the old and new types of cottage, often to be found in the same parish. The old type had often:

... overcrowding in the sleeping rooms, low ceilings, small windows, rickety stairs; while down stairs the living room is often a small kitchen possessing no back door, where the cooking and washing have to be done. The discomfort in case of illness in such places can be imagined. Add to this, dampness on the ground floor, general want of repair, little or no garden, no proper outhouse or sanitary arrangements, and water to be fetched from some distance, and occasionally nothing but pond water to be obtained, and you get some of the influences which make the agricultural labourer not disinclined to move elsewhere when he gets the chance.

The new type of cottage, by contrast, had often three bedrooms, a kitchen and scullery or pantry; a parlour, a washhouse with a copper or a bakehouse, and a garden and pigsty. This sort of cottage could really be a home: there 'health, decency, cleanliness, and comfort can be obtained; the wife need not be a slut, nor the husband a drunkard, nor the children "little hooligans"'.[51]

Although the latter type of new cottage was becoming more general, the improvement in the average quality of the rural housing stock was a slow and patchy process. William C. Little's report to the Royal Commission on Labour noted that although large or wealthy landowners might 'continue from philanthropic motives or from a sense of duty to indulge in unremunerative investments', the ordinary owner of land could not afford to do so. Further, in many places, local sanitary authorities were prevented from taking steps to have insanitary dwellings remedied because of their knowledge that the owners had not the means of complying. Large numbers of old cottages, indeed, belonged not to hardhearted capitalists but were owned in ones and twos by struggling small farmers, by petty tradesmen and craftsmen, by retired persons and widows who had inherited them, even by labourers themselves. What was needed was some means of making cottages more worthwhile as an investment, and of giving all property owners the financial means and incentive to make improvements or go in for building new cottages. This might be done by adopting the most economical plans and materials to reduce the original cost of building; by providing loans at a low rate of interest; by adjusting rents to the character and size of accommodation provided; and by attaching larger gardens than were usual, which would also justify a higher rent.[52]

The solution which might appear now to have been the most obvious one, an increase in the wages paid to agricultural and other low-paid country labourers, was not suggested. This no doubt was thought to be too sensitive a subject, given the hostility of the farmers and the failure of agricultural workers' unions. In fact, wages of agricultural workers had risen slowly but quite substantially since the 1860s, in money terms by some 25 per cent, in real terms even more. This must have been a factor helping large landowners to build more roomy and better-equipped cottages to let at somewhat higher rents than could have been charged previously. Precisely how much agricultural workers earned in the years preceding the First World War was a subject of dispute at that time, and certainly the figures were complicated by regional and local variations and by the extent of piece-work earnings, especially important at harvest time. However, it seems from the evidence collected by the Central Land Association that the average earnings of ordinary labourers had risen from 17s 6d a week in 1907 to 19s 10d in 1912–13. The figures included payments in kind, such as a free cottage, free fuel carted to the cottage by the farmer, and potato ground, to mention but some of them. However, at the end of the nineteenth century Wilson Fox had valued such payments as averaging only between 2s 3d and 3s a week, though subsequently the Land Agents' Society argued that the average cash value of £4 a year allowed for a free cottage and garden by the Board of Trade did not do justice to the true market rent. In addition to the men's earnings, there were many instances where the wife and older children were able to earn a useful supplement by helping in the fields and orchards, by going out charring and running errands, keeping chickens, taking in washing, and making such things as jams and pies at home for sale. By this time most of the formerly important cottage industries for women, like straw-plaiting, lace-making and gloves, had declined or completely disappeared, and there were few replacements. Nevertheless, some cottages continued to house a lodger which helped at least pay the rent, and many families grew a considerable part of their food on their gardens or allotments.

But clearly even the pound a week earnings of 1913 would not allow for more than 2s–4s a week to be paid in rent, and the higher figure, representing a fifth of earnings, would often have caused hardship. Rowntree in his study of 1913 set the farm labourer's poverty line at 20s 6d a week for a family of two adults and three children. He applied the 'physical efficiency' criterion which he had already used in his examination of poverty in York, and similarly allowed nothing for tobacco, beer, newspapers, railway fares, emergencies, or luxuries of any kind. Nor did he allow for the higher cost of goods in village shops than in towns, nor yet for errors or carelessness in the wife's management of the home. Of his total figure, 13s 9d was allowed for food, 1s 4d for fuel, 2s 3d for clothing, 4d for insurance, and 10d for sundries. Only 2s a week was allowed for rent.[53] of course, as we have seen, there were many other types of workers in the countryside other than agricultural labourers, even though in many villages farmworkers formed the largest group: railwaymen, policemen, postmen, workers in country factories, engineering works, quarries and brickyards, council road men and others, estate employees, village craftsmen and their assistants—the variety was diverse, and the majority earned more, if only a little more, than the ordinary farmworker. Consequently, they were able to pay rather higher rents, and this had the effect of pushing the farmworker down into the cheapest and worst accommodation, unless he were fortunate enough to be relatively well-housed in a subsidised estate cottage.

If Rowntree's estimate is valid, then few ordinary farmworkers (as distinct from the somewhat better-paid bailiffs, shepherds and men looking after cattle and horses) could have afforded any house which would not be let for about £5 a year or less. The Land Agents' Society suggested in 1913 that the cost of erecting eight cottages on an acre of land worked out at about £200 each, including the cost of the land.[54] To produce a 5 per cent return on the expenditure the rent would have to be £10 a year, double the figure that Rowntree allowed, and of course from the £10 would have to be deducted rates, repairs, insurance and management. The yield on Consols in 1913 was a trouble-free 3.4 per cent (although throughout the period 1889–1906 it had been below 3 per cent), so it was not unreasonable that cottage property, with its outgoings and possible difficulties with tenants, should be expected to produce an additional margin. We are back again to the problem that had bedevilled rural housing over the past century or more: it simply was not possible to build adequate houses for the poorest-paid rural workers unless the landlord was willing to accept an unprofitably low return, or one that was even negative.

Of course, it may be argued that the rate of interest was of greater relevance to building by private speculators than to owners of landed estates. Most landowners accepted the necessity of providing cottages as part of the fixed capital of a farm, just as much as were the farmhouse, barns and cowsheds. And it had long been argued that good cottages helped in finding a good tenant for a farm since the farmer might expect to obtain a better class of worker. The cost of cottage building on landed estates, therefore, was covered by the higher farm rents paid than might otherwise be received. And insofar as the cottage rents were below commercial levels, the difference may be regarded as forming part of the earnings of the farmworkers. If cottage rents were to be raised to more economic levels then this would lead to an expectation of higher wages to be paid by the farmer, which in turn would lead to the farmer demanding a lower rent from the landlord.

Furthermore, landowners faced numerous discouragements to cottage building in the years between 1870 and 1914. Farm rents fell and many proprietors were consequently short of funds with which to build cottages. Moreover, the reduced incomes of landowners now became subject to higher rates of central and local government taxation, while at the same time the costs of building cottages were rising for a variety of reasons. Building costs themselves increased, new rural bye-laws imposed higher expenses than formerly, and the standards of accommodation expected were rising. The fall in the death rate created a request for the retention of cottages by the elderly, a request frequently allowed, and this was reinforced by the introduction of Old Age Pensions in 1908. A reduced turnover of cottage tenants affected the demand for new cottages, a partial offset to the effects of the out-migration of rural workers.[55]

Some of these factors—higher costs of building, rural bye-laws, higher standards and out-migration—must have adversely affected also the activities of speculative builders, even though, on the other hand, the longer lifespan and the rise in labourers' incomes helped to stimulate demand and favoured higher rents. It may be that the most active days of speculative cottage building were over by the end of the nineteenth century. The Land Agents' Society certainly assumed that the bulk of new cottage building was being done by estate owners.[56] There remained the possibility of the workers building their own houses. A number of small building societies had become established in rural areas, receiving deposits from members and advancing sums on mortgage to be used for house-building. One example was the Berkshire and Ascot Society, begun in 1881, which in 1914 had 262 members and had advances on mortgage totalling £8,332—enough perhaps to build some 50 houses. The scale of operation was usually very small, and some village building societies failed to survive. The Deddington, Oxfordshire, Society, incorporated in 1888, had by 1910 declined to only one member and annual receipts of £5, and this story could be repeated elsewhere.[57]

VI

Although landowners complained of the additional costs imposed on their building activity by the growth of rural bye-laws, the introduction of regulation was a much needed step towards preventing the uncontrolled jerry-building of the past, more especially in open villages. It was not so much the improved standards of construction that annoyed owners of estates—some of them had led the way in this respect; it was rather the bureaucratic complications and powers of intervention given to officials of elected District Councils. As Sir William Grantham, himself a builder of model cottages on his estate at Barcombe, wrote regarding the Chailey RDC in Sussex:

It is bad enough to have to wade through fifty bye-laws and to understand them (almost an impossibility) before you can begin to build a single cottage to let at 3s or 4s a week, but much worse if you have to comply with a fifty-first bye-law in such a way that an official of the District Council could trip you if he had a spite against you, because you had altered the position of a window or the aspect of an earth closet door.

Furthermore, the requirement to submit plans created a difficulty since few small builders were able to produce them. Very many houses, except perhaps where landowners took a particular pride in their appearance, were built totally without plans, but that did not necessarily mean that they were badly built.[58]

In the years before the First World War there was considerable discussion of the nature of the housing that should be provided for the rural

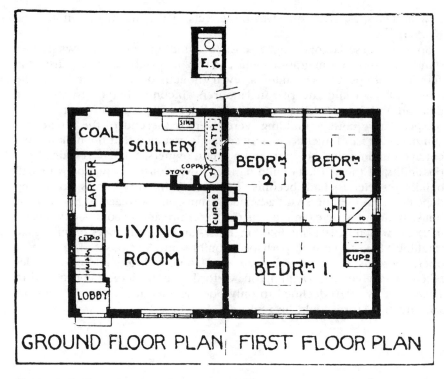

GROUND FLOOR PLAN | FIRST FLOOR PLAN

Figure 2.5 Plan of a pair of cottages of the accepted type, 1914.

worker. It was stated that:

By 1914 the accepted standard kind of new cottage consisted of a good-sized kitchen-living room, a small scullery, and a larder, on the ground floor, with coal-house and E.C. or W.C. either in an outbuilding or, less frequently, under the main roof. On the first floor three bedrooms are provided. The front door generally opens into a small lobby leading to the living room and staircase, or perhaps to the living room only, in which case the staircase is approached through the room. Occasionally the lobby gives direct access to the scullery also, but usually the scullery is approached through the living room, with a back door giving on the yard and leading to the outbuildings. The copper is commonly placed in the scullery, together with a small cooking stove intended for use in warm weather, though a separate wash-house is sometimes provided. A bath is often provided, either in the scullery or in one of the bedrooms.

The Departmental Committee on Buildings for Small Holdings recommended that the absolute minimum size for rooms should be 180 sq. ft for the living room, 80 sq. ft for the scullery, 24 sq. ft for the larder, and three bedrooms of 150, 100 and 65 sq. ft respectively. It accepted, however, that it might be allowable in some cases to have smaller dimensions, though the smallest house should have a living room of at least 165 sq. ft, a scullery of 65 sq. ft, the best bedroom 144 sq. ft and the smallest 65 sq. ft.[59]

Whatever the intentions of the Departmental Committee and of actual cottage builders, the use made of the accommodation by the families was often at odds with what was intended. Where, for reasons of economy, the third bedroom was placed on the ground floor, it was almost invariably used as a parlour, converting a three-bedroom home into a two-bedroom one. Again, the assumption that the scullery would be reserved for the dirty work of the house was unjustified, as in practice the scullery, however small, was frequently used as both living room and work room, while the living room was considered as a parlour and used only on Sunday or for receiving occasional visitors. If the scullery were large enough to hold a small table, this was invariably the case. The Departmental Committee went so far as to recommend that the scullery should be made so small as to be uncomfortable to live in.

There was, however, some opinion in favour of providing a separate parlour and that it should not be ruled out as an unnecessary luxury. Future advances in education would make it desirable to have a room in which children could work at their books. Or, if the parlour was not required by the family, it could be used as an additional bedroom or let to a lodger. Cottagers, it was argued, would seldom have any difficulty in getting a tenant for a spare room in view of the demand for accommodation of single men such as railway porters, shop assistants, postmen and builders' workers.

Another convenience, though one not always provided, was a sink with an open trapped gully outside to take the waste; its omission was a 'temptation to a slovenly woman to throw greasy water and household slops just outside the door, thus rendering the ground immediately about the house foul and unpleasant'. It would be better also if the staircase rose from inside the back door instead of from the front door. The front door was seldom used by labouring families, as was shown by the difficulty experienced by inmates drawing the bolts and opening the door when an unexpected visitor called. From the back door the staircase would give direct access to the bedrooms without going through the living room, with the further advantage of making it possible to carry the bedroom slops straight to the back of the house.

It was considered doubtful whether a bath should be provided. In many places the water supply was inadequate, and there being in general no demand for baths, the bath itself, when provided, was used for storing coal or potatoes. For use as a bath it was inconvenient when placed in the scullery, and even more so in a bedroom, where the water had to be carried upstairs and then baled out and carried downstairs again. 'The general practice seems to obtain of bathing the children in a portable bath before the kitchen fire on Saturday nights, and there does not seem to be much reason why much more than this should be required.'[60]

The question of having a parlour, the siting of the staircase, and the location of a bath were all academic questions for families who still occupied old unimproved cottages of the kind still commonly found in the countryside of 1914. Space was so cramped that the craftsman having no separate workshop used his bench and tools just outside the door as long as the weather allowed. For lack of storage room his products were to be seen stacked against the cottage walls or railings—chair legs, barrel hoops, wooden hay-rakes, birch brooms, trugs and baskets. To take the air on a nice day housewives put their wooden wash-troughs on a kitchen chair by the door or sat knitting jerseys or making bone-lace while chatting with the neighbours.

The most common amenities were often lacking. Hannah, wife of Joseph Ashby of Tysoe in Warwickshire, came as a bride to a tiny house with only two small rooms downstairs and two equally small above. She had no range for cooking, only an open fire with an ancient shallow oven; many other housewives nearby were even worse off—they could only boil and fry.[61] And Edwin Grey, in his recollections of cottage life in Harpenden, Hertfordshire, remembered houses where the water was drawn from wells, and which lacked anything in the way of a scullery, washhouse, copper, sink, or even drains. In large families six children shared one bed, and lads were still hired out at an early age to relieve the miseries of overcrowding. Despite the numbers sleeping there, bedroom chimneys were kept stuffed up to avoid draughts, and windows were tightly shut at night. In the dark people still used candles, rushlights, or the more recent paraffin lamps. No gas was laid on to the houses, though the gasworks itself was close at hand. And no privacy was possible when one closet had to serve six houses.[62]

Yet these were by no means the worst homes, not really slums as people then thought of them. The district nurse could not help but be familiar with the true slums—uneven earth floor, walls stained and broken, one single room downstairs to be used for all purposes, and furniture consisting of three hard wooden chairs and a bare table. There families lived out their lives in discomfort and squalor, there the elderly hung on lacking work, complaining of rheumatism, and dreading the approaching shadow of the workhouse. Water was still one of the most potent hazards to health, and a necessity often difficult to obtain. As one district nurse recalled in 1909:

I have known water used for cooking and drinking when it smelled so strongly that the same persons could not endure using it to wash the kitchen floor. Almost the first question one asks a cottage patient is, 'where do you get water?', and a frequent reply is, 'we take it from the roadside in the winter, and in the summer they let us have it at the farm, but it's a dreadful long way to send, and the pump's out of order this year'.[63]

The reports made by medical officers of health in the years before the First World War brought out the many various aspects of the rural housing problems. There were references at Smallburgh in Norfolk to porous walls, lack of gutters and damp-courses, many of the older cottages 'having been converted from barns or stables': in Linton rural district, Cambridgeshire, over three-quarters of the houses had fewer than three bedrooms, 57 having only one; at Chester-le-Street in Durham 469 out of 812 houses were scheduled as unfit for human habitation; in Essex there were many cottages 'barely fit for human habitation, and which owners would rather close than radically improve', while young people

Figure 2.6 Example of badly-built houses: houses built without gutters, the rainwater running off the roof and causing dampness at the base of the walls, 1915.

Figure 2.7 Example of a house built directly into a hillside with the soil rising on the back wall to the level of the roof, an inevitable cause of dampness.

who wished to marry were driven away for lack of a home; at Hartley Wintney, Hampshire, very few cottages were let at a rent within reach of the agricultural labourer, and 'to close even some meant driving the tenants to the workhouse'; and a final despairing note from Oundle in Northamptonshire: 'If a house is condemned there is no other for people to go to . . . It is impossible to work the [1909] Act simply by demolishing houses'.[64]

The Land, the 1913 report of the unofficial Land Enquiry Committee, which launched a comprehensive attack on the landowners, included a lengthy section on the scarcity and condition of cottages, as well as possible remedies for the situation. An investigator reporting from Leicestershire wrote of 'a back kitchen as dark as a coal pit . . . paper and plaster coming off the walls through dampness . . . Some twenty were condemned by medical officer and people still living in them'. A schoolmaster in Hampshire stated that in some cottages the walls were so damp that the pictures hanging on them were 'quite rotten', in one the rain dripped on the bed, three were without back doors. The deaths of two children in one cottage were attributed to the dampness. In Surrey, reported a County Councillor, many of the cottages were old, without damp-courses, and very dilapidated, with small windows which in some cases did not open. In Oxfordshire, wrote a schoolmaster, four cottages had been condemned, but an extension of time was allowed as there were no other cottages for the inhabitants to move into. (One had to have its outside walls supported by props.) In Suffolk cases of consumption and other complaints were attributed to overcrowding in small, badly ventilated bedrooms. In Wiltshire one or two of the mud cottages had holes right through the walls and the rain came through the roof and ran down the stairs. The majority had holes in the floors upstairs, and when the floors were scrubbed the water ran through. 'In one old lady's pantry the floor bricks are raised with mud and fungus coming through.'

And so on and on. In Suffolk three cottages used one open privy, and a group of four cottages had open privies within a few feet of the back door. 'The drainage of the village street of 113 houses falls into the stream.' In Pembrokeshire only five of the labourers' cottages had two rooms upstairs, the others having merely a loft over one end. The majority of the windows were fixtures, and most houses had only one door. There were numerous cases of gross overcrowding: in Lincolnshire a one-bedroom house held a man aged eighty, his grown-up daughter, granddaughter and grandson, and a male lodger. In Nottinghamshire a daughter of sixteen slept in a lean-to outhouse, the roof sloping down from 5 ft to as low as 4 ft high, the one window having wire netting and a curtain, but no glass. In Staffordshire a house with two bedrooms was occupied by two married couples besides children of both sexes. 'Notice has been given four months ago to clear one family out, but the people are still there, and say they cannot get a house with three rooms under 5s and won't go. And there seems an end of it.'[65]

Figure 2.8 Insanitary cottages at Biscovery, Cornwall.

Figure 2.9 A pair of neglected cottages on the Duke of Norfolk's estate, 1912.

Figure 2.10 Defective housing: a house built on an odd piece of ground with road front and back, 1913.

VII

The First World War brought an end to the controversy, at least for a few years. And after the war the continued drain of farm-workers off the land brought some easing of the situation, while further legislation accelerated progress in building new cottages, and in improving those that were worth saving. But the familiar problems did not go away. Among the many old houses there were still a great number without a piped water supply and having nothing more than an earth closet. In 1939 over 3,000 parishes, or about a quarter of the total, had no piped water supply. Rainwater was still widely used, as were wells 'of doubtful purity'. The lack of piped water, together with the scattered nature of the population, the small financial resources in terms of rateable value, and the opposition of the farmers, were factors discouraging local authorities from undertaking costly sewage schemes. Streams were still polluted with sewage and other rubbish, and those cottagers who had no garden still had nowhere to put their refuse. In an age of advancing education, motor cars, radios and universally-read newspapers, the cottage well, cesspool and earth closet seemed relics of a barbarous age. It was remarkable that in terms of epidemic disease and death rates the rural population still showed some margin of superiority, if a declining one, over townspeople. Nevertheless, bad housing was one of the several factors held by medical opinion to give rise to poor physique and under-nourishment among country children. Other factors included low incomes, which entailed a poor standard of diet, the migration of the more healthy to the towns, inter-marriage, and large families.[66]

New legislation after the First World War did relatively little to meet the need for an estimated 100,000 new houses in rural areas. Of the probable one million existing rural dwellings occupied by the working classes, between 60 and 70 per cent were occupied by people employed in agriculture. It was calculated that following the availability of subsidies provided by the Housing Acts of 1919 and 1924, nearly 83,000 new houses were built in rural areas, although only a moderate proportion of these were built in agricultural parishes. The world-wide economic depression of the early 1930s brought new building to a halt, and thereafter attention turned more towards the clearance of rural slums. In 1937 over 51,000 houses in the countryside were reported as unfit, and a survey of the previous year showed that about 3 per cent of rural houses were overcrowded. Subsidies were then provided specifically to relieve overcrowding, but the numbers of new cottages built as a result were extremely small.[67]

Altogether, between 1918 and 1938, 739,000 new houses were built in rural areas. Of this total, 266,000 were built with the aid of state subsidies (134,000 by local authorities, and 132,000 by private enterprise). As many as 473,000 were built by private enterprise without a subsidy, 64 per cent of the total. It is clear that subsidies played an important role in the provision of new rural housing, but it was still a role secondary to that of private building. No doubt the limitations and qualifications with which the subsidies were surrounded, as well as the inactivity of large numbers of Rural District Councils, had much to do with this. In any event, it is unlikely that more than a very small proportion of the 739,000 houses was built in agricultural parishes, and it is estimated that only 50,000 of new cottages, and probably many less, were occupied by the worst-paid and largest group of the rural poor, the farmworkers.[68]

Meanwhile, the number of small country dwellings which could be classed as slums was increasing as property owners failed to keep their cottages in repair, let alone make improvements. Partly this was because the cost of making repairs had risen greatly during the First World War, and between the wars was roughly double that of pre-1914, while cottage rents were controlled at low levels. Partly it was because landowners' rents and farmers' incomes had fallen sharply in real terms since the war, and indeed even in money terms, the rents of many estate owners were lower in 1938 than those received in the 1870s. New legislation offered state loans, and subsequently grants, to help owners to recondition their cottages, but little use was made of this assistance until late in the 1930s. By the end of 1937 reconditioning work had been completed on only 13,800 dwellings, and it is noteworthy that 26 out of the 134 Rural District Councils had made no grants at all. The legislation was intended primarily to help improve the housing of agricultural workers, but an analysis of the results in Devon, where 1,595 dwellings were reconditioned, showed that only 41 per cent of these houses were let at 3s a week or under, and as a result only 740 of the cottages, or 46 per cent, were in fact occupied by farmworkers.

The grants for reconditioning were surrounded by numerous requirements as well as restrictions on the rents that could be charged on completion. In particular, the cottages so improved had to have on completion of the work three bedrooms, a food store, wash-house, a renewed roof with gutters and down pipes, precautions taken against rising damp, and a separate water closet or earth closet provided for each cottage. The restrictions on the rent that could be charged were a discouragement to property owners, and the old problem of inability to pay an economic rent made both new and reconditioned cottages an almost impossible proposition for the poorest of rural inhabitants. In Devon 52 per cent of the houses reconditioned were let at rents of between 3s and 6s, and another 7 per cent at more than 6s, while in 1937 an official committee concluded that the maximum rent that could be expected from the worst-paid of rural inhabitants was only 3s exclusive of rates, or between 4s and 5s inclusive. And in 1930 the new subsidised houses built with the aid of assistance under the Act of 1924 rented at between 4s and 7s 6d. There was also some doubt whether many of the cottages reconditioned with the help of public money were worth the outlay. The basic structure remained old, the rooms small, and the house as a whole old-fashioned and inconvenient. Since the average cost of reconditioning was £215 per cottage, it might well have been better to have added another £100 and built a new house. As a report of the Ministry of Health commented, 'There are many country cottages the reconditioning of which would merely serve to perpetuate housing conditions which can no longer be tolerated'.[69]

While country occupations, especially in farming, were generally healthy, and even low-paid farmworkers lived to a relatively high age (even slightly longer than the farmers and their relations), few ended their days as hale and hearty old men and women.[70] A chesty, rheumatic old age owed a good deal to a lifetime spent in cold, damp and draughty cottages. And the level of infant mortality, though lower in rural districts than in urban ones and cities, was affected by overcrowding and impure water, as well as by large families, poverty and inadequate hygiene. The rural slum exacted a terrible toll of lives cut short and lives made miserable by chronic and disabling diseases. There were also the moral effects of overcrowding and lack of privacy, the young adults of both sexes sharing bedrooms, or sharing a bedroom with their parents—the situation which so horrified Victorian and Edwardian investigators. It was to relieve this situation that families were broken up at an early stage, the boys sent out when old enough to work, living with a relation, or a farmer or other employer, the girls to a nearby town to become live-in domestic servants.

Despite the horrifying revelations, the efforts of reformers, and the example set by some landowners who built model cottages, the rural slum was inescapable, given the condition of a free market in housing, where the poor tenant could not afford to be properly housed and those with the means of providing housing could do so only by building instant slums or providing a subsidy from their own pockets. The answer might be thought to lie in legislation and the provision of state subsidies. But even these measures, as the record shows, failed to provide the whole answer. The spending of public money had to be surrounded by qualifications and limitations, and the initiative lay with local bodies whose interest was frequently more in keeping down the rates of property owners than in improving the lot of the unpropertied. And, indeed, the dilemma continues: there are still in this year of writing rural families who cannot pay the rent of a subsidised council house without some further help from the tax-payer. The rural slum itself has now very largely disappeared, and the vast majority of country houses are ample and sanitary, but the fundamental problem of housing the rural poor remains one that future generations will still have to grapple with.

Notes

1. B. Seebohm Rowntree and May Kendall, *How the Labourer Lives*, Thomas Nelson, 1913.
2. John Woodforde, *The Truth about Cottages*, Routledge & Kegan Paul, 1969, pp.73–80.
3. Ibid., pp.85–6.

4. John Burnett, *A Social History of Housing, 1815-1970*, David & Charles, 1980, p.33.
5. Rowntree and Kendall, op.cit., p.330.
6. Burnett, op.cit., p.33.
7. C. Vancouver, *General View of the Agriculture of Devon*, Board of Agriculture, London, 1808, p.93.; A. Young, *General View of the Agriculture of Lincolnshire*, Board of Agriculture, London, 1813, p.40.
8. Woodforde, op.cit., pp.91-4.
9. Quoted by Burnett, op.cit., p.33.
10. Richard Heath, *The English Peasant*, T. Fisher Unwin, London, 1893, *passim*.
11. Woodforde, op.cit., p.39.
12. Peter Roebuck (ed.), *Constable of Everingham Estate Correspondence, 1726-43*, Yorkshire Archaeological Society, Record Series CXXXVI, 1976, pp.39, 59, 65, 67.
13. Vancouver, op.cit., pp.93-8.
14. A. Young, *General View of the Agriculture of Suffolk*, Board of Agriculture, London, 1813, pp.11-12.
15. A. Young, *General View of the Agriculture of Lincolnshire*, Board of Agriculture, London, 1813, pp.39-41.
16. Burnett, op.cit., p.39.
17. G.E. Mingay (ed.), *Agrarian History of England and Wales, VI 1750-1850*, Cambridge University Press, Cambridge, 1988, pp.1093, 1096, 1098, 1100, 1104.
18. Burnett, op.cit., p.41.
19. Ibid., p.43.
20. Duke of Bedford, 'On Labourers' Cottages', *Journal of the Royal Agricultural Society of England* (subsequently *JRASE*), X, 1849, pp.185-7.
21. George Nicholls, 'On the Condition of the Agricultural Labourer with Suggestions for its Improvement', *JRASE*, VII, 1846, p.17; Henry Goddard, 'On the Construction of a Pair of Cottages for Agricultural Labourers', *JRASE*, X, 1849, pp.232-4, 242; J. Young MacVicar, 'Labourers' Cottages', ibid., pp.404, 419.
22. T.W.P. Isaac, 'On the Construction of Labourers' Cottages', *JRASE*, XVIII, 1856, pp.495-7, 499, 500, 504-5.
23. E. Chadwick, *Report on the Sanitary Condition of the Labouring Population of Great Britain*, new edition M.W. Flinn (ed.), Edinburgh University Press, Edinburgh, 1965, pp.80-3, 86-9.
24. Ibid., pp.82, 84.
25. Barrie Trinder, *Victorian Banbury*, Banbury Historical Society, XIV, 1982, pp.9, 11, 13-14, 77.
26. *JRASE*, 2nd ser., VI 1870, pp.209, 213, 216-7, 220-3, 226, 230, 242-3.
27. Clare Sewell Read, 'The Disposal of Sewage by Small Towns and Villages', *JRASE*, I, 1890, pp.86-7, 89-95.
28. Woodforde, op.cit., pp.60-1.
29. Burnett, op.cit., p.52.
30. H. Taine, *Notes on England*, trans E. Hyams, Thames & Hudson, London, 1957, pp.134-5, 137.
31. Gillian Darley, *Villages of Vision*, Architectural Press, 1975, pp.26-7.
32. Ibid., pp.50, 52.
33. Burnett, op.cit., p.133.
34. Ibid., pp.125-6.
35. BPP 1865, XXVI, pp.148-51.

36. Beds. RO, X 344/3.
37. Burnett, op.cit., pp.127–9.
38. Beds. RO, RDBV 4.
39. Burnett, op.cit., pp.135–6.
40. R. Heath, *The English Peasant*, T. Fisher Unwin, London, 1893; W.G. Savage, *Rural Housing*, T. Fisher Unwin, London, 1915.
41. *The Land*: the Report of the Land Enquiry Committee, 1913; Land Agents' Society, *Facts about Land: a Reply to "The Land", the Report of the Unofficial Land Enquiry Committee*, 1916.
42. Burnett, op.cit., p.131.
43. Ibid., p.132.
44. This material from the Census of 1901 was kindly provided by Dr A.D.M. Phillips of the University of Keele.
45. Hugh Aronson, *Our Village Homes*, T. Murby, London, 1913, pp.78–9, 82–3; F.E. Green, *The Tyranny of the Countryside*, T. Fisher Unwin, London, 1913, pp.135–50.
46. Land Agents' Society, *Facts about Land*, 1916, pp.87–9, 94.
47. Ibid., pp.90–1.
48. See Dennis Clarke and Anthony Stoyel, *Otford in Kent—A History*, Otford and District Historical Society, 1975, pp.228–31.
49. *An English Rural Community: Batheaston with St Catherine*, Bath University Press, 1969, pp.73–4.
50. H. Rider Haggard, *Rural England*, 2nd edn., Longman, London, 1902, II, pp.61–4.
51. *Journal Royal Statistical Society*, LXVI, 2, 1903, p.305.
52. BPP 1893–94, XXXV, R.C. Labour, *The Agricultural Labourer*, V, pt. 1, General Report by William C. Little, Nelson, London, p.89.
53. Rowntree and Kendall, op.cit., pp.28–33.
54. *Facts about Land*, op.cit., p.107.
55. Ibid., pp.46–8.
56. Ibid., p.46.
57. A.W. Ashby, 'Village Clubs and Associations', *JRASE*, LXXXV, 1914, pp.11–12.
58. A. Dudley Clarke, 'Cottages for Rural Labourers', *JRASE*, LXV, 1904, pp.129–30.
59. C. Winckworth Allen, 'The Housing of the Agricultural Labourer', *JRASE*, LXXXV, 1914, pp.21–2.
60. Ibid., pp.22–3, 26–9.
61. M.K. Ashby, *Joseph Ashby of Tysoe, 1859–1919: a study of English Village Life*, Cambridge University Press, Cambridge, 1961, p.105.
62. Edwin Grey, *Cottage Life in a Hertfordshire Village*, 1934, new edn., Harpenden and District Local History Society, 1977, pp.44–51.
63. Woodforde, op.cit., pp.64–5.
64. Aronson, op.cit., pp.141–50.
65. *The Land: the Report of the Land Enquiry Committee*, I, 1913, pp.93–100.
66. W.H. Pedley, *Labour on the Land*, P.S. King & Staples, London, 1942, pp.94, 96, 99–100, 102–4.
67. Ibid., pp.79–81.
68. Ibid., p.82.
69. Ibid., pp.72, 85–90; R.T. Shears, 'Housing the Agricultural Labourer', *JRASE*, XCVII, 1936, pp.8–10.
70. Pedley, op.cit., p.106.

3 Beyond the Georgian facade: The Avon Street district of Bath

Graham Davis

The visitor, however, is not to suppose that Bath is all beauty. On the low-lying lands on the bank of the river to the west there is a region of filth, squalor, and demoralisation, where poverty and crime lurk in miserable companionship, and where, by a perversion of language, they may be said to enjoy, a kind of sanctuary free from the intrusion of respectability.

(Bath Revisited, *The Leisure Hour*, 22 July 1852)

The late H.J. Dyos has shown that the term 'slum' has no precise meaning, and our notions of what constituted the classic Victorian slum have shifted to incorporate changing attitudes to the urban condition.[1] From its invention at a time of social protest in the late nineteenth-century, the slum has been rediscovered periodically at other times of social concern. In the process, new forms and varieties have been added to what was once regarded as simply an area of squalid housing conditions.

Our images of Victorian slums and of slum-dwellers have been built up from the pioneering work of Edwin Chadwick and Friedrich Engels, from the reformist literature of Andrew Mearns, Octavia Hill, and William Booth, from the social surveys of Henry Mayhew, Charles Booth and Seebohm Rowntree, and from the popular literature of George Sims, George Gissing, and of Arthur Morrison.[2] Taken together, the picture that emerges from Victorian writers about the urban slum is drawn from a mixture of fear, outrage, contempt and despair. Contemporary ideas on religious values, in the emerging sciences, in the field of economics and politics were the guiding assumptions with which to observe and record the spectacle of the poor in slum communities. Powerful imagery was employed to sweep all the inhabitants of slum courts and low streets into one all-embracing concept of an outcast society. Contemporary commentators, despite bursts of humanitarian feeling and genuine concern, operated within an unshakeable moral framework.[3]

Dyos was attracted to an identification of slums that encompassed the work of geographers, sociologists and historians in a multi-disciplinary approach to urban study. Without settling on a comprehensive definition, he employed a variety of labels; areas of cheap housing, a market for casual labour, a reception tank for migrant workers and a focus for crime and disorder. Raphael Samuel has pointed to the unsavoury character of common lodging-house districts. Other slum communities were found in dockland districts or those bordering quays and waterfronts, usually with a high density of pubs and low taverns.[4] Also, high concentrations of ethnic minorities earmarked an area as one of low esteem. In these cases, the associations with particular occupation groups, such as tramps, sailors or bargees, and the presence of the Irish or the Jews were sufficient to condemn a district.

Our understanding of what constituted a slum and its importance in the urban process may be advanced by what characterised the attitudes and perspectives of those who lived in them, in addition to what fuelled the fears and consternation of those who viewed them from outside. Indeed the term itself is a label devised by outsiders and based on standards and values that simply did not apply to much of the urban working class in the nineteenth-century. In a sense, it could be argued that a district became a slum only when it acquired some form of notoriety. Once established, the reputation survived in serving as a focal point for all that was considered squalid and immoral in relation to contemporary codes of respectability. A definition of the Victorian urban slum needs to incorporate the standards and values of the time, and to recognise the different perspectives of those within and without Gissing's 'forbidden walls' that represented both physical and mental barriers to mutual comprehension.

Behind the elegant facade of Georgian Bath lay a sordid world of gambling, pornography and vice.[5] In attracting the fashionable company, the city found itself prey to a host of undesirables who found rich pickings there during the season. Pickpockets, beggars, tramps and prostitutes formed an integral part of the Bath scene and increasingly as the city expanded, they occupied discrete areas of the city.

The Avon Street district was defined not merely by the pattern of urban development in the city, which took place largely in the eighteenth century, but by its transformation from a fashionable resort to a residential city. It was during this transformation that the Avon Street district acquired its notorious reputation, one that starkly contrasted with the new 'genteel image' which the city had adopted.

In 1700, the city of Bath still remained a medieval city in size and appearance, with narrow streets and cramped buildings, dominated by the Abbey Church, a monument to its monastic past. By 1801, the population had grown from around 3,000 to some 33,000 to become the tenth largest city in England. In the process, a new Georgian city was created where terraces and squares formed an elegant setting for the pleasures of the nobility and gentry. Physical expansion brought a greater social segregation. After the building of Queen Square (1728–36), the

Figure 3.1 Early Georgian houses in Avon Street, Bath, 1900.

focus of fashionable lodgings moved northwards into Gay Street, the King's Circus and the Royal Crescent (1767–75). With the building of Pulteney Bridge (1769–74), a new town was opened up on the Bathwick estate to the eastern side of the city. Its centre piece was Great Pulteney Street leading majestically to Sydney Gardens. These developments to the north and east of the old medieval city created new fashionable quarters that were to dictate further building of squares, crescents and villa residences into the Victorian period. Lansdown and Bathwick became the two wealthiest suburbs of Bath, a process that began in the eighteenth and matured into the nineteenth century.

The early attempts to establish fashionable lodgings on the south-west of the old city were less successful. The building of Avon Street in the 1730s formed part of the first phase of expansion outside the city walls, connecting up with Kingsmead Square and designed by the same architect, Strahan, who built Beaufort Square. The northern half of Avon Street was designed to provide fashionable lodgings for visitors to the city. Yet within a generation, Avon Street lost its fashionable clientele to the new developments being built north of Queen Square. Gradually, the area between the Abbey and the River Avon, in a low-lying part of the city, frequently inundated by flood water, featured small-scale industry and working-class housing. An increasing population and higher numbers of visitors meant a heavy traffic in goods entering the city. The main entrance from the south for carriages and wagons was over the St Lawrence Bridge into Southgate Street. The slip at the bottom of Avon Street leading to the River Avon became a principal watering place for teams of horses after unloading had taken place. To meet the needs of the drivers, public houses grew up in Avon Street as it became a busy thoroughfare down to the river. By 1776, one in eight of the houses in Avon Street were public houses. With the concentration of traffic and the proliferation of ale-houses, Avon Street took on a new character.[6] Replacing the fashionable visitors was the army of building workers who were involved in the extensive building schemes of the late eighteenth century.

Indications of the street's later notoriety were already apparent in the 1770s and 1780s. Tobias Smollett refers to the 'nymphs of Avon Street' in 1771, a pointer to the infamous red-light district it was to become.[7] Evidence of squalor and neglect, an all too familiar picture in the Victorian period, is identified by a resident writing to the Improvement Commissioners in 1786:

I am sorry that present circumstances makes your attention necessary in Avon Street, which with the large quantities of all kinds of nastiness thrown out by its inhabitants for a whole week together and the interspersion of here and there a group of pigs makes a perfect dung muckson from one end to the other. Because 'tis Avon Street once a week is thought sufficient for the scavenger to cleanse it but from the disorderly practices of most of its inhabitants makes it necessary it should be well swept etc. every day, which I shall leave to your consideration.[8]

A physical deterioration accompanied a process of social descent as whole families crowded into single rooms with multi-occupancy turning once fashionable houses into tenements. Rooms were let out on the three or four storeys to separate families, or converted for use as common lodging-houses. Ground floor front rooms were commonly converted into shops and this meant families crowded into the backroom which served as kitchen, bedroom, living room and stockroom. The yards, gardens and stables belonging to the houses were built on in the nineteenth century. Cottages, outhouses, warehouses and workshops invaded any vacant space. Costermongers, hawkers and chimney-sweeps required room for their donkeys and carts and somewhere to store their produce and equipment. Those dependent on close proximity to the wholesale market to obtain their supplies early in the morning were compelled to live in an inner-city area. Washerwomen, laundresses and dressmakers needed to be within walking distance of their customers in the city, and their generally uncertain income confined them to poor lodgings. This occupational characteristic was central to the notion of a Victorian slum. 'A slum', in a word, 'represents the presence of a market for local casual labour.'[9]

Yet in another sense, the physical decline of the area, which was compounded by the overcrowding among the labouring poor who inhabited it, preceded the public recognition of what a slum represented. Arguably, the idea of Avon Street as a slum district only became established when in the 1820s and 1830s it began to offend against the image of the new 'genteel' Bath. To appreciate this fully requires some attention to what has been called the social decline of Bath but what was in fact a major economic transformation.

By 1830, the great heyday of fashionable Bath was at an end. The balls, the theatre, the Pump Room, and the libraries were all in decline. The decline of the city as a fashionable resort had been a gradual process since the 'reign' of 'Beau' Nash. No adequate successor was found as Master of Ceremonies and alternative attractions in the form of seaside resorts and rival watering places challenged Bath's supremacy. The Prince Regent's patronage of Brighton, and the rapid development of Cheltenham and Leamington in the early nineteenth century, undermined Bath's claim as the premier resort of fashion.

Private entertaining began to replace some of the old public amusements. When the Lower Assembly Rooms were destroyed by fire in 1820, it was decided not to rebuild them but to erect a Scientific and Literary Institution on the site. This decision symbolised the change from the indulgent pleasures of the eighteenth century to the more earnest activity of the nineteenth. Captain Roland Mainwaring caught the new mood of the time in proclaiming that 'Bath stands redeemed from the imputation of being a city devoted to pleasure and dissipation'.[10] The city was being transformed from the mecca of the rich in search of amusement to a retreat for the pensioners and annuitants of the aspiring middle classes. Where in the eighteenth century Bath had courted the 'quality' for the season, in the Victorian age it sought to tempt the 'gentility' to take up permanent residence in the city. What did remain throughout the Victorian period, in the language of the Bath Guides and in the utterances of local dignitaries, was a sense of its unique quality, informed by the legacy of history.

The ancient legend of Bladud and the healing waters, the link with classical antiquity through the Roman Baths, the architectural heritage of the Georgian masterpieces were a living embodiment of past glories. Famous literary and artistic associations brought the kudos of high culture. Pope, Fielding, Sheridan and Jane Austen, Gainsborough, Garrick, Smollett and Sarah Siddons are a few of the eighteenth-century figures Bath claimed for its own. They provided a rich tapestry of the cultural tradition of the city. And with due pride and reverence the list of star names was wheeled out to do yeomen service in the Bath Guides of the Victorian period to advertise the virtues of the city of Bath.

A reverence for the past, mingled with a certain smugness and complacency, may have proved attractive to elderly residents newly settled in the city. Indeed Bath revered age, not only in its buildings and ruins, but also in the comforts it afforded to its elderly population.

It is indeed a wonderful place of resort for very old people, of whom you see scores creeping placidly in the sunshine, or doddering about in corners sheltered from the wind . . . Of these veterans, the large majority are composed of the retired military, among whom still linger the black stock with its satin 'fall', the pipe clayed buckskin gloves, the bamboo cane, and the 'choleric word', which is a remarkably good imitation of flat blasphemy.[11]

Victorian Bath was frequently portrayed as 'the cradle of old age', a sleepy, conservative, provincial backwater, unaffected by the storms that marked the progress of the great industrial cities. These sentiments, combined with the official view of Bath, informed by its historic and cultural tradition, produced a genteel image of the city that was to endure.

Characteristic of the refined and altogether respectable image Bath projected was the comment found in magazine articles from the Victorian period:

The visitant is well aware that Bath is not a city of trade. No manufactures worthy of notice are carried on within its limits, nor is it the resort of commerce . . . Of all places in the Kingdom, Bath is best fitted for the retirement of individuals with independent incomes, whether small or large. For those past the meridian in life, its quietness, beautiful neighbourhood, and warmth of climate, particularly recommend it . . . Trade in Bath consists principally in the sale of articles connected with the refinements rather than the necessities of life.'[12]

This was an unashamed piece of window-dressing that was deliberately misleading about the commercial and industrial character of the city but in the process of selling Victorian Bath as a health resort and place of residence, certain features of living in the city were given particular prominence. Naturally, Bath advertised the unique qualities of its hot springs, through good times and bad, in healing rheumatic disorders. Added attractions included the mild winters, good railway communications with every part of the kingdom, and the agreeable combination of high quality shops and the provision of cheap food, coal and lodging. Indeed, one virtue that Bath proclaimed unfailingly in attracting new residents, was the very low level of its municipal, poor and water rates. Bath could offer fine buildings and parks, an increasing range of private schools, amenities such as a municipal water supply or the diversion of a City Art Gallery, but invariably one quality was consistently trumpeted aloud. Perhaps the most compelling reason of all for deciding to settle in Bath or to spend time visiting it, was that it attracted so many other people of refinement. In short, Bath became, through the advertisement of its attractions, a last refuge for polite society, set apart from the vulgar commercial world that appeared triumphant elsewhere.

In proclaiming such virtues, Bath wanted to forget its 'old dissipation' of the eighteenth century and established a 'genteel image' more in keeping with the spirit of the Victorian age. Even the commercial life of the city was subjected to careful camouflage.

The tone of a city can generally be ascertained from the character of its shops: in Milsom Street we see at once that Bath is entirely a place of 'genteel' resort and independent residents. The perfumers, milliners, tailors, printsellers, circulating libraries, etc., which occupy the principal streets, proclaim it a city of easy and elegant life.[13]

The old world courtesy of the place, 'the uncommon civility of attendants at the Baths', was especially appealing to a class of people anxious to preserve the traditions of a paternalistic society.[14] The social elite in Bath formed a series of exclusive networks that relied on personal contact and recommendation from among their own kind in and around the city. The Bath and County Club was described in 1876 as 'one of the idlest and gossipy of lounges'.[15] The county set were a reminder that Bath was both a market town and a regional shopping centre for the West of England. They were easily recognised in the city's most fashionable shopping centre.

The overflowing tide of Milsom Street has a distinctly 'County' stamp: apple-faced, white-haired, hard riding old squires—frank, fresh-coloured, healthy girls; half-military, whole-hunting young men, with hair just fresh from a turn under the mowing machine, and white cravats crossed and pinned with an accuracy only known in former days to the late Mr Ginger Stubbs. All very well acquainted with each other, all very much astonished at the presence among them of any one they do not know.[16]

Society at Bath, 'ramifies into four distinct classes—with great assiduity and skill a native may continue to belong to three of them; but even this would require some amount of ingenuity. There is a High Church, a Low Church set, a literary set, and a fashionable set'.[17]

Exclusiveness was practised in public entertainment to preserve the right social tone. A guinea was paid for a season of Subscription Balls, with five shillings extra for the Card Assembly, while sixpence was all the charge for tea. These were indeed 'moderate prices for admittance to

one of the most polite assemblies in the kingdom'. '"Nobodies",
however, must not expect to mingle with the "somebodies" of high life
on such easy terms. Certain rules are drawn up, by which all retail
traders, articled clerks of the city, theatrical and other public performers,
are excluded from its saloons.'[18]

Tradesmen, themselves, aped their social superiors. In a letter, written
in 1840 when times were hard, they were charged with their own down-
fall. 'The misfortunes of this city are to be attributed solely to the besot-
ted pride of the tradespeople and the narrow-sighted bigotry and
illiberality of the clergy.'[19] Similar sentiments were directed at the
tradesmen and clergy of the city in a pamphlet published in 1841. 'I
behold the most sectarian bigotry in those high places which should be
occupied by the benevolent and philanthropic. I witness even in the
dispensation of charity a narrow-minded exlusiveness worthy alone of a
trafficking junto.'[20]

The religiosity of the early Victorian period in Bath marked another
change from the frivolity and decadence of the Georgian age. The spate
of church and chapel building and the growth of charitable societies
reflected the new moral earnestness that dominated 'probably one of the
most religious cities in the kingdom, at least externally'.[21]

What has been observed to date has been the image of the city of Bath,
exclusively identified with its social elite. The changed economic
circumstances of the city in the early Victorian period created the need
for its virtues to be advertised in a bid to replace the loss of visitors with
permanent residents. Thus a genteel external image of Bath was established that emphasised refinement and economy, designed to appeal
especially to actual or aspiring members of the gentry, whether on large
or limited incomes. The increasing presence of a resident gentrified class
promoted exclusiveness in the institutions and social practices in the
city.

In the selling of Bath as a place of refinement and ease, the industrial
and commercial sectors of the city's economy and the existence of the
working-class majority of the population were largely ignored. Here one
can distinguish between the public and private faces of the city. Indeed,
throughout the Victorian period in Bath, beneath the image of social
tranquillity carefully fostered for the tourist trade, conflict between
classes and conflicts between generations formed part of everyday life.
Throughout the country, fear and anxiety were important elements in
the relationship between social classes. A profound anxiety existed about
the moral condition of the mass of the labouring poor. In Bath, this was
given another dimension with the potential threat posed to the newly
established social tone of the city which supported professional and
commercial middle-class interests. Doctors, lawyers, shopkeepers, and
property agencies all had vested interests in attracting people to reside
in the city. Yet what they read in the local newspapers about the
reported disorder in particular districts of the city gave cause for
concern. Among those brought before the magistrates' bench every
week, the people of the Avon Street district were all too frequently

represented. Moreover, there was an unending series of complaints from respectable citizens, drawing the attention of the Watch Committee to such nuisances as the noise from street hawkers and musicians, vandalism against public property, disreputable behaviour in the form of urinating and obscene graffiti in public places, frequent disorder and foul language among young people and prostitutes, especially on Saturday nights. An unstated desire behind many complaints was the preservation of property and trade, which could only suffer if visitors and respectable residents were to be frightened away by disorder.

We the undersigned being owners of Property and Inhabitants of Hat and Feather Yard, Walcot, also inhabitants near thereto, most respectfully call your attention to the great nuisances that have a long time existed, and are increasing in the upper part of the yard.

At the present time it is a harbour of thieves, prostitutes & characters of the worst description, and a receptacle for stolen property. These characters congregate together, their language is most offensive to persons passing by, particularly on Sabbath days—there being several places of worship in the neighbourhood. It is a great annoyance to the inhabitants of the lower part of the Court and a serious injury to the owners of property as no respectable person will live there.[22]

Noisy and disorderly children were a common target for complaint from their elders whether in crowding the pavements, using obscene language or forming groups of delinquents.

Mr Edwards and others, occupiers of shops at the Lower End of the Market Place attended the Committee and stated a great nuisance existing by the obscene and disgusting language used by girls standing on the foot & carriage way there, and requested the assistance of the committee.

The Memorialists beg to call your attention to the nuisance daily carried on by children and others congregating on the space of ground in Trinity Street and Kingsmead Square belonging to the Midlands Railway Company which is also a cause for fear to the said inhabitants from boys continually throwing stones and breaking windows. Mr Uriah Moore of 4 Kingsmead Street claimed to have had 50 panes of glass broken!!![23]

Such complaints appear to have come from every quarter of the city and to have continued unabated throughout the Victorian period. What was particularly significant about the Avon Street district was that it acquired a notorious reputation as the 'plague spot' of the city and this became a source of embarrassment in preserving the 'genteel' image of the city. Municipal policy was influenced not only by the desire to project an external image of the city but by a fear of the external reputation of a slum district. In both cases, there was an element of myth-making and a departure from the conditions that existed at the time.

In disentangling myth and reality on the subject of the Avon Street district, regard has to be paid to the nature of the evidence to hand. Much of it was written by high-minded clergymen and council officials who by education and culture were bound to condemn what they saw or chose to see. Wherever possible objective reports have been set against the views of those who lived in the district, and extensive use has been made of the census data to provide a structural framework. Lastly, consideration is given to changes that occurred over time in relation to the persistence of a slum reputation.

Natural and physical boundaries gave the Avon Street district its definition—the river to the south, the open wasteland to the west, the commercial thoroughfares of Southgate Street, Lower Borough Walls and Westgate Buildings, and the open spaces of Saw Close and Kingsmead Square along its eastern and northern limits. When the population of the city of Bath was about 50,000 in the mid-Victorian period, something of the order of 10,000 people lived within the Avon Street district. It was anything but a constant figure, not merely over time, but fluctuating with the seasons and the flow of migration both ways—urban workers drifting into the countryside for seasonal employment, and assorted travellers, hawkers, tramps, beggars and thieves taking temporary lodgings in the district. From the 1830s it succeeded the Holloway district as the city's main reception area for travellers.

The various kinds of vagrant added up to a very numerous group of unofficial visitors to the city, possibly as many as 20,000 a year in the 1840s.[24] They usually spent a day or two in Bath, obtaining cheap lodgings in the area or at one of the Refuges for the Destitute in Abbey Green or in Avon Street, and making use of the soup kitchens situated in Avon Street and Chatham Row. The police directed some of them, with a ticket obtained from the Station House, to the workhouse at Odd Down or suggested they apply for relief at the Monmouth Street Society which provided charity for poor travellers. In providing charitable relief and cheap lodgings, Bath was a popular centre on the tramp circuit. For the lodging-house keepers of Avon Street, tramps and hawkers were a source of income but they were commonly associated with infectious diseases which assumed epidemic proportions in an insanitary and overcrowded district. Avon Street was regarded as one of the unhealthiest parts of the city.[25] Many of the epidemics that visited the city in the Victorian period were attributed by the Medical Officers of Health to the influx of tramps coming from other towns.

Other health hazards were posed by the presence of donkeys, carts, rotting fruit and vegetables, the stock-in-trade of costermongers and hawkers, amidst an overcrowded population. These problems were aggravated by the migrants into the city who brought their rural habits with them, keeping their pigs and chickens in the yards at the back of houses or on any open space nearby. The central location of the Avon Street area meant it was also ideally placed for the slaughterhouses that served the many butchers among its shopkeepers. In the 1860s, there were 53 slaughterhouses in central Bath, concentrated along the riverside and not subject to any regulation or inspection. Diseased sheep and cattle were slaughtered daily and the blood, guts and animal dung were swept into the river Avon. On warm days in the summer, the stench from the river was a matter of complaint by residents who expected

Figure 3.2 A general view of Avon Street, Bath, looking towards Kingsmead Square and showing groups of inhabitants who include European immigrants, 1885.

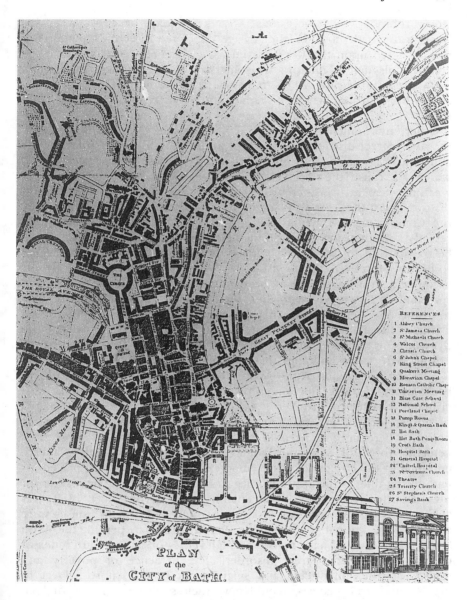

Figure 3.3 A plan of the City of Bath, Meyler, 1846.

higher standards in a health resort.[26]

The close proximity of the river marking the southern boundary of the Avon Street area was a further threat to health and the cause of great discomfort. Underneath Avon Street ran a sewer that discharged into the river Avon. Every few years this low-lying area was inundated by floods. The water covered the streets and invaded the ground floors of the houses. The residents became accustomed to crowding into the upper storey rooms on such occasions. After a few days or weeks when the flood water had subsided, the sewage deposited directly into the river was revisited upon the flood victims. One tangible result was that the area was plagued by rats of a fearsome size. Bill Cottle, who grew up in Corn Street in the early 1900s, remembers 'rats as big as cats' scampering across his bedroom when the family took refuge upstairs during flood times.

Other environmental hazards contributed to the poor quality of life in the Avon Street district. The constant pollution of the river from sewage and industrial waste from breweries and tanneries, the use of the river water to 'cleanse' the streets, as well as frequent inundations from floods was one element. Another was irregular refuse collection. The poorest districts were the least well served by the private contractors, hired by the Council, against whom there were constant complaints but little remedy.[27] Dungheaps, piled up in the streets until of a sufficient size to be transported to local farms for use as fertiliser, represented a danger to health. Moreover, the air itself was less than wholesome with people living next to slaughterhouses, breweries, ginger-beer manufactories, and surrounding themselves with their own assorted animal husbandry. Add to these the belching chimneys from a pipe factory in Kingsmead Terrace, the Baths and laundries in Milk Street, the ironworks and dyeworks on the Quay, and the thick encrustations of black grime on the porous Bath stone buildings that still survive are then explained.

The physical layout of the Avon Street district, with its multitude of back streets, courts and alleyways, had the classic dimensions of a criminal quarter or rookery. Criminals were attracted to isolated premises, situated in close-knit communities united in hostility to the police, where entrances could be watched and witnesses were conveniently forgetful. As a poor lodging-house centre, close both to a main entrance to the city and to its commercial centre, it was well placed for harbouring thieves, pickpockets, beggars and prostitutes. The market for these assorted 'traders' was conveniently close. Avon Street, itself, was at the heart of the vice trade. Among its pubs and lodging-houses were brothels well known to the police. In the Victorian period, the Avon Street district would have registered high scores on any modern index of crime, violence and street disorder. The evidence of poverty and domestic strife, infanticide and suicide, not by its nature subject to precise statistical analysis, would nevertheless suggest an area of high stress.[28] Furthermore, like the modern urban ghetto, it contained within its boundaries, the known categories of despair—young girls with illegitimate children, the sick, the old, the unemployed and ethnic minorities, notably the Irish and the Jews, obliged to take the cheapest available lodgings. To contemporary writers like Dickens, their presence marked out such areas as slum quarters.

Certainly the people of Victorian Bath needed no convincing about the nature of the Avon Street district. Not all of it could be described as a slum quarter, but at the heart of it and what determined its essential character, Avon Street and its offshoots were recognised as the worst part of the city. The question of reputation is clearly not a tangible commodity, nor a subject for precise measurement, but its elusive qualities do not prevent some discussion of it. An aspect of the question readily identified is the consistent reference made to Avon Street in the debates on contemporary issues. These form a chronological pattern extending over most of the century. In successive decades there was a different emphasis upon specific social problems. With each issue the neighbourhood centred on Avon Street commonly featured as a focus of public attention. The consequence of such consistent publicity was that the reputation of Avon Street became a byword for all that was thought evil among the respectable people of Bath. Moreover, once established, its notoriety made it the obvious choice next time round when examples of conduct or conditions to be deplored were required. Indeed, it is a curious irony that both sides in the continuing debate over social policy looked to Avon Street to provide ammunition, either to advance the cause of reform in pointing to the extent of existing evils or conversely to point to the hopelessness of reform in the depraved condition of its inhabitants who successfully resisted all attempts to raise them up. Even though different conclusions were drawn from the same condition, both views were those of outsiders who could only agree on the appalling state of the place.

Yet the view from inside the slum district presented an altogether different perspective. So many of the comments made about the condition of the poor reflected the values of the educated, God-fearing middle classes. These were not shared by the poor themselves, or even by respectable traders from the working-class community. Wherever possible it is instructive to find evidence from within the community: the voices of the people who actually lived there and who varied in status, income and in outlook. Outsiders of whatever persuasion found it easier to deal in blanket condemnations, in the creation of stereotypes and in generalisations that carried the weight of universal application. Variations and qualifications would serve only to confuse the picture presented and to undermine the force of argument behind it. Much of this, no doubt, was done unconsciously by those unable to free themselves from preconceived notions. But, in addition, there was an element of deliberate propaganda used for political ends both by those seeking change and those determined to oppose it. The reputation of the Avon Street district was forged out of political conflict.

Once established, this reputation became an entity in its own right, rooted in past associations, yet not always to be taken as an accurate reflection of the condition of the area and not at all related to it in time. Indeed, it became more a reflection of public concern and awareness rather than the conditions it claimed to represent. Charles Booth, in his pioneer survey of poverty in London, recognised that the level of public awareness did not necessarily coincide with the state of the social conditions in question: 'the impression of horror that the condition of this class makes upon the public mind today is out of all proportion to that made when its actual condition was far worse, and consequently the need to deal with the evils involved becomes more pressing.'[29] So it was with the reputation of Avon Street.

To give substance to the argument specific examples are taken from the evidence. The case advanced is that the reputation of the Avon Street district grew through a process of repetition and reinforcement as succeeding decades brought different issues to public attention, all of which featured the district as exemplifying some form of social disorder. In the 1820s, 1830s and 1840s, the issues which commanded attention were crime and poverty. Avon Street was consequently depicted as the haunt of thieves, prostitutes, tramps and beggars. From the 1860s to the end of the century, in addition to associations with crime and poverty, much greater emphasis was placed on issues affecting public health and on schemes of municipal improvement.

Throughout the 1820s Avon Street was described as the home of 'at least 300 persons who obtain a livelihood by begging, thieving, or on the miserable wages of prostitution'.[30] Shops were open on Sundays, public houses were open almost the whole of the day and street corner gambling and obscene language were usual. In July 1820, six residents of the street were sentenced to gaol for terms of one to six months for keeping brothels, and in September 1821, seven Avon Street juveniles aged 17 to 19 were sentenced to death for various cases of assault, robbery, and highway robbery at the Somerset Assizes. In the newspaper report of the Somerset Assizes, Avon Street was singled out for mention, confirming its known reputation for villainy.

The association of the Avon Street district with disorder was evident throughout the nineteenth century and affected even the most respectable parts such as Southgate Street, its chief commercial street.

Southgate Street, which in the old coaching time resounded throughout the day with rattle of stages and mails running between London and the West, gives the stranger no idea of the beauty of the modern town. The gable ends of the houses, the country-town like character of the shops, and the appearance of the inhabitants, presents another world to that which exhibits itself in Milsom Street.[31]

By day, Southgate Street presented a picture of commercial bustle: its shops, pubs, eating-houses and hotels catered for most needs across a broad section of the population from the middle classes down. All but the wealthiest tradesmen of Southgate Street lived over the shop premises, with resident servants and apprentices forming part of the household. Here dwelt the Victorian 'shopocracy', newly enfranchised in 1832, now guardians of the poor ratepayers and self-styled leaders of the working-class community.

By night, particularly on a Saturday evening, Southgate Street served as the entertainment centre for the densely packed working-class population on either side of the courts and alleyways leading off from the street. It was the place to go for a night out. Pleasure and entertainment were looked for in the pubs and in the street. Escapism from the overcrowded courts and slum tenements was found in bouts of beer-drinking lasting several hours at a time, with music and gambling as other diversions, or solace looked for in the arms of one of the 'Girls of the Town' who worked the pubs, often by arrangement with the landlord. Publicans found prostitutes good for business and some made rooms available upstairs for them to practise their trade. Other girls walked the streets until the early hours of the morning, commonly fortified against the elements by liquor and liable to be picked up when causing a nuisance and charged with being drunk and disorderly.[32] The better class traders, in their role as churchwardens, continually deplored the vice and rowdyism that occurred in Southgate Street, but their complaints did not meet with conspicuous success. Throughout the century the disorder continued.[33]

At the top end of Southgate Street lay St James's Church, with its Italianate tower a curious landmark in a poor parish. It faced the common problem of failing to attract the working class among its congregation. In 1845, a move was made to provide more generous free accommodation by enlarging the church in the cause of combating 'crime and immorality', which as the memorialists put it, 'must abound where even the ordinary advantages of church accommodation possessed in every parish are wanting'.[34] To the west of St James's Church and Southgate Street was a shorter commercial street, Lower Borough Walls which marked the boundary of the medieval city. Just inside the street stood the Bell Inn, guarding the entrance to St James's Court. In the 1880s, this was the scene of a spirited anti-vice campaign by the newly appointed Rector of St James's, the Reverend W.J. Bolton. To his horror, he found in St James's Court within a few yards of his parish church, a nest of brothels with upwards of 60 prostitutes operating from the 20 houses in the court and immediate neighbourhood, encouraging each other in drunkenness, debauchery and profanity. 'By day, even on Sundays, and within a stone's throw of St James's Church, dissolute women, half dressed, would stand in groups, soliciting passers by. At night, riots, fighting and piano playing disturbed the whole neighbourhood. Respectable people were ashamed to live in or pass through such a district.' The Bell Inn, investigations revealed, was the hub of prostitution. Bolton's activities were very much resented by the landlord, who claimed when failing to get his licence renewed that he had lost £400 in takings.[35]

Many of the properties built as houses in Lower Borough Walls had their ground floor turned into shop premises. Artisans and petty tradesmen made up the composition of the twenty separate occupiers in what was essentially a commercial thoroughfare. On one side of the street, the United Hospital was frequently visited by the sick poor attending the dispensary or treatment was received as a result of domestic quarrels or fighting in the street. More or less opposite was the venue for an interesting complaint brought against Crook, a shopkeeper who adapted his style of business to attract the passing trade. In a sense his methods were too successful as the crowds that gathered in front of his premises caused congestion and disturbances in the street. The memorial

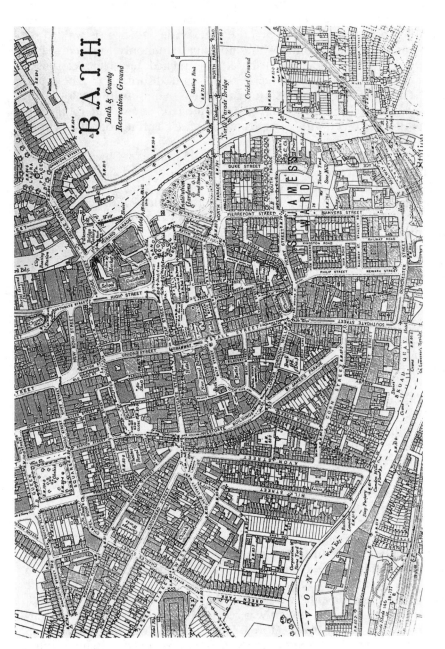

Figure 3.4 A map of Bath, 1902, showing the lower part of the city, including the Avon Street district.

presented to the Watch Committee was led by a chemist whose premises were at the top of Southgate Street, who no doubt deplored Crook's success as much as the methods used to obtain it.

Mr Alderman Bright, one of the Churchwardens of St James's attended, accompanied by inhabitants of Stall Street, Lower Borough Walls, and neighbourhood, and presented a numerously signed memorial from the inhabitants of that district complaining of the great nuisance existing at 19 Lower Borough Walls (where a person named Rufus Crook carries on his business of Fishmonger and Meat Salesman) caused by his continual shouting and filthy language, the same being quite unfit for anyone to hear and also to the great obstruction of the thoroughfare.[36]

Crook was auctioning off his produce in the style of market trading and evidently had a good line in vulgar, comic patter, the stock-in-trade of the stallholders at markets and fairs. Ted Ashman in his eighties remembered as a boy being frightened by Crook's beery, blue-veined nose and fierce features. However, Crook was something of a celebrated character with a popular local following. On his death in 1914, his body was laid out on a slab in his butcher's shop. The crowd who paid their respects stretched from the Old Bridge at the bottom of Southgate Street to Lower Borough Walls. Mounted police lined the streets for what was described as the most popular funeral seen in Bath for years. His success suggests that his customers in the area found his patter to their taste. Only the respectable inhabitants and traders made objection.

Lower Borough Walls joined up with Westgate Buildings, where lived mostly artisans and tradesmen amidst a smattering of professional people. Westgate Buildings and its continuation into St James's Parade had seen better days. In the eighteenth century, St James's Parade had been a respectable cul-de-sac. By Victorian times, the venetian windows and classical pediments over the doorways were less than representative of its inhabitants. Cultivated intellectuals like Edmund Rack, the Quaker founder of the Bath and West of England Society, were no longer resident in the street. Similarly, Westgate Buildings referred to coyly by Jane Austen in *Persuasion* at the turn of the century, though well beneath the presence of carriage folk, had clearly been respectable.[37] The older tradition of fading gentility was represented by a surgeon, three accountants and a schoolmistress employed at the Ladies Academy in the 1850s. Among 33 separate occupiers, one public house and a Primitive Methodist chapel competed for custom. Not surprisingly, some of the Georgian houses had also become converted into shops serving a wide range of customers in a thoroughfare leading on to Saw Close and Kingsmead Square.

Westgate Buildings led past St John's Place, once the address of 'Beau' Nash, now insanitary and overcrowded, to Saw Close. On the western side stood the Theatre Royal, gutted by fire in 1862 and rebuilt with an entrance in Saw Close. Famous for its associations with David Garrick and Sarah Siddons, it was in decline by Victorian times. Amateur night appeared to be the popular attraction or indeed any preposterous extravaganza that provided superficial delights.[38] On the eastern side of the Close, the Lyric Music Hall provided popular entertainment for working people. Those who, in all probability, did not frequent either establishment made their own entertainment in the open arena of Saw Close.

On Saturday nights, market traders set up their stalls there, selling assorted 'bargains', their raucous cries competing amid the comic banter of the travelling 'cheap jacks'. Crates, horses, carts and dogs added to the busy congestion. A popular sport among young boys was to untie the horses, as a diversion, and to 'pinch' anything from the stalls before the dogs got to them in the resulting chaos. As the pubs emptied, new voices were heard bellowing out a challenge to any 'townies' man enough to fight the pride of the Radstock colliers. Men and boys from the colliery districts sped down Wellsway on horseback into Bath at weekends to pursue their favourite pastimes—drinking and fighting. Brawling in Saw Close on Saturday nights provided open air entertainment for the slum-dwellers of the district. It invariably ended in one or another party sobering up at the police station or in one of the horse troughs in Saw Close, conveniently placed for the purpose.[39] Other open air entertainment of a kind could be had in the form of political meetings when such as Fergus O'Connor came to rally the Bath Chartists, or later in the century with the Salvation Army band attempting to bring religion to the untutored masses. In doing so, it only succeeded in attracting complaints from the respectable churchgoing citizens that their noise was a breach of Sabbath observance.[40]

Similar events took place around the corner in another open space, Kingsmead Square, once the scene of fashionable residents, as Bishop Butler's house reminds us. For a time in the Victorian period it was used as a warehouse. A similar fall from grace occurred with Strahan's fine Georgian terrace on the southern side of the square, when marked by the presence of two public houses. The open square, complete with drinking fountain, was the playground of the children of Avon Street. The climbing boys, employed by the master sweeps who lived there, enjoyed a game of pitch and toss in their leisure time or in the slack summer season. They were among the most wretched of the street urchins in Victorian Bath. Children in the criminal quarter of the Avon Street area were brought up to steal from the shops in the square. For the shopkeepers it was an occupational hazard in such a district but they exacted their revenge in the form of higher prices for the rest of the community.[41] The most likely victims of petty thieving were the butcher, the baker, the grocer and, for the more experienced of juvenile thieves, the watchmaker, among the sixteen traders in the square. Others included an apothecary, an oil man, a wine merchant, a tallow chandler, and a marine store dealer.[42]

Local newspapers commonly featured Avon Street specifically. In this case, the incidence of violence, the involvement of the Irish and the whole episode taking place on a Saturday night in Avon Street, made it a prime subject for a detailed piece with headline treatment. There would have been little point in using such a headline unless the words 'Avon Street Riot' conjured up a whole range of preconceived images in the minds of the readership.

MON.—AN AVON STREET RIOT—

Richard Barret, an Irishman, was charged with being drunk and disorderly in Avon St., on Saturday night.

It appeared that a crowd of people were assembled before the door of the Fountain public-house, in consequence of some outrage committed by the prisoner, while he was at a window, upstairs, threatening the mob outside. Presently afterwards some woman connected with him, hurled a lump of coal upon their heads. Some of the crowd, in retaliation, smashed the window, when the prisoner rushed out of the house, furiously wielding a poker, and followed the people down the street, attempting to strike indiscriminately, as he proceeded.

Patrick Sweeney, a labourer, with a head bandaged from recent injuries, stated that, as he was standing at the door of the Fountain, about half past nine o'clock on Saturday night he heard the cry of 'murder' and went to the prisoner's house, a little further down the street, from which the cry issued. He had not been there but a few minutes, when the prisoner took up a fender and struck him on the head inflicting several wounds, from the bleeding of which he fell to the ground insensible. He attributed the assault as an old grudge of the prisoner against him . . . [43]

At the bottom of Avon Street and Milk Street, parallel with each other and commonly bracketed together as terrible twins, lay the New Quay, an extension of Broad Quay that fronted the riverside as far as the Old Bridge and the entrance to the city into Southgate Street. Any illusion that this was the haven of a pleasant riverside walk would be dispelled by the condition of the footpath, soiled by the practice of 'persons constantly making use of the river path adjoining the Baths and Launderies in Milk Street as a privy'.[44] In the Victorian period, the whole Quay area was a scruffy mixture of workshops, stables, warehouses, cranes and weighing engines, examples of small-scale industry and trade. Industrial activity included stone-yards, coachbuilders, maltsters, the Pickwick Ironworks and Marshall and Banks Steam Dye Works. Among the traders were corn factors, general carriers and a marine store dealer. Two pubs and a handful of cottages crowded in between them. This concentration of economic activity, often of an unsavoury kind and alongside densely populated housing, was characteristic of Victorian slums. In Bath, it attracted the attention of the early sanitary reformers: 'Rev. Woodward referred to the offensive portion of the Quay, where sheepskins intended for parchment, were exposed in order for them to become dry, inflicted on the opposite houses the nuisance of a slaughter-house.'[45] Such environmental hazards were part of the price paid by those unable to afford anything but the cheapest housing.

The riverside area had a social usage besides its obvious economic function. Opportunity was there for the curious or mischievous child to find something of interest. By day, the movement of goods always carried the possibility of petty theft. At night, a hay loft could provide shelter for homeless juveniles or drunks incapable of making it home. A favourite pastime for the youths of Avon Street and Milk Street was to throw stones across the river. No doubt, the pleasure was in the collective sense of bravado, made the more exquisite with the sound of breaking glass in the windows of Stothert & Pitt's Engineering Works on the far bank of the river.[46] Younger children found their pleasure in climbing over and balancing on the sewage pipes which poured pollution and disease from the bottom of Avon Street into the river. At low tide, there was a gap between the end pipes and the water to which the children were irresistibly drawn.[47]

A rather different attraction for youngsters was the annual visit to Bath of Wombwell's Menagerie which by the end of the century found a temporary home in the open space adjacent to the Old Bridge. Lions and tigers still retained a marvellous novelty value in an age which had 'discovered' Africa. Then animal savagery may have found a mirror image among some of the wilder spirits in that riverside district. A rumour, only credible in such a context and recalled from boyhood, reveals that children believed a man from the menagerie stalked the courts, alleyways and riverbank at night with a big sack. Apparently, he was looking for stray cats and dogs to satisfy the voracious appetite of Wombwell's big cats.[48]

A curious irony is that just below the Old Bridge, the main entrance to the city, lay the spot where the most desperate of its people took their leave, not only of the city but of life itself. Here the melancholy scene, beloved of Victorian novelettes, was enacted. It was suicide row. There is, however, little sentiment to be found in the chilling accounts of the coroners' inquests which record the deaths of those wretched individuals for whom urban slum life became intolerable. Each entry represents a monumental human tragedy, usually featuring some ingredient of poverty, prostitution or drink. Two individual cases, each with their own powerful imagery, highlight the human tragedy of social distress. David Price, labourer, gave evidence before the coroner in 1816 that he had known the deceased, 18-year-old Franny Dayer, for two months:

On Saturday evening last he was sitting in the kitchen at the Ship and Nelson in Horse Street (Southgate Street after 1827) and she came in and drank with him. While there they agreed to go and sleep together. As they were going from thence to Avon Street along the Quay she complained her friends had behaved very ill to her in consequence of her going to Bristol with a man. They went to Mrs Yearsley's in Avon Street and went up the stairs into a Room where she took off her clothes and sat on the bed crying very much. He asked what she was crying about but she would not tell him and said he knew nothing about her trouble. She continued crying and he told her if she did not leave off that he would go away. He was attempting to go when she said if he did not stay and sleep with her she would make away with herself. He went downstairs and she followed him as soon as she had put her clothes on. She was very much in liquor. They went down the street together and at the bottom of Avon Street as he was going home to the Ship and Nelson, he wished her goodnight and they parted. It was about 10 o'clock. She often talked of destroying herself. She appeared very uncomfortable about having left her friends and if it had not been for them she would not have been on the Town. She drank 2 glasses of rum and water, 1 glass of gin and water and a part of a quart of beer.

Franny Dayer, who had left home in Twerton, just outside the city, only a few months before, was found drowned in the River Avon.[49]

In 1819, the surgeon gave his verdict on the death of an unknown woman of about 70 years of age, who died from 'infirmity of old age and the inclemency of the weather' in the Watch House, the Market Place, Bath. Elizabeth Palmer, a lodging-house keeper of 57 Avon Street, was the chief witness:

That the deceased came to this house about 4 o'clock on Thursday last and engaged a Lodging there and said that she came from Bristol. That she slept there Thursday and Friday Nights in their House. That Friday morning Deponent told her that she should not sleep there after that night. That she did not return home Friday Night till 10 o'clock at night. That she came to her house last night about 10 o'clock, that she has always walked with sticks since Deponent has known her. That when she came to her house last night Examinant refused to let her have a Bed at her house when she sat down at the Step of the Door. That Examinant desired her husband to go for a Constable to remove her. That she received only 3d from her for the time she lodged with her.

Alice Morgan, who had lodged about five weeks in the same house, provided further details:

That the Deceased came into their house on Thursday last between 1 and 2 o'clock and appeared much fatigued and sleepy. That she said she had come from Bristol about 12 o'clock the preceding night. That she said she belonged to Camarthen. That she slept there on Thursday and Friday nights. That she went out Friday Morning about 7 o'clock and did not come home until about 9 o'clock at Night. That she appeared very weak. That she went out Saturday Morning about 7 o'clock and Examinant did not see her after but heard that she was sitting at the Street Door about 9 o'clock that night. That she does not know her name . . .

John Mitchell, one of the city's Watchmen on duty in Avon Street at about 10.15, was called to No. 57 and asked to take the deceased who was sitting on the step to the Watch House:

That he could not get her to stand up when with the assistance of Thomas Applegate and Thomas Hook two other Watchmen they put her into a Wheel Barrow and conveyed her to the Watch House and delivered her into the Care of the night Constables. That her Cloathes were very wet and dirty. That she did not speak and appeared weak and feeble.

Described as 'very weak and infirm', the deceased was further removed about 12 o'clock to the upper Watch House and put by the fire. She appeared in a dying state and the surgeon was sent for. The old lady died about one o'clock in the presence of the surgeon. The coroner's verdict was death by the 'Visitation of God'.[50]

What might be described as life on the streets presented a grim picture of continuous depravity and sporadic disorder, a cause of deep anxiety on the part of the respectable middle classes. The legal term invoking the work of the Almighty carried a certain conviction when it came to the location of epidemic disease. Like many other cities, Bath suffered from the first major epidemic of Asiatic Cholera in 1832. As the cause of cholera was unknown and no certain cure existed, blame could be attributed after the epidemic to suit popular prejudice. The Bath Board of Health report identified drunkenness and dissolute behaviour among the poor as major factors in the incidence of the disease. With 33 of the 74 recorded cases occurring in Avon Street, the experience of its victims there invited the full blast of moral condemnation.

Nos. 40, 41 and 42—Ann Payne, Ann Howell and Rebecca Manley, residing in the immediate neighbourhood of Avon-Street . . . They were . . . habitual drunkards. Ann Howell, co-habited with Thomas Hayward, (No. 22) who died of the disease in Avon-Street; she obtained money, as compensation for the destruction of his clothes, left her house, and sought refuge in the apartment of her friend Payne, in Milk Street. There the money was spent in liquor, and under the influence of intoxication, these wretched women were attacked with the disease . . . Now mark the benevolent interposition of Providence.

With broken constitutions, contracted by loose habits, and a continual course in inebriety, were these poor women attacked, with a malignant and dangerous disorder, in expectation each succeeding hour of being called to the presence of their Maker! And, yet it pleased the Almighty to spare their lives . . . [51]

In 1837, Avon Street was again the most affected area in another epidemic in Bath. The Reverend Whitwell Elwin, chaplain to the Bath Union, wrote this account which achieved maximum publicity with inclusion in Chadwick's monumental work on the sanitary condition of the labouring poor published in 1842.

An epidemic small-pox raged at the end of the year 1837, and carried off upwards of 300 persons—yet of all this number I do not think there was a single gentleman, and not above two or three tradesmen. The residences of the labouring classes were pretty equally visited, disease showing here and there a predilection for particular spots, and settling with full virulence in Avon Street and its offsets. I went through the registers from the commencement, and observed that, whatever contagious or epidemic diseases prevailed—fever, small-pox, influenza—this was the scene of its principal ravages—and it is the very place of which every person acquainted with Bath would have predicted this result. Everything vile and offensive is congregated there. All the scum of Bath—its low prostitutes, its thieves, its beggars—are piled up in the dens rather than houses of which the street consists. Its population is the most disproportioned to the accommodation of any I have ever heard; and to aggravate the mischief, the refuse is commonly thrown under the staircase—and water more scarce than in any quarter of the town. It would hardly be an hyperbole to say that there is less water consumed than beer; and altogether it would be more difficult to exaggerate the description of this dreadful spot than to convey an adequate notion to those who have never seen it. [52]

Clearly the moving force behind such a description was moral indignation. There was a complete ignorance of the origins of epidemic disease and a powerful misunderstanding of the cultural values inherent in a slum community. To the outsider it was uniformly abhorrent but in a sense, too, perhaps a shade comforting. To those who looked down from their villa residences on the city slopes, it was assuring to be safe in the knowledge that they deservedly enjoyed the Almighty's approval.

When agitation for improvements in public health gathered strength in the 1860s in Bath, Avon Street and the neighbourhood around it, became a prime target for highlighting the inadequate sanitary provision in the city. The self-styled champion of public health in Bath was Samuel Sneade Brown. In the first of his many pamphlets, he quoted from a memorial of the Monmouth Street Society in 1864:

The west side of Avon Street and the east side of Milk Street form a long parallelogram, and the space between, which may be stated to be about twenty yards in breadth, was originally reserved and used for the back offices of both buildings, but in process of time some thirty smaller houses and courts have, in addition, been built in the said space or interval. These are only accessible through the houses of the above street; though they stand on a much lower level, and being shut in on all sides, they are wanting in proper ventilation, and the back offices of all three lines of buildings, including the privies, refuse yards and cellars closely adjoin the dwelling-houses in the intermediate row. In addition to the above obvious drawback to the health and cleanliness of the neighbourhood, pig-keeping has also been extensively resorted to by the inhabitants, and twenty or more pigstyes have been made in the already crowded space close to the dwelling-houses.[53]

Sneade Brown, a skilful propagandist, was happy to use this account to highlight the condition of Avon Street and Milk Street. Pigs were kept in other parts of the city but they received less publicity. In the municipal politics of Bath, the reputation of Avon Street was a weapon with which to spearhead the attack on the Town Council. As a representative of the social elite living in Tory-controlled Lansdown in the upper part of the city, Sneade Brown employed the condition of Avon Street as an embarrassment to the Liberal-dominated Council that depended on its electoral support in the lower part of the city.[54]

Following two severe droughts in 1864 and 1865, and the worst epidemic of the century, the city appointed its first medical officer of health, Dr C.S. Barter. Even so it was a tentative beginning. The MOH walked something of a tightrope. On the one hand, as a medically trained official he was concerned with the health of the whole community; on the other hand, he was the servant of the council that employed him. Unwittingly or not, he was a public relations official as well as a medical officer of health.[55] In 1867, Barter was clearly discomfited by a complaint that a false picture was being presented of Bath's sanitary condition in comparing the mortality figures of Bath with those of much larger cities. Yet in his annual report he conceded that the death rate was high for a city like Bath and he continued to argue for sanitary improvement. Barter thus had one voice urging better health provision, which was adopted for the sanitary committee, and another in support of the healthy image of Bath, which was adopted for public consumption.

In reporting to the sanitary committee, Barter was sensitive to the reputation of the Avon Street district and the most graphic of his early reports feature the unsavoury conditions revealed by his investigations. Dog Lane formed the western boundary of the district running parallel with Kingsmead Terrace down to the river. Beyond it lay an open space that acted as a barrier between the slums and the servant-keeping Green Park Buildings. Early in the century that open space was used both as a playground and a dumping ground for those around it. Later, the Corporation stone yard took over from the scrubland. Open space in close proximity to dense population quickly came under pressure. In this case, to the discomfort and disapproval of the MOH, it was an invasion of pigs.

In Dog Lane there are several large pig styes with 13 pigs in them belonging to Ferris, Butcher, Westfield Place. These styes are very dirty, ill-paved, and drain apparently into cesspools which are open air. The pigs are fed on blood and offal, and the stench is most offensive. Adjoining these styes is a large shed with a small room attached in which live 3 persons, a man, his wife and a boy: in the shed a horse is kept and in the yard behind is a pig stye without a drain containing the pig. There was also a large heap of pig and horse dung. This house in its present state is *most unfit* for habitation the people being surrounded by filth of all descriptions. I consider this locality quite unfit for pigs, and should recommend that they be prohibited. Upon enquiry I found that the inhabitants of Kingsmead Terrace are much annoyed by the smell from the styes; and that the blood and offal are conveyed from Ferris's slaughter house behind New Westgate Buildings to Dog Lane in tubs, and that occasionally the street is sprinkled with the drippings from the tub. The distance from Dog Lane to Kingsmead Terrace is in a direct line about 40 yards.[56]

Other examples of insanitary conditions on which the MOH reported were prompted by an unexpected death. In the following case, the MOH visited No. 8 Chapel Court, St John's Hospital, after a man had died from pneumonia in both lungs:

From information received I visited the house and found it inhabited by an Hungarian Jew, a herb doctor. There are 4 very small rooms on one floor, averaging 10 ft. by 8 ft. and 7 ft. high. There is a small and very wet yard on one side of the house, in which under an archway is the closet, used by 5 houses, which opens on to the yard. The tap from which the water supply comes leaks and the yard is always wet. The surface drain is insufficient and the paving bad. The house is most ill adapted for habitation. The rooms being very close and ill-ventilated and dirty.[57]

The worst housing conditions, as Engels found in Manchester, were usually tucked away behind the commercial streets in Victorian cities, in the courts and back streets that led off them. Such conditions were not always revealed unless they advertised themselves by association with deaths or, as in the following case, with the intransigence of a landlord in neighbouring Hetling Court:

I visited 10 Hetling Court, previously visited, owned by Mr Barry. Nothing done except a bit of whitewash. Same insanitary conditions as to open cistern, close to foul dustheap, a filthy water closet unsupplied with water, a shed in the back yard dangerous from its rottenness—paving of courtyard broken up—room adjoining that in which a case of smallpox had occurred not cleaned since being disinfected. In one apartment at top of house, with no proper bed to lay on or sufficient clothing to cover them—with filthy walls, I found a man & wife & 4 children occupying a space hardly sufficient for 2, for this they paid a rent of 1/6 per week. House occupied from cellar to attic by a total of about 14 souls, men, women & children. This landlord laughs in his sleeve at sanitary legislation. Promises but never does anything worth noticing.[58]

The closure of a house by the MOH was a weapon of the last resort and consequently used very sparingly. Ironically, this particular property was within a few yards of the United Hospital in the yard of the Lamb and Lion public house in Lower Borough Walls:

I found here a building occupied by two families sublet by the owner of the Public House adjoining. The conditions of the house were simply abominable. The staircase was rotten and tumbling down as was the flooring of the rooms. The walls had not been papered or coloured for years apparently and were covered with an accumulation of dirt.

In its present condition, I unhesitatingly report the house unfit for human habitation and recommend it to be closed until necessary repairs are carried out.[59]

The closure of property did not by itself ease the problem of over-crowding in the poor districts as those removed invariably moved round the corner so adding to the overcrowded accommodation elsewhere. The MOH also had to be sensitive to the interests of property owners who were prominently represented on the Town Council. Where he had a clear responsibility to act was in the regulation of the registered common lodging-houses in the city. These were principally located in Avon Street which was the main reception area for the tramps, vagrants and itinerant workers who passed through the city. With the association between tramps and epidemic disease strongly fixed in the public mind, the state of the lodging-houses was a recurring political issue. The same political motives applied in the constant critical references made to the condition of the Avon Street lodging-houses as a way of embarrassing the ruling party on the Town Council. Yet it is quite clear that, as in other cities, something of a minor miracle was achieved in improving the state of the registered lodgings in Bath. Dr Barter's own description of 17 Avon Street, one of the first and probably the worst of the common lodging-houses he visited, records the poor conditions that existed soon after he was appointed.

I was quite unprepared for the scenes which I beheld in this habitation & could scarcely have believed that such a state of things could exist in a city like our own. The house is *foul & dirty* to the last degree, & some of the rooms are almost in ruins. The Day room for travellers & lodgers is immediately inside the doorway; it is a close, small apartment, exceedingly dirty; there is one window which *does not open* and many of the panes of glass are absent & their places supplied with paper. On one of the seats I observed a pile of broken victuals— bread, meat, vegetables, etc. I was informed that it is the custom when the lodgers arrive at night for each to furnish the supply of food in his possession which is then mixed up and distributed amongst those present, and any leavings are sold to a neighbour who feeds his dogs with them. So much for the food. On the first floor are two rooms, the front one—the largest, containing 3 beds in a filthy condition; the window was closed & could only be kept open by support, there being no weight: the air was highly oppressive & very impure. In this & in all the rooms a pan was placed for general use, & in every instance was full of urine. The back room on this floor is 9 ft. by 8 ft. & 8 ft. high = 576 cubic feet; in this are 3 bedsteads & there is only room to turn round; the beds very dirty, the window closed, the air most impure. It is needless to enter into a minute description of the upper rooms—which were worse than these two; the ceiling having fallen down in large patches forming holes opening into a loft under the roof in which were several holes, so that on a wet night the rain must penetrate into the rooms. The water supply to the house is from a pipe situated in a cellar under the street, to obtain access to which it is necessary to go through an underground kitchen—the ceiling of which is ruinous & the dirt & litter astonishing. At the rear of this house is a smaller one containing two rooms the state of which is beyond description. Foul bedding, rotten bedsteads, closed dirty windows, unwashed rooms, floors covered with filth & rotten ruinous ceilings, impure air, combine to render this house *unfit for habitation*.[60]

A system of regular inspection raised the standard of the registered lodging-houses within a few years of Barter's appointment. When he inspected the lodging-houses in June 1867, 17 Avon Street had been closed down, and he found them 'generally in a much better condition than at my last visit'.[61] By April 1870, the condition of 17 Avon Street had been improved sufficiently for a licence to be granted to it. 'This building has been recently altered and improved', Barter reported, 'and is clean, and the rooms fairly ventilated as well as the staircase. The kitchen is in a cottage at the rear. There is a water closet in the yard & good supply of drinking water'. The MOH found the beds and bedding clean and recommended a licence to be granted for 12 lodgers, with a limit of 4 in any one room.[62]

The registered lodging-houses continued to be kept under regular supervision with quarterly inspections established under Barter's successor, Dr Brabazon. A report of his in 1882 refers to the inspection of 9 common lodging-houses in Avon Street. 'They have been recently coloured & whitewashed & I found them generally speaking, fairly clean & well kept & probably much better than the generality of such institutions in other towns.'[63] New bye-laws in 1887 restricted the number of permitted lodgers, thus restricting the scope for overcrowding, and with a good report in subsequent inspections, all the evidence points to a gradually improving standard from the late 1860s to the end of the century during which time the number of tramps coming to Bath was increasing.

Yet public attention continued to focus on the Avon Street lodging-houses as the worst examples of insanitary conditions to be found in the city. Brabazon, in looking for ammunition to combat public anxiety on this issue, made a count of the number of lodgers staying overnight on 18 April 1881. The 9 registered lodging-houses in Avon Street were officially allowed to take 194 lodgers, but Brabazon found that the total number resident was only 104. His verdict was simply 'no overcrowding evidently takes place'. Ironically, the Avon Street lodging-houses attracted most adverse criticism when their condition was markedly superior to that of the unregistered tenements that were outside the jurisdiction of the MOH. Lodging-house keepers required the goodwill of the sanitary officials to stay in business and the registered lodging-houses were prominent as business premises. The worst housing conditions, as noted earlier, were to be found in the courts and alleys, tucked away behind the streets and obscured from view.

Indeed, during an inspection of the Avon Street district in 1890, Brabazon condemned the condition of Pickwick Mews, one of the courts off Avon Street, as 'insanitary and incapable of structural improvement'.[65] Other black spots identified were Hucklebridge's Court, Chapel and Hetling Courts off Westgate Buildings and the cottages on the Quay. Outside the Avon Street quarter, further black spots were reported in the courts off Walcot Street, Black Swan Court, Hen and Chicken Court and Hat and Feather Yard. Grove Street and the Dolemeads also contained poor quality housing.[66] These places had two things in common. They were situated away from busy commercial streets and were close to the River Avon.

Contemporary descriptions provided a series of images that were deeply disturbing on the condition of the Avon Street district. How far were these images supported by the data to be drawn from census enumerators books? This source offers the most complete snapshot of the community at two census dates, 1851 and 1871.[67] In the second half of the century, the population of the city of Bath remained more or less static at around 50,000 inhabitants. Yet within the overall figure, there was a relative expansion in the suburban parishes.[68] Consistent with inner-city decline in Bath was the long-term loss of population in Avon Street. In 1821, an estimated figure of 1,519 people lived in its 90 houses. In 1851, 1,284 people were living in 84 inhabited houses and in 1871, 959 people were living in 91 houses. This represents a decline of 15.5 per cent and 25.3 per cent between 1821 and 1851 and 1851 and 1871.

Accompanying this loss of population was a reduction in household size and in levels of overcrowding. Between 1821 and 1851, the average household size in Avon Street fell from 16.9 to 15.3 persons and by 1871, the figure had fallen to 10.5 persons.[69] In 1851 something of the order of a fifth of the inhabitants of the street lived in 'uncrowded' conditions, and by 1871 this had doubled to two-fifths. The numbers living in overcrowded conditions fell from 1,023 to 575 in the space of twenty years.

An analysis of the age structure, occupational distribution and birthplaces recorded in the census data reveals a mixture of the familiar and the unexpected in the trends identified. In the period 1851 to 1871 there was a loss of young people who were not fully replaced by further immigration from the surrounding areas or from Ireland. So what was a predominantly young population (almost half the 652 males were under

21 and nearly four-fifths were aged 40 or under in 1851) had become older by 1871. While the total number of males fell by 26.5 per cent to 479, those under 41 fell by more than a third and those aged over 60 increased by almost two-fifths. Among the females a similar pattern existed. All the younger age groups recorded higher percentage losses than the overall loss of 24.1 per cent and those aged over 41 recorded percentage increases. Both male and female populations were affected by the same influences—a disproportionate loss of young members of the labour force, leaving behind an ageing population.

The heavy loss of males and females aged 21 to 40 of 32.1 per cent and 28.7 per cent respectively suggests that casual employment opportunities were becoming more difficult in Bath. Correspondingly, the loss of young married couples was reflected in the lower numbers of children in the street. The numbers aged under 21 fell by about a third from 614 to 408 and by 1871 a higher proportion of those aged 3 to 15 were classed as scholars than had been the case twenty years before.

In 1851 male workers were principally engaged in two types of employment. Craftsmen and tradesmen formed just over a third (34.6 per cent) and labourers made up just under half (49.3 per cent) of the 428 specified male occupations. In 1871 the corresponding figures on male employment show a significant reduction in the number of labourers from 211 to 118 to form only a third of the total while the proportion employed as craftsmen and tradesmen fell slightly to less than a third of the 333 recorded male occupations. Significantly, there was an increase in the recorded numbers of hawkers and costermongers in the street. Their numbers more than trebled to become the third largest group with nearly a quarter of the male labour force. A similar diversification took place in female employment. Three groups, servants and laundresses (43.2 per cent), dressmakers, milliners and sempstresses (25 per cent) and hawkers (20.5 per cent) made up 88.7 per cent of the 220 specified female jobs in 1851. By 1871, with the addition of dealers and lodging-house keepers, four groups formed 94.8 per cent of recorded female employment. Within these groupings there was an important shift away from those employed as needlewomen of various kinds and into employment as tradeswomen. Women in the latter category supported their husbands in business or indeed as widows ran businesses themselves. The great majority of occupied females living in Avon Street were either married (41.7 per cent) or widowed (22.9 per cent), leaving just over a third (35.3 per cent) unmarried. The low level of earnings among the labouring poor meant that female work of some kind was essential in maintaining a household.

Taken together, the variables of age structure, birthplace and occupational distribution highlight the most significant changes. In 1851 occupied males aged under 41 years formed 70.6 per cent of the male labour force. This figure had fallen to 58.5 per cent by 1871. The male labour force had become significantly older. There was also a change with some of the young males lost to the schools. In 1851 many of the boys had jobs as messengers or hawkers. By 1871 the number of male hawkers had more than trebled from 24 to 76 and the proportion aged 41 to 60 had risen tenfold to form 40 per cent of the total. This growth in the number of hawkers and the accompanying age structural changes are evidence of a process of social descent in that the street contained a higher proportion of low-status occupations. Declining occupations (shoemakers 19 down to 5), chimney-sweeps (29 down to 8), masons (19 down to 5) and labourers (211 down to 118) confirm the trend towards more low-grade jobs. Some workers, deprived of their traditional livelihood, could only make a living as self-employed hawkers. Others, as the age structure evidence suggests, were forced to leave the district.

In the middle decades of the century, Avon Street became the centre for hawkers and costermongers in the city of Bath. Males and females engaged in the various forms of street selling formed a combined total of 122 people and the largest category of workers. In fact, 46 of the 79 female hawkers in Bath lived in Avon Street. In 1851, a third of the 45 female hawkers had been born in Ireland and only 13.8 per cent were aged over 40 years. By 1871, the proportion of Irish-born had fallen to less than a quarter and more than two-fifths were aged over 40 years. The new recruits to street selling were predominantly older women, either born in the surrounding counties or in the rest of England and Wales. The greater mobility of the Irish took them away from Bath in search of employment and they were replaced by rural migrants from Somerset, Wiltshire and Gloucestershire.

The casual labour market had a built-in surplus with hawkers acting as a reserve army and movement between them and better paid employment fluctuating with demand. It seems likely that some female hawkers may have been employed formerly as needlewomen. They were another depressed class losing clientele among the middle classes who drifted into the suburbs. Their numbers more than halved from 55 to 26 between 1851 and 1871. Among servants and laundresses, numbers fell only slightly from 95 to 85 but those aged 41–60 increased from under a quarter to over a third, giving further evidence of an ageing population not being replenished by young migrants. In fact, those born in Bath increased significantly from 45 per cent to 69 per cent and the Irish-born servants at 7 per cent were only a third of their former share. This was part of an overall trend towards a higher proportion of locally-born inhabitants. Males born in Bath rose from 45 per cent to 53 per cent and among the female population the increase was from 40 per cent to 61 per cent. This increase in locally-born inhabitants, particularly marked in the case of occupied women, points to an older and more matriarchal society. This suggests a comparison with Sultan Street in Camberwell where Professor Dyos interpreted such trends as evidence of the social decline of the street.

If there is reason to identify a pattern of social descent in Avon Street, it was not the experience of all those in the labour force. There were examples of upward social mobility both individually and among particular groups. For instance there was an increase in the number and proportion of females employed in crafts and as dealers. Also among this group were some Irish, who since coming to Bath had quite clearly prospered. A mere 2.7 per cent of craftsmen and dealers were Irish-born in 1851 and despite fewer numbers the proportion increased to 6.1 per cent by 1871. A few individuals among the immigrant community established themselves as respected figures in the slum district. For instance, Antonio Pierano, a lodging-house keeper of 84 Avon Street, was born in Italy in 1818, married an English girl from Barnstaple and became a British subject. His lodging-house, which he occupied for a generation, became a reception centre for other immigrants. Another example was Sarah Warren, a widow aged 66, at 83 Avon Street in 1851. She was born in Ireland in 1785 and styled herself as a laundress who took in lodgers and kept a resident servant.[70]

The presence of a sizeable colony of Irish immigrants in Avon Street reinforced the already notorious reputation of the district. Nationally the Irish aroused widespread alarm as they invaded British cities in the wake of the Great Famine in the late 1840s.[71] Many of them arrived in rags and tatters, half-starved and with few possessions. In 1851 over a thousand Irish-born people were recorded in the census in Bath and Avon Street alone claimed a fifth of the Irish population of the city. The prominence of Irish men and women as costermongers and hawkers shows that at first only the meanest of occupations were open to those who settled in a slum community. The keeping of animals and the storing of fish or vegetables were an integral part of such business activity but it scarcely endeared them to the public health authorities. Also as street traders, the Irish were inevitably in the public eye in the commercial heart of the city where they were destined to come into conflict with restrictive bye-laws and the harassment of the Bath police.[72]

Given the context of Irish poverty and the suspicion of the host community, it is worth recording that the Irish presence was less emphatic than it may have appeared. In 1851 there were 230 Irish-born residents in Avon Street, forming 17.9 per cent of the population. They lived in close proximity and possessed strong ties of kinship and county loyalty. Of the fifteen households with Irish-born heads, seven adjoined each other. Most of these households were situated at one end of the street, known as the Catholic end, and commonly Irish families congregated together in the same house. In one lodging-house, no fewer than 38 out of the 58 inhabitants were born in Ireland. Overwhelmingly, too, the Irish in Avon Street were natives of County Cork, the great majority of whom were from Cork city.[73]

If the Irish were set apart in their physical presence in the street, there were in fact only minimal differences in household structure compared to the rest of the community. Average household size in Avon Street in 1851 was 15.3 persons and among the Irish it was 14.2 and the average number of separate families per house was 3.2 for the Irish and 3.6 for the street as a whole. As far as one can tell, the Irish sent their children to school as readily as other families. So by all accounts, Irish immigrants were not an exception to the pattern of life characteristic of the host community. By reputation they were singled out for unfair treatment in the press and in the courts but in practice the measurable differences taken as a whole were insignificant.

Of course, by no means all the Irish in Bath lived in slum quarters or within the Avon Street district; for though the latter was universally described as inhabited by the poor, there were in fact various layers of wealth and status among its inhabitants. The majority of houses were within a rateable value of £5.9s (69.1 per cent). A further 12.3 per cent were rated at less than £5 per annum, but almost a fifth (18.5 per cent) were rated at over £10 per annum. In 1862, of the 90 recorded premises in Avon Street, 35 appear to have been owner-occupied.[74] Even allowing for sub-letting among the 21 owners, there must have been extensive ownership among a group of Avon Street residents. These people were not poor but were petty capitalists in their own right. Fifteen people owned two properties and a further eight owned between three and six houses. This hierarchy of property and ownership belied the poverty label attached by outsiders to the street. Landlords were not all outsiders, sustaining a suburban level of affluence on the 'ill-gotten gains' of slum rents as has been suggested in Victorian London.[75] Indeed, it was their presence and opportunism based on an intimate knowledge that fitted them best to take advantage of the local market.

It is clear that Avon Street had its own social elite; publicans, shopkeepers, master craftsmen and lodging-house keepers. With the £10 property qualification entitling them to vote, they were set above the other residents.[76] In addition to the income derived from their occupations, they received rents from their properties. Their relative affluence in a poor district and their economic power as employers, tradesmen and landlords made them the natural leaders of the working-class community. The persistence of certain surnames as occupiers and owners over at least a generation suggests that a nucleus of families survived and prospered in Avon Street.

At one end of the social spectrum were lodging-house keepers and tradesmen. At the other end were hawkers, costermongers, the invalid, unemployed and paupers, living on the edge of subsistence. Landlords, tenants, sub-tenants and lodgers all lived in the same house. Anglicans, dissenters and Roman Catholics, English, Irish, Germans, Italians, Jews and West Indians occupied the same street. Stereotyped images ignored the diversity within the Avon Street community. In reality, it was a patchwork quilt of humanity. Moreover, while there were criminals, beggars and prostitutes operating from Avon Street, the great majority of people appeared to live decent, respectable working lives as far as conditions allowed. Louie Stride, who grew up the neighbourhood, described it as a 'beehive' of frenetic activity and, as she was made painfully aware, illegitimacy, at least by the Edwardian period, had a powerful stigma attached to it.[77]

Most of the comment about the Avon Street district and its attendant 'evils' came inevitably from outsiders who passed judgement from a perspective of middle-class values, hence the consistent tone of moral indignation to be found in them. A few outsiders retained the capacity to be surprised even if unable to free themselves of their own preconceptions. A Cornish clergyman visiting Bath in the 1860s and eager to save souls was directed to Avon Street as an impossible challenge to his zeal. By his own account, he found the work a 'trial of faith', but in the process recorded for posterity both the predictable indignation of one of his profession and the discovery that all was not as he expected.[78] Having been told that it was a rough quarter where 'the policemen always went down there in couples', he was also reassured to find that the police seldom saw anything wrong. 'The moment they appear at the end of the street, a signal is given, and passed from one to another, so that the people are on their best and most demure behaviour.'

Escorted by the local Scripture reader, he set out on his mission to visit the people of Avon Street. He thought there were about one hundred houses in Avon Street alone and more than eighteen hundred people. 'Whole families lived in one room; consequently the staircase was common to all. The front door was always open, but the landlord of the house, or someone belonging to him, kept his eye upon it to see who came in, and more especially who went out, lest they should take away more than belonged to them. The filth and bad atmosphere were all beyond description. How human beings can live in such places, or be content to have them so, I cannot imagine.' He was surprised to find one old man, living in a cold, damp cellar, 'happy in his dirt, and quite satisfied with his lodging'. He was convinced that dirt, drink and disease went hand in hand. 'Bad and vile as these dwellings were, from attic to cellar, their occupants, with a few exceptions were far worse; their depravity was equal to their ignorance. It was easy to see that drink had a great effect in stupefying and drowning their senses. Twenty, thirty, and sometimes forty people, might be found living in one house, and that without any supply of water.'

This was all confirmation of the condition of a Godless people, yet he discovered that the people of Avon Street possessed unexpected qualities. On visiting one of the lodging-houses for beggars, he was surprised 'to see the cleanliness and order. I was told, however, that these places were open to the inspection of the police, and were only licensed on such conditions'. He was equally surprised to find the beggars quite unlike the miserable, whining creatures that infested the streets. They happily discarded their beggars' guise as blind, crippled or as limbless soldiers and sailors. 'A group were sitting round the fire as merry as crickets, telling of the day's exploits and gains with great glee . . . It appeared to me, and further observation confirmed the impression, that these men and women were far too clever for regular plodding work. They had sharp wits and much ingenuity, by which they imposed upon the public'.

Clearly, there was a social hierarchy among the inhabitants of the street. Now and then he found 'poor but comparatively respectable people', judged by their tidy appearance, with a sense of dignity and a strategy for survival despite their hand-to-mouth existence. 'One man told me he had eaten nothing for three days; yet he seemed lively enough. "Oh", he said, "I gets two penn'oth o' gin, yer see, and a little 'bacca, and that does for a day or two; and yer see", he continued unbuttoning his ragged coat, "I braces up all tight here; that's a wonderful thing to go on. The stomach don't want nothin' when it's done up close".' Our clergyman also made reference to the sweeps who were looked upon as 'the gentlemen' of the place, who professed to obtain their living 'honest'.

At the other end of the scale were the gypsies who travelled around the country and only wintered in Bath. In the spring they went travelling about the country and towards the end of the summer, with many others of the Avon Street people, they worked at hop-picking in Kent and Sussex. '"How do they get there?" I inquired. "Oh, bless yer, they walks. How do yer think we gets all over the country? We walks, to be sure, and in all weathers; and they does the same, there and back again."'

The gypsies kept much together. While some occupied themselves at home with tin and wire work, making lanterns and toasting-forks, others went out and sold their wares. 'One happy and intelligent man among them pointed to his family of boys and girls who were all busy chipping and cutting wood. "There they are", he said, "working away. That there", pointing to a faggot of willow or ash, "is our meat, drink, fire, bed, covering, and all."

"Indeed", I answered inquiringly.

"Yes", he replied, "we work at that, yer see; we sells the skewers and things for our bread, and with some of the chips we makes a fire, and the smallest on it we puts down for a bed. Look here", he said, drawing on one side a ragged curtain. There I beheld a boy fast asleep, on and under some of these veritable shavings. "A capital bed and blanket they makes, I can tell yer; and when it's werry cold we puts on our coats and things on the top, yer know, and there we sleeps as snug as can be, and the fire goes on burning all the night."

He and his family seemed perfectly content and happy with their lot.'

Other inside perspectives not mediated through the eyes of an outside observer, provide further evidence of different attitudes. Two examples, both from the 1880s, possess a distinct tone of indignation on the part of residents in being all condemned alike.

Letter from Ratepayer of St James's

Sir, I was much startled and began to rub my eyes on reading in one of the newspapers the remarks at the Council Meeting by Mr Alderman Bright, with reference to the proposed improvement in Avon Street. Surely this tribune of the people, as he prides himself on being, must have sadly forgotten the character he assumes when he exclaimed 'Fancy respectable people making the transit of Avon Street', and then following this up by insinuating that the residents of Avon Street are a set of thieves . . . inasmuch as he says he would not have advised two lady friends to walk up Avon Street with parcels in their hands at seven o'clock in the evening. I would tell Mr Bright that there are residents in Avon Street as honest and much to be trusted as there are in Southgate Street or other parts of the city. Mr Bright need not be afraid that they wish to thrust themselves between the wind and his nobility.[79]

In similar vein, a letter in 1887 complained about the description given by a Mr Howard J. Goldsmid of one of the Avon Street lodging-houses.[80] Goldsmid, an author of a book on London doss-houses had disguised himself as a tramp and spent the night in an Avon Street lodging-house. He then exposed what he saw in the Bath press. The incident caused a considerable storm, not least among the residents of Avon Street. Mr George Gould, of 3 Avon Street, was one of a number who complained about Goldsmid's article.

I have lived in the street for a number of years and know no such place in any respect either as regards the people he came in contact with or the description of any lodging-house in this street. It is a sad thing that people should go about the country in false colours doing all the harm they can to honest, hard-working people under the cloak of religion.[81]

These authors of letters to the *Bath Chronicle*, publicans, shopkeepers and lodging-house keepers, all regarded themselves as respectable working-class citizens.[82] They resented the imputations of dishonesty and disorderly conduct with which they had been publicly branded. Moreover, there was a clear sense of hostility to the kind of elected councillors who posed as friends of the working classes at election time but were quick to disociate themselves once safely returned to the more elevated platform of the council chamber. The clergy were also identified as enemies of the working class. It was no secret that the Reverend F.M. Caulfield, secretary of the Bath Vigilance Committee (for the detection and punishment of sensual offences), had invited Goldsmid into the city with a view to exposing the moral depravity that he believed existed in Avon Street. In the face of such attacks from outside, even to the extent of infiltrators being sent into the slums as 'spies', there was a well-developed sense of working-class solidarity in the community.

A common identity and alienation from other parts of the city was further demonstrated in a report on the presentation of a silver medal made to a local hero, Mr J. Linsley, a currier of New Quay, in commemoration of his having saved 13 people from drowning in the past seven years. In 1872, the Bath Humane Society had presented him with a handsomely bound volume of the 'Pictorial Gallery of Art' but he had not received the society's medal. So a fund was instituted to provide him with one. Subscriptions were confined to the Quay, Avon Street and Milk Street. 'Some other persons living in a wealthier neighbourhood offered to contribute, but their offers were declined, as it was wished that the gift should emanate exclusively from the poor of the neighbourhood bordering upon the river.'[83] This action reflects the view that the Humane Society's medal was earlier denied to Linsley on grounds of social discrimination because he lived in the slum district. Refusal of charitable donations from outside was a gesture of defiance and contempt for those who, in the minds of working-class people, represented a race apart.

For those who lived inside the slum quarter, Avon Street was by no means regarded as the worst part of it. To those like Bill Cottle, who grew up in the district in the early part of this century, Avon Street was the rich quarter, where the relatively wealthy lodging-house keepers and tradesmen lived, not a few of them owning their own property. Travellers who could not afford to pay 3d for a night's lodging in one of the registered lodging-houses in Avon Street, might have had to resort to cheaper, unregistered and altogether less wholesome accommodation elsewhere in the locality. Little Corn Street, for instance, harboured a rough set of itinerant tinkers and was known as 'Little 'Ell' for the frequent disorder among its inhabitants. Louie Stride, who lived in every slum part of the city, recalls in her memoirs that Avon Street was a cut above Corn Street and even within the street there were those who gave themselves airs. 'They mostly consisted of Pubs and Rag Merchants, but the very top ends were very respectable, they took in lodgers. A Mrs Harris at the top house was very superior, had a nice family of girls, and took in the players of the Theatre and Palace Music Halls from the Sawclose which was near.'[84]

Inside perspectives are few and far between but they demonstrate how misleading it is to depend entirely on the official view of outsiders, whose values and interests frequently coloured their descriptions. What emerges from within the slum district is a sense of community, a notion of class identity and a suspicion of officialdom. When required the assistance of policemen, clergymen or doctors was requested. There was also a compassion for fellow lodgers and neighbours and a toleration shown towards social casualties and those with physical disabilities. Despite the background of poverty and grim surroundings, the inhabitants of slums possessed a sense of fun and a capacity to enjoy life. George Orwell, writing in 1937, understood the spirit of slum communities: 'When you walk through the smoke-dim slums of Manchester, you think that nothing is needed except to tear down these abominations and build decent housing in their place. But the trouble is that in destroying the slum you destroy other things as well.'[85]

Avon Street became a pawn in the political game fought between powerful interests. The real condition of the street mattered less than its political value in conjuring up images of squalor and moral decay in the minds of self-styled champions of the poor and of the respectable ratepayers who lived well away from the district. From the tone of contemporary comments, it is clear that public anxiety about the Avon Street district became most acute from the late 1860s to the 1880s when, in fact, Bath was beginning to enjoy a revival in its popularity as a health resort. The cumulative effect of the district's association with successive evils—poverty, crime and prostitution, its identification with epidemic disease, drunkenness and disorder, and the state of its lodging-houses— all played their part in creating a rounded image of notoriety. Over the same period, it is plain that real conditions were steadily improving so that by the 1870s, a contemporary could confidently write that Avon Street was nothing like as bad as it had been in years gone by:

The Avon Street of today, bad as it is, is but a faint representation of what it was fifty years since. Vice in all its hideous forms was so rampant and so unblushing, that no respectable female ever thought of entering the street alone; very few persons above the baser sort ever entered it, except for benevolent purposes. The Methodists acting on Mr Wesley's advice, 'Go to those who need you most', looked upon the urchins of this street as the most destitute and the most needy.[86]

With the benefit of rather more hindsight, writing in the 1920s, the Master of St John's Hospital, which owned a substantial amount of property in the Avon Street area, compared the insanitary conditions of the 1860s with the improvements that had taken place since: 'This state of things has long been altered by the action of the officials, and also, all honour to them, by the inhabitants themselves, although the improvement is unrecognised by the public at large, for the place remains a cul-de-sac.'[87] Its physical isolation meant that myths replaced a knowledge of the area. He continued by lamenting the failure of the proposed street improvement scheme which would have effectively opened up the Avon Street area.

When a road was proposed to connect the Great Western and the Midland Stations in 1867, one councillor said 'he had no sympathy at all with Mr Jolly's scheme, as it would have the eminent advantage of landing visitors from Liverpool, America, and the Colonies, which the new line was to bring them, in Avon Street and the adjacent locality'.[88]

And that would serve as their impression of Bath. In a later letter, the Master of St John's firmly pinned the blame for council inaction on the bad reputation of Avon Street and the surrounding district.

Between the old city boundary and the river on the western side of Bath that is between the GWR and the Midland Railway Stations is a part of the city untrodden by any visitors and unknown save by repute to most of the residents of Bath, and never a week passes without some of its inhabitants appearing before the magistrates. It would be entirely changed if a good street were made connecting the two stations, but for many years this plan was opposed under the idea that if persons passing through Bath saw only its back streets, it would be prejudicial to its renown as a fashionable resort.[89]

A council scheme that was implemented, the Dill's Court Improvement Scheme of 1882, was preceded by much reporting and debate. One small part of the evidence submitted to the council referred directly to the reputation of Avon Street.

It may not be known to all the Members of the Council that throughout the whole length of Avon Street there is no lateral communication with any street or outlet. There are Courts leading off the main street but neither from the Courts nor the street itself is there any public means of exit eastward or westward. Avon Street leads from Kingsmead Street to the towing path by the side of the River Avon so that no main thoroughfare passes along it. It is old and dilapidated and its reputation is evil, the absence of traffic deprives it of any chance of amendment. The houses in the street have been denounced by Dr Brabazon, the MOH, as 'barely habitable—all alike in a state of decay, scarcely safe by miserable patching'—'the habitat of infectious disease'—'a blot on the fame of the City'.[90]

This is a clear example of the power of reputation as a factor in determining social policy. Once more the point is made that the Avon Street area was known to most of its citizens only by its reputation. In the minds of councillors and respectable citizens alike, the evil reputation of the Avon Street area was a powerful reality, threatening to undermine the carefully fostered image of refinement and gentility that had been so assiduously cultivated for the restoration of prosperity to the city of Bath.

In a profound sense the conditions that were created in the eighteenth-century expansion of Bath were only understood in terms of a classic slum in the Victorian period. Moreover, the Avon Street district was the focus of the greatest attention precisely when it appeared to threaten the newly-minted 'genteel image' of Bath in the 1820s and 1830s and again in the 1860s to 1880s, when the city was enjoying a resurgence as a health resort. The fabric of the slum was a product of urban development in Georgian Bath. The idea of the slum came with the search for a new identity in Victorian Bath. What the Avon Street district represented to those concerned to investigate and improve it was a 'region of filth, squalor, and demoralisation, where poverty and crime lurk in miserable companionship, and where by a perversion of language, they may be said to enjoy, a kind of sanctuary free from the intrusion of respectability'.[91] In other words, it offended against a middle-class code of morality through what Derek Fraser has termed 'social perceptions of reality'.[92] The grim, doom-laden descriptions about the moral degeneracy of poor slum-dwellers fed the fear, anxiety and guilt of middle-class onlookers. Yet it is argued in this study that slums were not as they were perceived to be from the outset. If Avon Street was at all representative, slums had a more diverse social structure, contained a more mobile population and possessed a greater sense of community than was ever appreciated at the time.

Notes

1. Dyos, H.J., 'The slums of Victorian London', in Cannadine, D. and Reeder, D. (eds), 1982, *Exploring the Urban Past: Essays in Urban History by Dyos, H.J.*, Cambridge University Press, Cambridge.
2. Chadwick, E., 1842, *The Sanitary Condition of the Labouring Population of Great Britain*, London; Engels, F., 1845, *The Condition of the Working Classes in England*, Basil Blackwell, Oxford (1958); Hill, O., 1883, *Homes of the London Poor*, Macmillan, London; Mearns, Rev. A., 1883, *A Bitter Cry of Outcast London: An Enquiry into the condition of the Abject Poor*, James Clarke & Co., London; Booth, W., 1890, *In Darkest England and the Way Out*, Salvation Army, London; Mayhew, H., 1851, *London Labour and the London Poor*, Frank Cass, London (1967); Booth, C., 1902-3, *Life and Labour of the People in London*, 17 vols, Macmillan, London; Rowntree, B.S.,

1901, *Poverty: A Study of Town Life*, Macmillan, London; Sims, G., 1889, *How the Poor Live and Horrible London*, Chatto & Windus, London; Gissing, G., 1886, *Demos*, Smith Elder, London; 1889, *The Nether World*, Smith Elder, London; 1894, *In the Year of Jubilee*, Lawrence and Bullen, London; Morrison, A., 1894, *Tales of Mean Streets*, Methuen, London; 1896, *A Child of the Jago*, Methuen, London; 1902, *The Hole in the Wall*, Methuen, London.

3. See Stedman Jones, G., 1971, *Outcast London: a study of the relationship between classes*, Oxford University Press, Oxford.

4. Samuel, R., 1973, 'Comers and Goers', in Dyos, H.J. and M. Wolff, *The Victorian City*, Routledge, London, vol 1, 126.

5. See Neale, R.S., 1981, *Bath, A Social History 1680–1850: A Valley of Pleasure, yet a sink of Iniquity*, Routledge, London, also Davis, G., 1986, 'Entertainments in Georgian Bath; Gambling and Vice', in *Bath History*, Alan Sutton, Gloucester, vol 1, 1–26; for a critique of Neale on Bath see Davis, G., 1989, 'The Scum of Bath: The Victorian Poor', in Stapleton, B., *Community and Conflict in Southern England*, Southern History Society Conference papers, Alan Sutton, Gloucester.

6. Ibid, Neale, 216.

7. Smollett, T., 1771, rep. 1983, *The Expedition of Humphry Clinker*, Penguin, Harmondsworth.

8. Op.cit., Neale, p.217, J. Mansford to Improvement Commissioners, January 1786, Improvement Commission Records.

9. Dyos, H.J., Reeder, D.A., 'Slums and Suburbs', in op.cit., Dyos and Wolff, 369.

10. Mainwaring, R., 1838, *Annals of Bath*, Bath, 262.

11. Yates, E., 8 April 1891, 'A Week at Bath', in *The World*.

12. Gibbs, S., 1844, *The Bath Visitant*, Bath, 56–7.

13. *Bath Miscellanies*, Bath, 14.

14. Op.cit., Yates.

15. 20 April 1876, *Bath Chronicle*.

16. Op.cit., Yates.

17. 20 April 1876, *Bath Chronicle*.

18. *Bath Miscellanies*, Bath, 15.

19. A letter to the Mayor of Bath on the causes of the Present declining condition of the City, 1840, *Lud Hudibras*, Bath.

20. Correspondence of Smallarms, Capt., and T. Broadlands, 1841, Bath.

21. 1864, *Bodies and Souls: a discursive paper with Glimpses of the City of Bath*, Bath.

22. 14 October 1841, 'Memorial from the inhabitants near Hat and Feather Yard, praying for the establishment of a Police Station House there', Bath Watch Committee Memorials.

23. 21 July 1853, Bath Watch Committee Minutes; Undated Memorial on 'Nuisances committed by children in Trinity Street and Kingsmead Square'.

24. De la Bèche, Sir Henry, 1845, *Report on the Sanitary Condition of the City of Bath*, Health of Towns Commission, 32.

25. Avon Street, although notorious for its associations with epidemic disease, did not always have the highest recorded mortality in Bath. In 1845, Lampards Buildings and Ballance Street, a poor district off Lansdown Hill, had a gross mortality rate of 27.2 deaths per 1,000 pop. compared with a figure of 24.8 per 1,000 pop. in Avon Street and Milk Street, ibid., De la Bèche, 39. For fuller details, see Davis, G.P., 'Image and Reality in a

Victorian Provincial city: A working class area of Bath 1830-1900', unpub. Ph.D thesis, University of Bath, 1981, (after referred to as Davis thesis) chapter 6, 'Dirt, Disease and Death', 379-348.

26. Barter, C.S., 1869, *A Report on the Sanitary Condition of the City and Borough of Bath during the years 1867 and 1868*, Bath, 29-30.
27. 27 August 1866, *Bath Medical Officer of Health Report books*, vol 1.
28. 1798-1835, *Coroners Inquests*, City of Bath, 3 vols.
29. Keating, P., 1976, *Into Unknown England 1866-1913*, Fontana/Collins, Glasgow, 139, from Booth, C., 1889, *Life and Labour of the People in London*, vol 1.
30. 20 November 1821, *Bath and Cheltenham Gazette*.
31. *Bath Miscellanies*, 12.
32. 1820-27, 3 January 1825, *Information concerning Vagrants*; 6 March 1815, *Bath Coroners Inquests*, Examinations before Coroners, Inquest on Mary Brown.
33. 1 May 1885, 11 February 1887, 26 September 1890, 21 November 1890. *Bath Watch Committee Minutes*.
34. 1845, Miscellaneous Memorials to the Town Council, St James's Church.
35. Bolton, W.J., 1883, *St James's Court: a narrative of events*, Bath.
36. 12 October 1894, 5 April, 11 April, 3 May 1895, *Bath Watch Committee Minutes*.
37. Armytage-Green, E., 1968, *A Map in the time of Jane Austen with comments and descriptions from her letters and novels*, Pitman Press, Bath.
38. Wroughton, J., 1972, *Bath in the Age of Reform*, Morgan Books, Bath, 55-66.
39. Recalled by Bill Cottle of Bath; see also 27 January 1888, *Bath Watch Committee Minutes*.
40. 1 July 1887, ibid.
41. Recalled by Bill Cottle.
42. 1858-59, *Bath Directory*, Bath.
43. 22 January 1852, *Bath Chronicle*.
44. 17 February 1871, *Bath Watch Committee Minutes*.
45. Health of Towns Association, 2nd annual meeting, 19 October 1848, *Bath Chronicle*.
46. 28 May 1880, *Bath Watch Committee Minutes*.
47. Vol. 1, 30 June 1866, vol. 3, 28 April 1880, vol. 5, 6 August 1884, vol. 6., 13 October 1886, *Bath MOH Report books*.
48. Recalled by Bill Cottle.
49. Inquest on Frances Dayer, 1 March 1816, Examination before Coroners, *Bath Coroners Inquests*.
50. Inquest on Unknown woman, 17 January 1819, ibid.
51. Mainwaring, Capt. R., 1833, *A narrative of the progress of an epidemic disease which appeared in Bath in the autumn of 1832*, Bath.
52. Chadwick, op.cit., 235-6.
53. Sneade Brown, S., 1867, *The Wants of Bath*, Bath, 32.
54. For further details on the political dimension, see Davis thesis, chapter 8, 'The Politics of Improvement', 503-92.
55. For a fuller account of the role of the MOH, see Davis thesis, chapter 7, 'Public Health and Public Relations: The work of the Medical Officers of Health', 449-502.
56. Vol. 1, 1 July 1867, *Bath MOH Report books*.
57. Vol. 1, 11 June 1866, ibid.

58. Vol. 3, 14 April 1880, ibid.
59. Vol. 3, 23 July 1879, ibid.
60. Vol. 1, 26 April 1866, ibid.
61. Vol. 1, 15 June 1867, ibid.
62. Vol. 2, 8 April, 7 November 1870, ibid.
63. Vol. 4, 19 April 1882, ibid.
64. Vol. 3, 4 May 1881, ibid.
65. Vol. 7, 3 December 1890, ibid.
66. Vol. 1, 6 January, 17 August, 28 September, 12 October 1868; vol. 8, 2 May, 13 June, 3 October, 14 November, 12 December 1894, ibid.
67. Census Enumerators books, Bath, Walcot Parish, 1851 HO 107 1943 9630, 1871 RG 10 2492 9630. For fuller details on the interpretation of census data on Avon Street, see Davis thesis, chapter 3, 'The Social Structure of Avon Street', 164–230.
68. Davis thesis, tables 1 and 2, 64.
69. For a comparison on levels of overcrowding, see the conditions in Sultan Street, Camberwell, op.cit., Dyos and Reeder, 374–5.
70. Sarah Warren also had a son and daughter living with her and another son and his family who lived at 85 Avon Street. The births of Patrick Warren's children indicate that the family had been in Cardiff, Ireland and France between 1833 and 1845.
71. Swift, R., and S. Gilley, 1985, *The Irish in the Victorian City*, Croom Helm, London.
72. For examples of press reporting on the Irish in Bath, see Davis thesis, 352–6.
73. The Cork Irish migrated via South Wales to Bristol, Bath and to London often in a process of step migration.
74. 1862, Walcot Parish Valuation List.
75. Dyos and Reeder, 'Slums and Suburbs', op.cit.
76. For voting behaviour and the significance of Avon Street voters in the municipal politics of Bath, see Davis thesis, 210–16.
77. Stride, Louie, 1985, *Memoirs of a Street Urchin*, edited by Davis, G., Bath University Press, Bath, 6.
78. Haslam, Rev. W., 1882, *Yet Not I*, 9–22. I am indebted to Paul Cresswell of Bath History Research Group for directing me to this source.
79. 20 October 1881, *Bath Chronicle*.
80. For a short account of the Avon Street Lodging-House scandal, see Davis, G., 1988, *Bath beyond the Guide Book: Scenes from Victorian life*, Redcliffe Press, Bristol, 59–62.
81. 27 January 1887, *Bath Daily Chronicle*.
82. 26 January 1887, letters of J.J. Baker, 10 Avon Street and Antonio Pierano, 84 Avon Street, *Bath Daily Chronicle*.
83. 19 December 1878, *Bath Daily Chronicle*.
84. Stride, Louie, 1985, 22. In talking to a number of old people in Bath who can recall the life of slum communities before 1914, I have been impressed by their ability to recite the names of people who lived in all the houses in a street and the strong sense of community in such districts.
85. Orwell, George, 1937, rep. 1969, *The Road to Wigan Pier*, Penguin, Harmondsworth, 62–3.
86. Turner, John, 1872, *The Bath Sunday Schools*, 42–3.
87. Vol. 1, St John the Baptist Notes, Item 81, 'Letter of Master', *Bath Charities*.
88. Ibid.
89. Item 82, Letter of Master, ibid.

90. Supplement to the Special Committee Report after the Council Meeting, 11 October 1881, Dills Court Improvement Scheme, MS, 1882.
91. 22 July 1852, 'Bath Revisited', *The Leisure Hour*.
92. Fraser, D., 1979, 'Politics and the Victorian City', *Urban History Yearbook*, Leicester University Press, Leicester, 37.

4 The Metropolitan slum: London 1918-51

Jim Yelling

Introduction

During the period under consideration the question of slums occupied the attention of contemporaries to at least the same extent as did new suburban development. This has not been true, however, of subsequent academic attention, which has largely focused on suburbs and new towns. The one major exception to this, as far as London is concerned, is Jerry White's recent book *The Worst Street in North London*.[1] Otherwise, accounts of the period have still to be derived from contemporary works, most of which largely concentrate on the action proposed or taken to remedy the slum problem.[2] Nonetheless, there were some useful descriptions of housing conditions, particularly in the local surveys carried out by Irene Barclay and Evelyn Perry.[3] More disappointing is the material available to discuss the sociological aspects of slums. *The New Survey of London Life and Labour* (1929–31) should occupy a prominent place here, but for all its wealth of data, it has none of the freshness of Booth's survey, and adds little to the type of observation that he made. Only with Marie Paneth's *Branch Street* (1943) did studies begin that have entered the modern sociological tradition.[4]

It will be readily agreed that slums are characterised by poor housing and social conditions; the question of degree is, however, constantly present. Moreover, whilst an extreme level of one measure may in itself justify the use of the term, often it refers to an association of several conditions. References to slums may therefore not only vary in the degree of intensity of the conditions they portray, but also in the range of elements they emphasise. There may, for example, be a differing emphasis on unfit housing or overcrowding, but particularly important is the distinction between housing or environmental elements as a whole and those of a sociological nature. It has been argued that sociologically the slum 'represents a sub-culture with its own set of norms and values', and that 'slum residents have become isolated from the general power structure of the community and are looked upon as being inferior'.[5] Certainly, there is always some social distance between those living in slums, of whatever kind, and the principal definers of slums who largely —and certainly in our period—form part of quite a different social group. However, the judgements passed on social life vary considerably, and do not necessarily coincide with those passed on slum housing. This was especially important in our period, when the New Survey claimed that 'the level of real incomes of London workpeople have risen very much faster than their housing accommodation has improved', and that therefore 'it is very hazardous to draw definite conclusions as to the predominant standard of life of the inhabitants of a street from the standard of their house accommodation'.[6] Indeed, the feeling that a relatively wide section of the population lived in unacceptable housing conditions was an essential element in the contemporary importance of housing as a political issue.

However slums are defined, they cannot be explained purely by their internal conditions; external relations and wider processes of social and economic differentiation are essential factors. Such is the range of elements and processes involved that some academic specialisation is undoubtedly necessary. In this study the primary concentration is upon the factors most closely connected with housing, reflecting the nature of my own research interests. My essay therefore contains sections on unfit housing and on multi-occupation and overcrowding, these following a brief consideration of metropolitan urban structure. However, I have also sought to relate these conditions to some aspects of the social structure and social life. A section is therefore devoted to income groups and social classes, mainly using the results of the New Survey. These are regarded, in the circumstances of inter-war Britain, as the primary indicators of economic and social power in the community, and thus important in terms of social relations as well as for the command they offer over housing resources. I have also attempted in a final section to bring together contemporary accounts of social life and culture and to relate them to the rest of my discussion.

In dealing with housing conditions it is often useful to concentrate on the individual house or dwelling. Usually, however, there is an emphasis on spatial association, and this is invariably the case in sociological accounts of slums. There are a number of reasons for the concentration of attention on slum areas. In part, the clustering of slum conditions may be simply an observed feature, which might be explained by such factors as the nature of the building process, externalities in the property market, local employment opportunities or the advantages to the poor of mutual social support. Also important are processes of recognition and labelling of social areas, with consequent effects on social ecology. However, the presumed remedies for the slum have also been a major factor. There has been much preoccupation with concentrations of poor housing or poor people, often with the assumption that problems of housing, health or social behaviour are worsened by the presence together of numbers of poor houses or poor people. Attention to slum areas has also been powerfully reinforced by the practicalities of housing action designed to replace unfit dwellings or relieve overcrowding.

Whatever its origins, the territorial connotations of the term slum have important consequences. If one considers some particular index of slum conditions—such as overcrowding—it is possible that the bulk of this could lie outside the areas commonly defined as slums, whilst some of these areas may not be subject to overcrowding. Another feature of note is that slum areas have often been far from uniform internally, either in housing or social character, and may be over-contrasted with districts outside. To some extent this is an inevitable product of generalisation, acceptable for many purposes, but it does have dangers in promoting a view of slum as a thing apart, requiring special remedies. Most importantly, however, divergent or inaccurate conclusions may be derived from the confusion of different scales of analysis, given that in most studies the nature and intensity of physical and social variables is not strictly controlled. The term slum has been applied to territories of very different extent, as the following examples show:

A street, court or alley which reflects the social condition of a poor, thriftless, irregularly employed and rough class of inhabitant. The site of the slum is generally a pocket off a main street or a nest of streets where through traffic has been made impossible.

G. Duckworth, 1926[7]

The long line of slums lying by the northern shores of Battersea, Lambeth and Southwark and stretching through Bermondsey, Rotherhithe and Deptford into the riverside parts of Greenwich and Woolwich form a region fairly prolific in juvenile offenders.

C. Burt, 1925[8]

Slums are of all types, shapes and forms. New York has its Harlem and its Lower East Side, Chicago has its Black belt, London has its well-known East End . . .

M. Clinard, 1968[9]

Duckworth's definition refers specifically to the concentrations of poverty mapped originally by Booth, and in our own period by the New Survey. This emphasis on the street or street block may be said to be the primary one in contemporary designations of slum, certainly in London. It concentrates on the most intense conditions and corresponds, in general terms, with the kind of scale of areas designated for slum clearance. It is a scale at which poor housing and social conditions are often associated, and at which most studies of 'outcast' populations are located, including that of White.[10] A second type of scale reference is, however, also very characteristic. The essence of it is the designation of large areas, zones, or sectors within which slums especially flourished. Sometimes, this means simply that the distribution of slum blocks has been considered on a larger scale, bringing out the point that they cluster in certain wider territories. Very often, however, slums are seen to be more prevalent within such a structure, and the pattern of slum blocks standing out against a more normal background may be reversed. This is so in Mrs Chesterton's account of Southwark where, 'North Southwark . . . residentially speaking, is pure slum, with occasional tracts of better class houses'.[11] Such a view, seen at the zonal scale, is most classically expressed in Simon and Inman's description of Manchester (1935): 'Round the commercial centre lies the slum belt . . . it forms a ring, for the most part about one and a half to two miles wide'.[12] The zonal division of cities is particularly relevant to a polarity between central districts in which work is concentrated and a suburban fringe in which new housing can most easily be developed. Housing reformers and town planners of our period were particularly exercised by this polarity, developing zonal models of slum distribution in response. At first such a view was most attractive to the advocates of a 'suburban solution' to urban problems, including Charles Booth in his later writings.[13] In the mid-1930s, however, it was taken up by the advocates of redevelopment. Redevelopment Areas, introduced in the 1935 Housing Act, were intended to lead to 'the reconstruction to a large extent of the bad old cores of the inner areas of our towns'.[14] Afterwards, zonal or sectorial descriptions of slums received even greater emphasis, notably in Forshaw and Abercrombie's County of London Plan (1943). Indeed, they became the norm in planning studies and, correspondingly, attacks on the planners' view of slums also often relate to large urban areas. Thus the influential work of Jane Jacobs paid special attention to the North End 'considered Boston's worst slum and civic shame', which she says contained 15,000 people, or 30,000 when overcrowding was at its peak.[15]

In discussing such matters I do not intend to imply that any particular remedies were appropriate forms of action—that could only be assessed in terms of a much wider discussion involving political constraints and actual outcomes. The concern here is merely with the way in which such proposals related to the manner in which slums were defined and depicted. This relationship is not confined to the more explicit contributions to public policy. All discussions of slums are affected by the causal factors explicit or implied, and hence related remedies, and this is necessarily connected to appropriate forms of description. Although in this essay it is the empirical basis of slum descriptions which is under examination, it is necessary to bear in mind that it is always interconnected to some degree with policy choices and ideological orientations.

In some cases, data are available to survey complete populations in London. This is true for the various measures of population density, and there are less precise statistics about the whole number of unfit houses, or the numbers in certain income groups. These can all be usefully compared with the data for slum areas, bringing out on the one hand the more intense forms of social deprivation, and on the other the degree of coincidence of various conditions and their wider spread through the community. I have generally used the word slum when referring to the more intense conditions, including those at the level of street blocks. These of course include a range of conditions which need to be distinguished. I have sometimes used the term 'wider slum' to refer to the greater range of housing and social difficulties, of which the more intense conditions form a smaller and related part. These scale references form a general framework for the study, within which the various topical sections can be set and related to each other.

Urban structure

The metropolitan character of London was shown in the scale of the commercial core, and its dominance of the city's economy, society and spatial structure. The City alone, on its 677 acres, generated some 430,000 jobs in 1921, and three other central boroughs of Holborn, Westminster, and Finsbury added another 500,000.[16] Beyond this core, employment generation per unit area fell steeply, but it remained relatively high in boroughs included in the Victorian manufacturing belt recognised by Hall,[17] and reached its lowest level within the county in such outlying parts as Lewisham, Woolwich and Wandsworth. Land values, rateable values, and rents per unit area were all closely related to this structure. Slum property was no exception. Even on the basis of special compensation, it cost in the late 1930s some £38,000 per acre in Finsbury, £20–30,000 in parts of Bethnal Green and Stepney closest to the City and £10,000 in Poplar. This was at a time when development land on the suburban fringe rarely sold for more than £1,000.[18]

This paradox, that poor families were often housed on high value land, had been recognised by Charles Booth. Whilst the poor had to live close to their work, and much of this was centrally located, then they had to compete with other users for whom access to the centre was also an advantage. In particular, business usages of various kinds were expanding around the central core and raising land values. Historically, they had secured room for development by penetrating into surrounding slum areas, removing some bad property but adding to the congestion of other parts. However, the inter-war period which saw these processes theorised in the ecological concept of 'zone in transition' also saw the first real check to their development. By 1938 the Town Planning Institute was telling the Barlow Inquiry that the greater ease of development on the fringe 'has caused substantial areas around the inmost cores of towns to become semi-derelict, whole neighbourhoods tend to become slums, not only housing but business and industrial slums'.[19]

In discussing this changing industrial geography of London, some contemporaries stressed the operation of the new Rent Restrictions Acts, which increased security of tenure. This factor, highlighted because of its role in current political debate, formed a small part of a set of problems involving obsolescence, constriction of sites, and poor vehicle access, which reduced the advantage of central location. The preference of industry for suburban sites was a phenomenon which affected large cities in North America as well as Britain, and Homer Hoyt saw it as a long-run change beginning about 1930.[20] In London the impact was probably earlier, and it was quite clear by the early 1930s that the spread of business usages in the inner parts of the city would not be as important a process as hitherto envisaged. However, industry continued to spread into areas like Hackney, whilst in Southwark complaint was made in 1935 that 'at present there is a haphazard encroachment of industrial on residential areas, while part of the former industrial area is left derelict'.[21] Here the varied nature of London industries has to be borne in mind, consisting not only of clothing and furniture, but of the miscellaneous activities described by the New Survey in north Lambeth:

There are candle and toilet-soap works, beer and vinegar breweries, printing works, laundries, a flour mill, a lead smelting works, potteries and factories for the production of boot polishes, sauces and meat essences, hydraulic packing and emery paper and polishes.[22]

There was plenty of scope here for varying locational factors and fortunes; for dereliction of some sites, further expansion of some activities. Most of these industries were, however, in the more favoured consumer sector, and there does not appear to have been any dramatic collapse. Inner London industries continued to offer employment to the working classes and to repel the middle classes. Raymond Unwin, in 1933, still thought that 'it is the casual intrusion of business or industrial buildings into residential areas which is responsible for most of the depreciation of residential property',[23] and the concentration of industry in the centre continued to be the main stumbling block to decentralist solutions to housing problems.

London had spread well beyond the boundaries of the county in the late nineteenth century, particularly in the north-east. In only twenty years between the wars, however, its built-up area doubled in size, and even in terms of population the Outer Ring of Greater London, as defined by the census, reached the size of the county itself. New housing areas were created at lower densities with cottage-style dwellings and modern amenities. This naturally had a profound effect on London property as a whole, and produced a heightened contrast with the older dwellings in the inner areas. Most of the expansion of middle-class and better-off working-class residence occurred in this outer zone partly by continuing migration from the older areas themselves. Thus the New Survey found that 'the predominant movement of the "residential" middle class population has been outwards across the boundary, not only of the County but of the Survey area as a whole'.[24]

The exception to this concentration of more dynamic elements in the suburbs lay in the centre itself, which was attractive residentially as well as for business. One of the most interesting findings of the New Survey was that the sectorial contrast between West End and the East End had been reinforced since Booth's day. Such a conclusion can only be inferred very roughly since the New Survey definition of middle class (M) was very different from Booth's. It must however be significant that the middle-class population thus defined had doubled in Holborn, Westminster and St Marylebone and risen significantly in Hampstead, Kensington, Paddington, Chelsea and Battersea, whereas it halved in Bermondsey, Bethnal Green, Camberwell, Fulham, Hammersmith,

Islington, Lambeth, Poplar and Southwark.[25] The middle classes were not only moving outwards, but consolidating their territory around the West End, whilst further east whole boroughs like Shoreditch and Bermondsey contained, it was found, not a single middle-class residential street.

In some cases this changing class composition of districts became politicised. Thus the Hampstead Labour Party and Trades Council complained that the demolition of unfit property in Town Ward was being used 'to drive out the present occupiers'[26] and similar complaints were made about the Portman Town district of St Marylebone.[27] Mrs Chesterton castigated Westminster City Council for encouraging demolitions and conversions which led to the expulsion of working-class populations.[28] Conversely, middle-class opposition to the expansion of working-class residence on the suburban fringe is well known, and this was replicated on the 'inner frontier' as working-class inner London pushed out into middle-class suburbs. The Clapham and District Ratepayers Association strongly opposed LCC development at Poynders Lane and made it quite clear that 'it was the influx of a large working class population with the large numbers of children . . . to which objection is raised'.[29]

Forshaw and Abercrombie in their County of London Plan (1943) defined a tripartite division of London outside the central commercial core. First, they recognised an East Central group of residential areas which lay 'north of the river from Poplar to Kentish Town and bounded approximately by the Regents Canal, south of the river from Maze Hill Greenwich to Battersea and bounded by rising ground to the south'. This district contained 'the main areas of slums, obsolescent property and overcrowding as well as the worst examples of large scale 'peppering' of industries within residential districts'[30]

The boundaries of this zone were defined, particularly to the north and south, not only by land use but also by relief, and roughly they include the areas almost entirely built up by 1870, mostly by 1840. The East End was particularly infamous, but similar conditions applied north of the City and also south of the river, as described by Martin (1935):

The great plain south of the river, between Wandsworth and Deptford, originally flat marshy land . . . contains some of the worst property in the Metropolis . . . In Southwark and Bermondsey the riverside is flanked by great warehouses and factories; behind, a · chaotic jumble of narrow streets, alleys and courts, interspersed with large business premises . . .[31]

In statistical presentation the County Plan recognised seven boroughs as falling wholly within the East Central zone—Bermondsey, Bethnal Green, Finsbury, Poplar, Shoreditch, Stepney and Southwark. Others, however, fell partly within it—particularly north Lambeth, south Islington and St Pancras, and the riverside parts of Battersea, Deptford and Greenwich. I shall designate these 'Mixed Boroughs'. A further group of boroughs consists of Chelsea, Holborn, Kensington, Paddington, and St Marylebone, together with the Cities of London and Westminster.[32] This includes most of the County Plan's central core as well as its 'West

Table 4.1 Population, 1921–51

	1921	1931	1938	1951
Inner East	1,013,572	938,688	807,850	468,892
Inner West	686,469	661,696	626,160	549,583
Mixed	1,225,694	1,183,442	1,077,430	886,730
Outer	1,558,788	1,613,177	1,551,360	1,442,777
London AC	4,484,523	4,397,003	4,062,800	3,347,982
Middlesex	1,253,002	1,638,728	2,058,300	2,269,315

Sources: General Register Office, Censuses 1921, 1931, 1951, National Register, Statistics of Population, 1939, HMSO 1944.

Table 4.2 Population Densities, 1921–51

	Gross Densities per acre			
	1921	1931	1938	1951
Inner East	116.0	107.4	92.5	53.7
Inner West	73.3	70.6	66.9	58.7
Mixed	70.2	67.8	61.7	50.8
Outer	39.7	41.1	39.5	36.7
London AC	59.9	58.7	54.3	44.7
Middlesex	8.4	11.0	13.8	15.3

Sources: as Table 4.1

Central' area. Essentially it represents a central district of relative wealth in which the townscape was one of large structures (although mews and small cottages might be tucked in behind), and in which working-class housing difficulties were largely related to rents, overcrowding and multi-occupation. Finally, a fourth group of boroughs is called 'Outer Districts'. Tables 4.1 and 4.2 summarise the major contrasts in population growth and density in these four divisions, and use the County of Middlesex to indicate comparative conditions in suburbs of more recent development. The various boroughs and regional divisions are indicated in Figure 4.1.

Unfit housing

The 'unfitness' of houses is notoriously a question of degree. Local authority statistics vary in the standards they apply, partly in response to the scale and type of action they contemplate. Housing which remained unscathed in some northern cities would certainly have been represented in London, whilst within London some prosperous areas represented

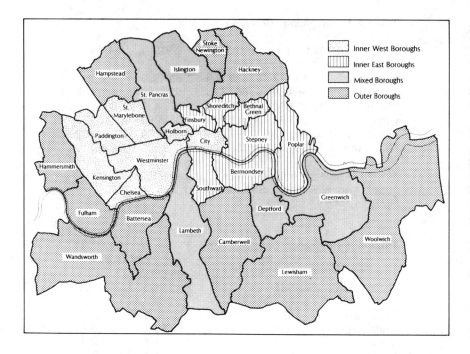

Figure 4.1 London Boroughs and Regional Divsions

houses which would have been excluded in other parts. In 1911, however, the LCC had undertaken a complete and detailed survey of unfit housing in the county under its medical officer Shirley Murphy.[33] This reduced some of the difficulties of comparison between boroughs, and is doubly important in that it formed the basis of slum clearance in London throughout the inter-war period. Groups of houses on the list were re-classified in 1922 according to degrees of urgency, and this was brought up to date from time to time, notably in 1931 and 1933. When Labour came to power in London its slum clearance programmes of 1934 and 1937 were essentially designed to remove these areas from the housing stock.

The 1911 list contained some 25,000 houses, amounting to only 4 per cent of the total properties in the county. Even in the Inner East, the list involved only some 10 per cent of properties, rising to 14 per cent in Stepney, 12 per cent in Bermondsey and Shoreditch, and 11 per cent in Bethnal Green. Forty-seven per cent of the properties on the list were in the Inner East and another 23 per cent in Mixed Boroughs (Table 4.3). When the houses in the First Division of the list were divided into three categories of urgency, the Inner East figured more strongly, containing two-thirds of the houses in this group in 1931.

It must be appreciated straightaway that these lists did not comprise all that was popularly referred to as 'slum' even under the narrowest

Table 4.3 Unfit Housing in London, 1911 and 1931

A   Number of houses
B   Percentage of unfit houses in the LCC area
C   Percentage of all buildings in the relevant area
D   Class 1.1(a) (most urgent)—percentage of the LCC total in this class, which comprised 5416 houses.

	1911 A	1911 B	1911 C	1931 A	1931 D
Inner East	12,079	47	10	9,279	67
Inner West	3,091	12	4	1,786	6
Mixed	5,939	23	4	4,427	15
Outer	4,625	18	2	3,735	12
LCC	25,734	100	4	19,227	100

Note: Figures exclude the City.
Sources: LCC Housing Committee, Presented Papers (HC) Dec. 1911 (3 vols.); LCC HC 19 Feb. 1931 (5).

definitions of the period. Instead, they involved those buildings whose condition was thought not to be remediable other than by demolition and replacement. Overcrowding, multi-occupation or the reputation of tenants were not important factors in this equation. So, Campbell Road, White's 'worst street in north London' was not included in any inter-war clearance programme.[34] When the St Pancras Housing Trust wanted to clear another notorious street, Litcham St., St Pancras, the LCC MOH refused, as these three-storey houses faced a 50 ft road and 'the external walls are sound, very little can be said against the arrangement, the light and ventilation is satisfactory and the property has by no means reached the end of its life'.[35]

The comparatively restricted scope of clearance legislation is especially well indicated by the treatment of basement rooms. Basements were a common feature of London property before 1840 in even relatively small houses, and occur frequently in property taken for clearance. Unfit basements were not in themselves, however, sufficient to condemn a whole house. A survey of 1929 revealed 121,575 underground rooms still extant in the county of which 30,500 were reckoned unfit.[36] For once the Inner East was not specially significant, having only 15 per cent of these rooms, which were most frequent in Islington, Kensington, Lambeth, St Pancras and Hackney. Unfit basements were particularly common in south-east London where many were subject to periodic flooding as well as dampness and lack of light. The MOH considered that 'not more than ¼ of the living rooms on an insanitary area are so grossly insanitary as the worst type of basement dwellings in London',[37] but local authorities were reluctant to take action against them because this created no replacement housing.

In the 1922 and 1931 classifications some 85 per cent of the property

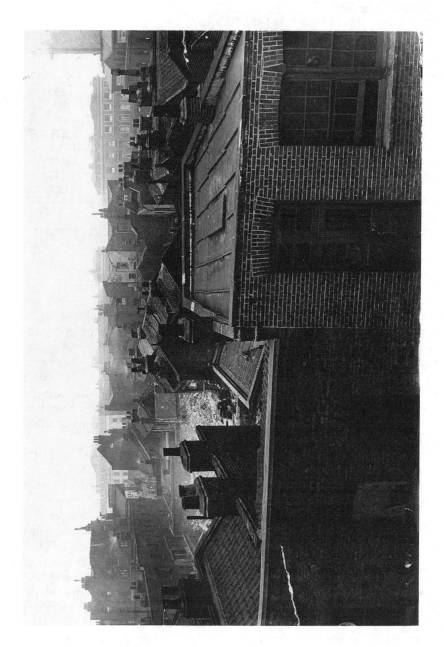

Figure 4.2 A 'congested area'—Brand Street, Islington, 1927.

Figure 4.3 A row of cottages—Victoria Place, Southwark, 1921

lay in Division 1: 'areas which have a common feature of "narrowness, closeness and bad arrangement" associated of course with other evils and sanitary defects'.[38] In Division 2 such bad overall arrangement was a subsidiary feature and 'insanitary properties are peculiar to the houses themselves'.[39] In this class were included only those houses already scheduled in 1911. It was noted as 'indefinitely expansible' but included relatively few houses because in 1911 'bad arrangement remediable only by clearance was a selective consideration'.[40] This priority dates back of course to the beginnings of this legislation in Cross's Act, and the following description of Drysdale Street, Shoreditch in 1931 shows the type of area that might have been represented at any time since 1875:

Drysdale St. is a small congested area, with badly arranged houses consisting of cul-de-sac or narrow passages. It is about 1½ acres in extent and contains some 120 houses; it is enclosed on three sides by industrial buildings, shops and a railway. The houses are two storeys in height.[41]

At 80 houses per acre Drysdale Street is an example of the crowding of houses which 'narrowness, closeness and bad arrangement' often involved. Although not exceptional, it nonetheless lay near the City and at the top end of the range. The LCC in 1918 compared the new standard of 12 houses per acre with existing conditions ranging from '40 to 80 houses per acre in insanitary areas to about 20 houses per acre in generously planned estates',[42] and this would appear to be essentially correct.

A 'congested area' in some parts of London might consist mainly of three storey houses. Thus at Gee St., Finsbury such houses lay 'in long terraces in narrow streets congested on all sides and in parts seriously overshadowed by large industrial buildings'.[43] Normally, however, the houses were smaller, and commentators in the period almost invariably associated such smallness with insubstantiality. As a general rule the larger the house the more likely it was to be structurally sound, free from damp and adequately provided with light and air. Thus Barclay and Perry in their surveys of Shoreditch and Southwark distinguish 'tenement houses' of 6–10 rooms from 'cottages', varying from two to four and sometimes five rooms. It was among the latter two storey buildings, built originally for a poorer clientele, that the conditions of 'unfitness' were concentrated.

Table 4.4 shows the distribution of dwellings among four different-sized groups. It refers to structurally separate dwellings, ignoring the question of multi-occupation. The 1921 Census is, however, particularly useful in separately itemising dwellings in purpose-built flats, or separate apartments in subdivided houses and above shops. The bulk of the smaller dwellings were thus contained in larger buildings, and relatively few consisted of small houses. Even in the Inner East, where small houses were most frequent, cottages of five rooms or less made up only some 29 per cent of the total separate dwellings. The figure was under 8 per cent in the Inner West. Given that slum clearance was heavily concentrated on this type of small dwelling, the proportion of such stock

Table 4.4 Types of Dwelling, 1921

A Houses
B Flats, and separate apartments over shops or in divided houses.

		Dwelling size (rooms)				Total
		1–3 per cent	4–5 per cent	6–7 per cent	9 + per cent	Dwellings Nos.
Inner East	A	6.7	22.0	31.2	2.7	152,056
	B	26.0	7.8	3.2	0.4	
Inner West	A	2.0	5.8	14.0	22.3	115,267
	B	27.8	14.0	11.7	2.4	
Mixed	A	2.5	14.8	44.6	12.6	180,238
	B	10.7	9.7	4.4	0.6	
Outer	A	2.4	19.6	44.0	11.3	272,473
	B	6.6	11.3	4.4	0.4	
London AC	A	3.2	16.7	36.6	11.5	720,004
	B	15.2	10.6	5.4	0.8	
Middlesex	A	2.7	32.5	42.7	7.8	243,669
	B	3.3	7.6	3.0	0.4	

Source: General Register Office, Census 1921, Table 10

declared unfit becomes more important. The number of unfit houses on the 1911 List was thus equivalent to nearly 18 per cent of London's stock of cottages under 6 rooms in size, and in the Inner East to some 28 per cent of this stock.

In most of the predominantly middle-class parts of London, properties, even if multi-occupied, were rarely in a condition to be condemned under the Housing Acts. There were patches of inherited 'old village' houses, and in other cases property had deteriorated through infilling with small cottages or industry which had altered its original spatial character. But one type of dwelling exceptionally concentrated in such areas was the mews. Gaddesden Mews, Kensington, condemned in 1933, is a good example. It contained:

. . . fourteen dwellings of the usual mews type comprising a ground floor stables, workshops stores etc and three living rooms over (with kitchens and closets). Bad arrangement is a marked feature, and there is some lack of light and air, the mews being back to back in principle and having skylights only in the rear bedrooms. The fabric is old and worn out and odour and flies from the stabling are a constant nuisance.[44]

Barclay and Perry (1932) recorded some 2,900 mews dwellings in Kensington, and noted that their character much depended on use and the presence of stables. Those in north Kensington were used 'largely by costermongers and a good deal of refuse is accumulated', whereas further south 'a few are converted into modern flats and made very attractive, others are kept in good repair and occupied largely by chauffeurs who have charge of the cars in the garages downstairs'.[45]

In the Inner East and corresponding parts of the Mixed Boroughs unfit properties were far more extensive, and less easily separated from the mass. Here, too, some of the condemned properties had been inherited from the pre-suburban past. Slums in Poplar in 1919 were thus described as 'portions of scattered villages or groups of houses existing at the beginning of the nineteenth century'.[46] Much of this was in a bad state, damaged by damp and rain penetration. But the medical officer also described 'little backways', 'reminiscent of a country village of which . . . they are frequently the surviving remnants, and in their quaint and obsolete structure, with their creeper clad walls and their little front gardens the semblance is sustained.'[47] The picturesque is suggested at Eastney St., Greenwich, where many houses were 'very ancient and typical of old riverside property with steep mansard roofs and heavy timbering'.[48] In Southwark, 'a few sixteenth and many seventeenth and early eighteenth century cottages survive'. They included 'Wagstaffe buildings, a picturesque row of ancient timbered cottages'.[49]

However, the vast majority of condemned houses in such areas dated from the late eighteenth and early nineteenth centuries. Dates ranging from 1800 to 1840 were particularly frequent. This was the period of rapid extension prior to the existence of new building bye-laws, and it was the period often referred to in official statements and reports (including Forshaw and Abercombie's) as essentially constituting the moment when the modern slum problem in British cities was created. This was not just a question of age, but of the character of building. Barclay and Perry thus say of Southwark 'The largest part of the property dates from the late eighteenth or early nineteenth century, but it was not so well built as the older houses . . . The cottage property of this date . . . is completely worn out'.[50] Poorer quality building in this period was often accompanied by the use of courts or alleys in which much of the worst property was to be found. Thus Nelson Place in the notorious Lant Street district of Southwark:

. . . consists of eight four-room cottages, worn out and dilapidated . . . Most of the roofs were found to be leaking, and in some cases plaster was falling from the ceilings, and paper hanging in strips from the soaked walls. There are . . . leaking w.c. pans, a room window out owing to the frame having rotted away, broken flooring, and large rat holes in every house.[51]

Barclay and Perry in their accounts of Shoreditch and Southwark describe the best type of four or five-room cottage as a two-up two-down with an entrance passage, a washroom and w.c. and a yard or garden, sometimes with an attic room or back addition room over the scullery. In some, economy on space was made by building a steep staircase between the front and back rooms. Streets of this type of cottage, when built in the last 50 years or so, were not unhealthy. A second type still contained four rooms, but had no entrance passage or separate scullery, the street door opening onto the living room, and a narrow staircase leading up to the bedrooms from the back kitchen or scullery. A third type had no second bedroom over the back kitchen/scullery, and finally the smallest cottage consisted of two rooms, with no scullery or backyard, the w.c. being placed in the front court. In all cases rooms were small—in Southwark figures varying from 8 x 10 ft to 11 x 12 ft were mentioned.[52]

George Row, Brand St. and Hope St., Islington, clearance schemes in the 1920s, involved some larger tenement houses, as well as two, three and four-room cottages, the latter with passages and without. They exemplified the twin problems of dampness and structural dilapidation which affected much condemned property and could only be aggravated by any congestion on site which cut out light and air. At George St. these problems were ascribed to 'bad footings, absence of damp courses, poor quality bricks, sagged and leaky roofs'.[53] It was noted that 'some walls are badly bulged, the bricks are old and porous, and the mortar has ceased to act as a deterrent against the weather, woodwork is generally defective . . . many rooms are small and low. Plaster is loose and broken, light and ventilation is bad'. At Brand St. three houses 'had been gutted, new partition walls, floors stairs roofs and windows provided, and the sites under the ground floors concreted over', but by 1919 these measures had not sufficed to remove the property from the local medical officer's attentions.[54] The New Survey noted that 'Many of the older houses are without damp proof courses or surface concrete, but these have been rendered obligatory for all houses built in the County since 1879, and wherever substantial repairs are undertaken to buildings owners are required to remedy these defects'.[55]

One of the most striking features of the unfit housing lists is that despite their concentration on groups of houses, these groups are surprisingly small. In 1911 the mean size of the group was only 13 houses. In the 'urgent' section of the 1931 list the mean size of group was 11 houses, rising to 13 in the Inner East. Over half the houses in the 1922 'urgent' list were found in groups of under 10. Slum clearance areas might be formed of more than one of these groups, as well as houses taken as 'added' or 'neighbouring' lands. In the 1920s the LCC concentrated on the largest blocks, most suitable for rehousing purposes. Even so, the mean size of clearance area was 6.7 acres or 270 buildings. Between 1930 and 1935 the mean size of clearance area was only 2.46 acres, including added lands and excluding the small areas dealt with by clearance orders.[56]

The scattered nature of unfit housing, distributed in small groups reflects the piecemeal nature of the building process. Larger-scale developments were rare, and probably concentrated on the better quality property. The worst housing was tucked away in patches behind main streets, rather than occurring over extensive areas. Moreover, a process which concentrated on the worst necessarily picked out points of unintended defect of site preparation or building, as well as differential histories of subsequent maintenance under a complicated structure of small-scale property ownership. The processes of the Housing Acts were,

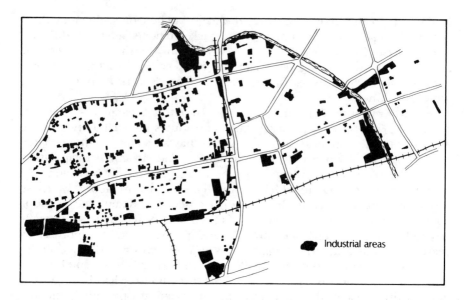

Figure 4.4 Industry in Bethnal Green, 1945. (Based on Glass and Frenkel 1945)

however, also very important in this respect. With the more severe treatment of unfit housing under the 1919 Act, the unfitness of individual properties was subject to very close attention, and the generally conservative nature of property condemnation was reinforced. The 1930 Act, which sought to retain a 'penal' basis of compensation, did so at the cost of re-emphasising the division between fit and unfit.

Amongst the mixture of better quality houses, railway lines, public buildings and other features which limited the extension of areas of unfit property, commercial and business usages were the most important. The way in which 'peppering' of residential areas with industry was highlighted as a problem in the period has already been noticed, figuring largely in the County Plan (1943). It particularly affected the Inner East and adjoining parts of Mixed Boroughs, and is illustrated in Figure 4.4. Generally speaking, the problem lessened as one moved away from the City and the docks, but even then slum areas were likely to be associated with various kinds of activity unwelcome elsewhere. Moreover, business usages did not simply border residential blocks but penetrated within them. In the more central parts there might be large overshadowing buildings, as well as shops and workshops in converted houses or backyards. On the far side of Bethnal Green, Doris Bailey had a fairly large factory complex at the bottom of her street, lived opposite cabinet makers, and next door to a clay pipe maker with a workshop in the front downstairs room and a kiln in the back garden.[57] Such mixed land uses often appear in autobiographical accounts as part of lively 'village' existence, recalling Jane Jacobs. However, the proximity of these premises might also bring vermin, ranging from rats to flies, encourage litter, and add to the general dust, gloom and grime in a period when

Londoners still lived 'under a roof of corrosive smoke'.[58]

From the official point of view, however, the most important feature of these activities was not their advantages and disadvantages in lived experience, but the manner in which their presence served to block attacks on unfit housing through slum clearance. It became difficult to identify parts consisting only of unfit housing, except on a small scale, producing problems of rehousing on site. In 1911 the Hoxton St. district of Shoreditch had been identified as containing the largest relatively compact area of unfit housing in London—843 houses distributed in various smaller groups. By 1934 it was recognised that most of the unfit property lay in small groups:

mostly courts and alleys of comparatively few houses, scattered and surrounded by business premises or better class property . . . There are so many smaller slum areas concentrated in this district that the question of some much larger scheme linking them up suggests itself . . . in the 80 acre area . . . there are about 25 areas scheduled since 1911 as unfit, involving at least 400 houses.[59]

These problems arising from intermixture of land uses were one important element in the increasing prominence given to the 'wider slum' as a programme of accelerated clearance began to be considered in the early 1930s. It took place across a wide range of the political spectrum. Howard Marshall, for instance, opposed council housing and supported Octavia Hill's methods of management, but nonetheless argued against piecemeal forms of redevelopment. 'The only way to achieve permanent results is to replan towns in large areas at a time.' Correspondingly, he talks of 'a great belt of slums encircling the heart of the city', and of 'miles of dilapidated cottage houses'.[60] These kinds of reference were also supported in the reports which the LCC was receiving from its officers. The MOH, reporting in 1933 on possible clearance schemes in Stepney noted that:

Stepney contains so many unfit houses and slums that the only real remedy would seem to be the reconstruction of the whole borough. Unfortunately, the many small areas are scattered and separated by industrial and business premises. The larger and more concentrated areas only are given.[61]

Not only were unfit houses difficult to bound within clearance areas, but related problems went well beyond the kind of property they defined. Barclay and Perry write of Southwark in 1929 that:

The amount of property which is hopelessly defective and altogether deplorable is very large. Damp, dilapidation of every kind, obsolete design and construction, vermin . . . abound throughout the whole borough, and impart to much of it a character of unrelieved defectiveness.[62]

Such a description did not mean, of course, that conditions in Southwark were uniform. On the contrary, Barclay and Perry, as we have noted, carefully distinguish various types of property, and they also stress the way in which conditions varied according to the quality of management. Apart from more deep-seated structural problems, damp penetration through defective flashings, gutterings, or window surrounds was a widespread problem. Difficulties arising from the general condition of the internal fabric are put well by the New Survey:

Dilapidated woodwork plaster and wallpaper, if less serious than structural faults, are also much more general. Few except the most modern working class dwellings are entirely free of these defects. They are responsible for much dirt and discomfort and for the depressing atmosphere of squalor associated with so many working class homes. The most serious effect, however, is that they harbour vermin of all sorts and especially bugs.[63]

The survey went on to say that such problems existed in many houses in Fulham which were 'sound and outwardly in fair condition', whereas in the poorer area of Somers Town (St Pancras) 'it is stated that hardly any room in the old tenement houses is free of bugs'.[64] Massey reported that rats were frequent in older houses in Stepney, and the 'thousands of people are in the habit in summer time of pulling their beds into the street in order to escape from the bugs'.[65] The LCC was advised that 'in many of the slum areas at the very least some 80 per cent [of dwellings] are badly infested with vermin'.[66] Two features stand out in the accounts of this problem given in autobiographies. One is that the apparent frequency of bug infestation nonetheless went side by side with a distinct social stigma.[67] The other is the amount of work needed to keep bugs down: 'a never-ending onslaught of soap, carbolic and sulphur'.[68] The problem of vermin appears more strongly in the slum literature of the inter-war period than it had before 1914. Between the wars, of course, the model suburban home with its electric cleanliness, was constantly brought before the public eye. The presence of bugs or rats, extending well outside the most degraded houses or areas, formed part of a heightened contrast between the old and the new.

Certainly, the maintenance and reconditioning necessary to bring housing standards closer to the current norm in new building was a central problem of the inter-war period. Space does not permit a detailed discussion of this subject, including the large problems which exist in relating the economics of house property to the effects of the Rent Acts or the suburban building boom. Although most property demolished in the period had already been condemned in 1911, these matters are particularly relevant to the 'wider slum'. However, attention should also be directed to the more general foundations of the property market, and to features which were not new to the period. The widespread economic obsolescence of property was related to rising costs of maintenance and of improvement of amenities as housing in the inner areas increasingly aged. In the absence of any sinking fund this was bound to affect profitability and lead to a reluctance to invest. Slum housing conditions were a normal feature of the market under such conditions. The only alternatives were redevelopment or conversion to a higher class of user, or otherwise a major increase in the rent-paying ability of the existing tenants. Neither of these was forthcoming, except in special circumstances.

I have attempted elsewhere to show the significance of the Moyne Report in drawing attention to these and other problems and in shifting the focus of political action from reconditioning to much more widespread clearance and rehousing programmes.[69] From this point, and particularly after the Housing Act of 1935, the 'wider slum' becomes more prominent in public debate and official action. The LCC cooperated with the Ministry in preparing the Redevelopment Areas section of this Act, and in May 1935 it presented plans for redeveloping—

. . . a large area covering some 700 acres in the Boroughs of Stepney, Shoreditch and Bethnal Green, stretching between London Docks in the south and the Regents Canal in the north . . . and forming a corridor some 1 ¾ miles in length and ¾ mile in width.[70]

Two parts of this extensive district were declared as Redevelopment Areas before the war. Bethnal Green no. 1 Area of 45 acres (later reduced to 39) and some 5,000 people, lay in the north of the borough. The larger Redevelopment Area no 2, comprising 128 acres and nearly 20,000 people, stretched across south Bethnal Green from the Boundary Street estate to the Cambridge Heath Road, These areas, of course, contained a wider range of property than did the clearance areas that were embedded within them. Area no. 1 included 891 premises divided into 646 houses, 134 shops with dwellings over, 38 other commercial premises, 61 factories or industrial premises and 12 pubs; 62 per cent of its houses were regarded as unfit, a figure reducing to 44 per cent in the larger Area no. 2.[71] Redevelopment procedures meant, in effect, an attempt to solve problems arising in the clearance of unfit housing by demolishing further housing in the immediate surrounds, and re-zoning industry and commerce.

Later, the concept of the redevelopment area was adapted in the County of London Plan (1943) to include a large measure of decentralisation. The much wider view of the slum was, however, retained, as it was in housing and planning circles generally. A survey of Stepney by Avery in 1942 placed 32 per cent of its dwellings in a category 'ready for immediate demolition' and a further 35 per cent as 'old and usually incapable of being put into habitable condition according to modern standards'.[72] The large 'decentralisation area' of the County Plan, discussed earlier, was also that part for which comprehensive redevelopment was advocated and in which 'a great majority of the houses might be regarded as slum dwellings'.[73] The pre-war location of redevelopment areas was changed to take account of bomb damage, and by 1951 two large areas had been declared of 1,500 acres in Stepney-Poplar (1946) and 170 acres in Bermondsey (1947).

Income groups and social classes

The New Survey attempted to replicate Booth, and to discover the proportion of the population in 1929–30 which was still below the poverty line he had established in 1889. It was inferred from cost of living indices that an income of 40s a week in 1929 would be equivalent to the 21s which Booth thought to mark the poverty line for a moderate household. In the street survey, households whose head earned less than this amount were placed in Class P. A further line of division, at 60s a week for a moderate household separated classes labelled Unskilled (U) and Skilled (S). With the middle classes (M), at over 100s a week, a basic structure of four income groups was therefore used, and this corresponded to a classification of streets in map form in which P,U,S and M were represented by blue, purple, pink and red respectively, although this was complicated by the award of blue or red stripes to indicate the more mixed streets. Certain streets were also awarded black stripes or, exceptionally, coloured wholly black. This designation did not refer to an income group, but was intended to give a general indication of a high degree of 'moral subnormality' in the form of 'crime, disorder, drunkenness, gambling and vice'[74] It was not separately included in the statistical analyses of the survey.

The results of the street survey showed that some 9.6 per cent of the population in the County of London fell into Class P, thus representing only one third of the proportion in poverty in the Booth survey. It was an important result, reflecting a rise in the general standard of living, the effects of the war in redistributing income, and new social provisions. However, in its determination to emphasise the fall in the level of absolute poverty since 1889, the New Survey explicitly violated Booth's poverty standard. This had required 'the satisfaction of primary physical needs of clothing, shelter and warmth according to the customary standards and conventions which prevail at the time and place.'[75] Customary standards and conventions were certainly higher in 1929 than in 1889, so that Rowntree in his second survey of York (1936)[76] used a minimum standard for a five person family of 43s 6d. after payment of rent and rates, a figure which applied to London would include the larger part of Class U. The New Survey, however, made no attempt to establish a contemporary poverty line even though it also included a sample survey of working-class households which collected data on incomes and household composition.[77]

The tables of income class and street category compiled from the street survey (Tables 4.5–6) show striking regional contrasts which parallel those of land use and physical structure discussed in the last section. The Inner East stood out in its high proportion of P and indeed of U, these two classes making up some 60 per cent of its population. P was particularly high in Poplar (24 per cent), Shoreditch (18 per cent), Bethnal Green (18 per cent) and Bermondsey (18 per cent). Conversely, P and U were of considerably less importance in the Inner West and Outer Districts, dominated by income groups M and S respectively. In the Inner East over one third were also in class S. The top income group was more strongly segregated, some 85 per cent of its population occupying red or red-striped streets. The virtual absence of this class from the Inner East was largely connected with the reputation of the area. Indeed, given that

Table 4.5 Income Groups, 1929–31 (Street Survey)

	Total Population Nos.	Percentage in Income Groups			
		P	U	S	M
Inner East	918,300	17.1	42.6	37.5	2.8
Inner West	555,200	5.8	16.5	36.2	41.5
Mixed	1,132,300	10.1	30.8	47.5	11.6
Outer	1,534,900	6.2	20.6	48.9	24.3
LCC Area	4,140,700	9.6	27.7	44.3	18.3

Source: Smith, H. Llewellyn, New Survey of London Life and Labour, London: 1931–35. Figures are calculated from the Borough Summaries, vol. 3, 345–388 and vol. 6, 381–449. They exclude the City.

Table 4.6 Categories of Street, 1929–31 (New Survey)

	Blue/ Blue Stripe (%)	Purple (%)	Pink (%)	Red/ Red Stripe (%)
Inner East	19.3	41.9	34.1	4.7
Inner West	4.7	14.8	28.1	52.3
Mixed	8.9	29.7	44.0	17.4
Outer	3.9	17.8	46.3	32.1
LCC Area	8.8	26.0	40.5	24.7

Source: As Table 4.5

the Mixed Boroughs were explicitly divided in character, it is clear the whole of the County Plan's decentralisation zone was characterised by an absence of the M income group, and that this was interrelated with the apparent meanness of the physical environment. Three quarters of all the blue and blue-striped streets in London lay in the Inner East and Mixed Boroughs, a figure which corresponds well with the regional figures for unfit housing.

The New Survey continued to use Booth's notion of 'poverty trap' to characterise smaller-scale concentrations of poverty. These 'nuclei of poverty' were often, but not invariably, 'districts where the free circulation of population is impeded by some physical obstacles'. For instance, it says that 'some of the most dismal slums of Bethnal Green are in the immediate vicinity of the railways and Regents Canal'.[78] The Survey claimed to find, however, that:

what remains of 'poverty' (in the sense in which Charles Booth used the word) is ... less concentrated than was the case forty years ago. No doubt slum clearances have had something to do with this process of dispersion, which is certainly beneficial from a social point of view, since 'pockets' of poverty and degradation . . . tend to perpetuate themselves by in-breeding and the contamination of environment.[79]

It went on to say:

Sometimes it is suggested that slum clearances are futile because their denizens only spread themselves and their habits over a wider area. But all experience negatives this conclusion and confirms the verdict of Charles Booth in 1889: 'The inhabitants of the slums have been scattered, and though they must carry contamination with them wherever they go, it seems certain that such hotbeds of vice, misery and disease as those from which they have been ousted are not again created'.[80]

Leaving aside for the moment the language of this report, was it the case that poverty had become more dispersed since 1889? In some cases large slum areas had certainly been cleared, and we might connect this with the difficulties in identifying large scale slums for the official clearance programme in the early 1930s. However, the dispersion which the New Survey claimed to find is almost certainly a product of its confusion over poverty 'in the sense in which Charles Booth used the word'. The main evidence for dispersion was that 'the population of streets which are fully coloured blue (i.e. streets in which the predominant grade of inhabitants is below the poverty line) is only about one fifth of the total persons recorded as living in poverty. This is a great change since Charles Booth's time when the corresponding proportion was over three-fifths'.[81] Booth, however, had attempted to identify those who were poor by contemporary standards. The New Survey P Class bore a much closer resemblance in numbers and relative position to Booth's 'very poor' (Classes A and B). Using the sample streets given by Booth[82] it can be calculated that some 9 per cent of his Classes AB probably lived in streets where these classes comprised over 50 per cent of the population, whereas some 73 per cent of the 'poor' (Classes ABCD) lived in streets where the majority were from this group. Similarly, from the New Survey it can be calculated that some 12 per cent of the very poor (P) lived in streets where they comprised the majority of the population, and 73 per cent of the poor (UP) did so.

Hence, although there is no evidence of change in the spatial concentration of poverty since 1889, an emphasis on the scattered nature of the lowest income group is certainly justified. The 'blue' streets in the New Survey, contained only two per cent of the population of the county, eight boroughs having none of these streets at all. They contained only 6 per cent of the population of Bethnal Green, reaching a maximum of eight per cent in Poplar. Correspondingly, only 32 per cent of those in Class P in the County lived in blue or blue striped streets, the latter having between a quarter and half of their inhabitants in the P Class. Some 35 per cent of Class P lived in purple streets, 28 per cent in pink streets and 6 per cent in red or red striped streets. Even in the Inner East the figures change only to 42 per cent, 37 per cent, 19 per cent and 2 per cent respectively.

In the course of its Borough Summaries the New Survey identifies many examples of slum. Thus in Paddington, near the Grand Junction Canal and the Harrow Road, 'there are many streets that have degenerated into poor class dwellings including some slums, notably Clarendon Street, Cirencester Street and Woodchester Street, where poverty and overcrowding are accompanied by crime and degradation'.[83] Describing Bethnal Green the Survey says that 'poor and overcrowded conditions are found in many parts of the borough. Perhaps the worst area is a group of streets . . . hemmed in between Cambridge Road and railway lines and sidings. Other bad patches are the Turin Street area . . . the line of streets immediately to the west of the railway behind Cambridge Road and the area north and west of . . . Meath Gardens'.[84] From these parts were taken such clearance areas as Pott St., Hollybush Gardens, and Turin St. They contain some blue streets, but their predominant colour coding is purple, although often qualified by black or blue strips. A few clearance areas, such as Teale Street are coded pink and purple. The redevelopment areas naturally comprise a much larger cross-section of income groups, including large tracts of the pink streets that occupied a major part of Bethnal Green, as of the Inner East as a whole.

The New Survey statistics do not take into account the homeless poor, including those living in common lodging-houses. The lodging-houses were, however, identified in colouring the maps, no doubt particularly in the use of black, or the award of black or blue stripes. The Survey says that, 'The unemployed, the aged, the mentally deficient and the criminals all contribute their quotas to the "homeless" group, which also includes quite a large proportion of the poorest grade of the street trading community'.[85] It calculated that at any one time there were about 15,000 inhabitants of common lodging-houses in London, about half the figure in Booth's time. This was seen as part of the general improvement in living standards, but it also reflected the increased regulation of lodging-houses, making them unviable as a commercial proposition. Conceivably, this might have increased the number of homeless living outside the lodging-houses. From the Survey this would appear not to be the case, but it would bear further examination.

The New Survey records the state of affairs at one of the most favourable times for employment in the inter-war period. After 1918 the County rate for unemployment amongst insured persons peaked at 14.1 per cent in 1921 and fell progressively to 6.4 per cent in June 1929. It subsequently rose to 12.5 per cent in June 1932 and then fell to 6.6 per cent in June 1937 before rising again in 1938. Because of relatively low rates of female and juvenile unemployment, unemployment amongst males over 18 was consistently higher, reaching 16.4 per cent in June 1932. Table 4.7 shows the distribution of unemployment at the time of the New Survey and at the later peak of unemployment in 1932. Not surprisingly, unemployment was most marked in the Inner East, although relatively it was not so concentrated there as certain other indices such as poverty, overcrowding or unfit housing. It is noticeable, too, that relatively this district performed better at the peak of unemployment when loss of work was more widely spread. Although the evidence is

Table 4.7 Unemployment in London, 1929 and 1932

A   Percentage of insured persons unemployed.
B   Percentage of insured males unemployed.

	June 1929	June 1932	
	A	A	B
Inner East	7.4	15.6	20.9
Inner West	3.2	11.5	16.9
Mixed	4.1	12.3	15.7
Outer	3.1	11.2	13.2
London AC	4.4	12.5	16.4

Source: London County Council, London Statistics
(annual)

extremely thin, it seems likely that similar effects were to be seen in the narrower slum. In one case, at Bronze Street Deptford, a survey taken by the LCC at the end of 1932 showed 19 per cent of 236 males were out of work, among a group whose main single occupations were labourers and hawkers, and 9 per cent of 88 occupied females.[86]

It is generally accepted that the apparently dramatic change of emphasis from casual work and irregular earnings in the Booth survey, to unemployment in the New Survey represented a smaller change in the real state of affairs. Compared with other industrial districts, fewer London industries were in structural decline, and long-term unemployment was a lesser proportion of the whole although an important factor amongst older people. Conversely, although the general market for casual labour was now much reduced, it still existed to some extent in industries such as the docks, where casual labour and short-term unemployment were overlapping categories.[87] Labourers were still often subject to seasonal irregularities of work, changed their employment more frequently than skilled men, and were subject to more frequent bouts of unemployment. It seems likely, therefore, that the picture at a single moment in time particularly emphasises unemployment as a factor reaching out widely into the working class, with a consequent impact on the income grades shown for different regions in the New Survey. Long-term and recurrent unemployment would have been much more prevalent in the cores of poverty represented by the slum.

Rowntree in his 1936 survey of York calculated that skilled workers formed some 10 per cent of his AB social classes, below the Poverty Line, whereas unskilled and semi-skilled workers formed 51 per cent of his top working-class group E. Unemployment and ill-health contributed to this pattern. However, he emphasised the importance of the 'poverty cycle' in causing 'a constant movement of families from lower classes to higher ones and vice versa'.[88] The New Survey showed surprisingly little interest in the poverty cycle, or in cross-correlating income class with other factors, except for the small group in Class P. Unemployment was the chief factor contributing to this class, but old age (despite old age pensions) and large numbers of dependants were important contributory factors. The Survey did show considerable interest in the extent to which supplementary earners contributed to working-class household incomes. It can be calculated that the single male breadwinner was characteristic of 49 per cent of London working-class households, ranging down to 43 per cent in the Inner East. Wives made some contribution, particularly in the Inner West, where there was also a high proportion of female-headed households. The main supplementary earners were, however, older children and young adults.[89]

In so far as the poverty cycle is dependent on the numbers of children, its significance must have been declining in the inter-war period, especially among the families of skilled workers. If, as expected, unskilled workers retained higher fertility rates and household sizes, then their living standards would fluctuate to a much greater extent. Bowley, in an independent paper, attempted to use the New Survey record cards to distinguish the family sizes of various income groups which he labelled skilled (head's income 61s +), unskilled (52–61s) and poor or casual (under 52s).[90] He found that among married couples the number of children in the household did vary with income at all ages, so that at age 40 it ranged form 2.38 in the skilled group to 2.60 in the unskilled and 2.86 among the poor. His figures also, however, show marked regional differences, so that in a district covering Bethnal Green, Shoreditch, Stepney and Bermondsey the average size of the skilled household at 3.44 was well above the whole London average for the poor and casual. Indeed, the New Survey shows that mean household size in the Inner East for all working-class families was 3.77 compared with a London average of 3.52 and an inner West average of 3.11.[91] These statistics indicate that income, although important, was not the only factor in determining household size, and that other factors of rent, work and local 'culture' were also at work. Gittins argues that women's paid work centred on the home, as was often the case in Bethnal Green, was less related to family limitation than paid work at a distance.[92] However, in the national context it is the low levels of household size in the Inner West that are unusual, yet indicative of future trends.

During the late 1930s the LCC collected data on the tenants rehoused from slum clearance schemes. Apart from general averages, available in the presented papers, an employee of the Council, A.R. Holmes, made an analysis of 1,602 rehoused families in Bethnal Green, Shoreditch and Southwark over the period 1934–35, comparing them with the New Survey family income categories.[93] The rehoused families included some 73 per cent of the original population of the clearance areas, a proportion normal for LCC clearances at this time. In the general statistics reported by the Council for the whole of London in the quarter to March 1935, rehoused families averaged 4.40 members and had an income of 63.67 shillings.[94] Holmes's figures for Bethnal Green (370 families), Shoreditch (508) and Southwark (724) give some indication of the

Table 4.8 Working-Class and Slum Rehousing Household Incomes: Bethnal Green, Shoreditch and Southwark (range)

A   Number of households
B   Percentage of households in each income range
C   Cumulative percentage of B

Weekly Income (shillings)	New Survey 1929-31			Rehousing Tenants 1934-5		
	A	B	C	A	B	C
Under 34s.	370	12.6	12.6	153	9.6	9.6
34/1-52/6	335	11.4	24.0	394	24.6	34.2
52/7-72/6	910	31.0	55.0	522	32.6	66.8
72/7-102/6	684	23.3	78.3	391	24.4	91.2
102/7-142/6	398	13.6	91.9	118	7.4	98.6
142/7-182/6	151	5.2	97.1	19	1.2	99.8
182/7 +	83	2.8	99.9	3	0.2	100.0

Source: Holmes, A.R., Investigation into the Effects of Rehousing by the LCC (1947), using data from the sample survey of working-class households contained in Smith, H. Llewellyn, New Survey of London Life and Labour, London: 1931-35.

Table 4.9 Working-Class and Slum Rehousing Household Incomes: Bethnal Green, Shoreditch and Southwark (means)

Mean weekly household incomes (shillings)

	New Survey 1929-31	Rehousing Tenants 1934-35
Bethnal Green	78-81	70-72.5
Shoreditch	80-83	60-62.5
Southwark	74-77	62.5

Source: as Table 4.8

distribution around this mean, and how it compared with the New Survey figures for the whole working-class population of the three boroughs (Table 4.8). Table 4.9 shows how the mean family incomes of slum tenants being rehoused compared with those of the survey sample.

The Tables show that the mean income of 'rehousing' families in these boroughs was less than the working-class average. Nonetheless, there was a considerable degree of overlap between the two categories. However, account must be taken of the 23 per cent of slum tenants not rehoused by the LCC, and of varying household sizes, matters in which Holmes, unfortunately, took little interest. It is certain that the families not rehoused were poorer than the average. Amongst these were many older households, particularly of single persons. This helps to account for the low percentage of slum rehousing tenants in the lowest category of family income. It may also mean that rehousing families were a little larger on average than those of clearance areas as a whole. In the clearance areas studied by Holmes, the mean family size at 4.05 was higher than that of the New Survey sample in the three boroughs at 3.69. The relative financial position of the two sets of families was, therefore, tilted further in favour of the New Survey sample. Nonetheless, an important degree of overlap between the two categories would still have existed.

The role of supplementary earnings in these figures is shown by later LCC reports which give the income of household heads as well as their families. In the quarter ending March 1938, representative of its period, the mean size of family in rehousing lettings (936) was 4.18, including 0.69 members under 10 years-old. The tenant's mean income was 46.08s, and that of his family 81.75s. The ordinary lettings (1,266) at this time, mostly in suburban cottage estates, went to families whose average size was smaller (3.69), but contained more children under 10 (1.11). Their family income was actually less, at 76.67s., but the tenant's income was higher at 64.33s.[95] A 1937 survey of working-class household incomes in North London produced an average of 74.6s with adult male incomes of 57s.[96] These comparisons emphasise the importance of the family life cycle. The reported earnings of slum rehousing tenants were very low, but they made up only 56 per cent of family earnings. Wives' income certainly contributed to this, no doubt to a greater extent than the average for working-class families. Nonetheless, the vital contribution of children to the family income necessarily meant greater fluctuations in prosperity over the life cycle.

If we accept that the degree of overlap between family incomes in the slum and wider slum owed much to the family life cycle, how important is that in terms of their general social characteristics? It would mean that there was less overlap if comparison was restricted to the income of the household head, and the nature of his/her occupation. The life cycle would be more important in the slum, with greater poverty in childhood and old age, but with a larger family income when children were earning. It would appear from White's account that some young people were able to use this window of opportunity to escape from even the worst conditions.[97] In general, however, childhood experience and the income and occupation of the father are likely to be preponderant determinants of life chances and of social behaviour. If this is so, the degree of overlap between slum and wider slum in terms of their general social character, although important, would be less than the overlap of family incomes. The same comment would apply to a comparison of the wider slum with working-class families living outside it, and even more strongly to any comparison with the middle classes.

Multi-occupancy and overcrowding

Of all housing indices, multi-occupation most clearly brings together the nature of the housing stock and that of the occupying households. In its most extreme and deleterious forms sharing of dwellings and amenities produced slums similar in scale and intensity to those produced by unfitness. They were not recognised as slums in official statistics only because the remedy was held to be different. However, when the LCC came to consider 'Improvement Areas' under the 1930 Housing Act, the medical officer had no hesitation in referring to them as slums. Yet such areas had been particularly chosen from properties far removed from those currently being represented as unfit: properties that were 'not less than three storeys in height, well built and of sound fabric, well arranged on site . . . originally designed for one family'.[98] Improvement at Clarendon Street in Paddington, referred to as 'this notorious slum' meant reducing overcrowding and closing the basements, where extra toilets were installed together with sinks in the rooms. Forty-seven per cent of the original population were removed, and the average household size reduced from 4.1 to 2.8.[99] This was the classic remedy for dealing with large buildings in which poor families with children shared staircases and other amenities.

Despite exterior neglect, large multi-occupied tenement houses in wide streets might still present a reasonable face to the outside world, concealing interior dilapidation, and the problems of noise and of common sharing and care. Although not usually counted as multi-occupied, some of the older blocks of flats showed similar characteristics, combined with a more forbidding exterior. Marshall presented a common middle class view on visiting such flats in Southwark: '. . . inhuman, rambling echoing warrens . . . I felt that to be crowded into one of these towering prisons, to be engulfed by those stone jaws would be living death indeed'.[100] One such block Wolseley Buildings, Bermondsey, was also considered as a potential Improvement Area. This was a six storey building with 180 two-roomed flats, reported in the New Survey as 'the enumeration district with the highest degree of overcrowding in the whole of London'.[101] Despite the small size of the flats, the average household size was 4.2 as late as 1938. Frequently, the disposal of refuse was a problem in such buildings, and here the dust chutes were inadequate and the small tarmac yard 'a dumping ground for all kinds of household refuse'. There were two lavatories and one cold water tap on each landing shared by four families.[102] Thorogood reported visiting a similar block in Bethnal Green where 'the dark stairs are unswept, unwashed, the plaster scabbing off the ugly walls. Many of the hundreds of windows . . . are broken and covered with board or paper'.[103] The Southwark Housing Association (1935) reported several examples of 'particularly objectionable' blocks of flats in Southwark.[104] H.J. Bennett recalled moving into a block in Ash Street in 1922–23: 'We were jammed up with insufficient accommodation, the neighbours were noisy and the people in the upstairs flats made a practice of throwing their rubbish out of their windows at night'.[105]

Table 4.10 Multi-Occupation in London, 1931

A The percentage of dwellings multi-occupied
B The percentage of dwellings shared by more
   than two households

	A	B
Inner East	43.7	14.5
Inner West	26.5	18.1
Mixed	28.0	22.1
Outer	36.2	9.2
London AC	40.1	14.7
Middlesex	19.9	2.9

Source: General Register Office, Census 1931,
Table 10

Table 4.11 Households in Shared Dwellings, 1921–51

A The percentage of households sharing a dwelling
B The percentage of working-class households living
   in a separate house
C The percentage of such households living in a
   separate flat

	1921	Census 1931	1951	New Survey 1929–31	
	A	A	A	B	C
Inner East	64.3	65.7	39.3	15.0	13.2
Inner West	53.3	55.2	33.6	6.7	17.2
Mixed	72.3	74.0	56.8	14.9	4.1
Outer	56.3	57.0	46.1	27.6	2.3
London AC	62.1	63.3	47.2	17.5	7.8
Middlesex	38.3	35.3	28.5	–	–

Sources: General Register Office, Censuses 1921, 1931
and 1951, Table 10. Smith, H. Llewellyn, The New
Survey of London Life and Labour, London: 1931–35.
Figures are calculated from the Borough Summaries, vol.
3, 345–388 and vol. 6, 381–449. They exclude the City.

However, multi-occupation of some kind was the norm for London
families in the inter-war period rather than the exception (Tables 4.10–
4.11). For any given category of dwelling size it was most frequent in the
Inner East, where 80 per cent of the tenement houses with 6 rooms or
more were shared as were 40 per cent of the 4–5 room buildings. Yet
working-class families had a higher chance of possessing a separate house
or flat there than in London as a whole, whereas an absence of flats made

multi-occupation surprisingly frequent in the Mixed Boroughs and Outer Districts. Sharing among more than two families increased markedly in 6–8 room houses and was most important in the largest buildings of more than 9 rooms. It was thus found particularly in the Mixed Boroughs and the Inner West, in such places as Kensington, Paddington, Islington, Lambeth and St Pancras.

Whilst much multi-occupancy was not associated with slums in any sense, its effects in more severe cases or when mixed with other problems were very important in the worst slum. Undoubtedly, the prevalence of multi-occupation was a major contributory factor to the maintenance problems of the period, and equally its decline after 1945 contributed to housing improvement. In the 1937 survey of working-class households in North London only 7 per cent had a separate bathroom and only 48 per cent a separate scullery.[106]. A few more shared these facilities, and others would have access to sinks. Another survey of 1,200 households reported by the Southwark Housing Association in 1935 found that one quarter of the families in cottages had only an outside water tap, but this applied also to one third of those in tenement houses, who were more likely to have to share. Only 20 per cent of the families in tenement houses had their own water closet.[107] In larger houses shared toilets might be located on upstairs landings, but more often they were to be found on the ground floor or in basements or backyards, sometimes out of repair, frequently with doors not possible to fasten. The Housing Association thought that: 'It is hard to stress too strongly the undesirability of dwellings which are not self-contained. They result in friction between tenants and endless unnecessary labour'.[108] Part of this labour came from the fetching and carrying of jugs and pails of water, of coal for the fires, the emptying of waste water and chamber pots, and disposal of refuse. It particularly affected the tenants on upper floors, and gave the ground floor and even basements a certain advantage. Basements were reported to be much in demand in Paddington, because they could more easily be made self-contained, with separate entrance and access to the backyard.[109] Similarly, in Southwark the best cottages were sought after for their 'easy access to the open air, being able to sit by an open door in warm weather, and the sense of having "a home of one's own"'.[110] Moreover, the Housing Association, noting that 'many tenants themselves do minor repairs and decorations', thought this 'particularly the case in cottage property and in houses occupied by few families'.[111]

The difficulties of sharing houses added to the overcrowding and multiple use of rooms. Household utensils and crockery might have to be stored in living or sleeping rooms, the washing and drying of clothes had to be done there, and storage space found for food. Very often, the latter consisted of a cupboard in a living room, and many dwellings had no special facilities for this at all. Although 40 per cent of working-class households in North London did not have electric lighting in 1937,[112] gas was now normally found and cookers were accommodated in the rooms, or sometimes on the landings. Constant re-arrangement was necessary to accommodate the multiple functions of living, sleeping cooking and washing in a few rooms, adding greatly to the woman's labour. As one housewife with five children told the New Survey 'we are all beds, so you can tell how awkward it is for cooking and eating'.[113] In such circumstances, cleanliness was always difficult, and sometimes conditions might deteriorate into squalor. Spinley, describing slum rooms at their worst in Paddington c.1950, says:

Clothes are drying over the back of the chair, and from a line stretched across the room. The most noticeable characteristics of the house is a strong and unpleasant smell . . . the smells of cooking, lavatory bucket, mattress wet in the night, a baby's vomit only hurriedly wiped up. Also, even when the housewife is extremely conscientious, the houses are so old and damp that they have a smell of their own which it is impossible to combat.[114]

Whilst the inter-war period saw increasing interest in the effects of over-crowding on cooking facilities, food storage and the preparation of meals, it was the arrangements for sleeping which continued to dominate discussion. Partly, this concerned the need to sleep in rooms that were used for living or eating. This was a widespread feature— it was claimed, for instance, that for working-class families in Kensington 'to enjoy possession of a living room which is not used as a bedroom is so exceptional as to be a rarity'.[115] The standard Census densities in 1931 involved counting every room in the house, including kitchens, but not sculleries, bathrooms or rooms shared with other families.[116] The New Survey applied a 'bedroom test' to its working-class household sample with interesting results. It counted as bedrooms all one room tenements and otherwise rooms structurally arranged for that purpose. It then applied the 'Manchester Standard', under which the percentage of children under 14 living in dwellings with a deficiency of bedrooms was 76 per cent in Holborn, 75 per cent in Southwark, 72 per cent in Stepney, 67 per cent in Shoreditch and over 60 per cent in Bermondsey, Bethnal Green, Fulham, Kensington, St Marylebone and St Pancras.[117]

However, the two features of key importance in contemporary debate were the separation of the sexes and the presence of children in the parents' bedroom. Such arrangements could be arrived at, of course, by the use of rooms for multiple functions. Whilst families did pay attention to separation of boys and girls, parents and children, this was impossible to achieve where large families occupied a small number of rooms. Thus Margery Spring Rice quoted the case of a Battersea woman living in two rooms with a family of seven:

I have a bed in the back for the two girls, and a bed for the boy which I take down every day . . . to make more room. We have our own food in this room, I do all my cooking here; in the other room is my bed, one bed I make up for the little boy on the settee, and the pram the baby sleeps in.[118]

Similarly, Barclay and Perry provide numerous examples of acute over-crowding in their surveys. In Shoreditch, a two-roomed cottage was occupied by a married couple with a boy of 10 and four younger girls.

The boy slept in the same bed as the parents, and all the girls in another bed in the same room.

The downstairs room is so small and congested (as well as being damp, dark and infested with rats) that sleeping in it is impossible. At meals there is just room for the father to sit at the table; the children sit on the stairs, and the mother walks about.[119]

The separation of the sexes, parents and children, continued to be largely seen as a moral matter, and in relation to the possibilities of incest. However, with the development of psychological studies the range of interest was later widened. Robb, in his survey of Bethnal Green carried out in 1947–49, noted that 'In the past it has been common . . . for babies to sleep in the parents' bed and almost unknown for them to sleep outside the parents' room'.[120] It produced, he thought, a close relationship with the mother and rapid gratification of wants, but later such security was lost as other children were born. For Spinley this was 'a sudden and violent change in circumstances' which produced 'marked feelings of insecurity'. Moreover, she believed that in the slum sexual disturbance 'is one of the most pronounced features of the life history' with marked effects on the development of personality.[121]

The effects of slum conditions on physical health became less important in the inter-war period from the technical point of view. That is to say, the formulation of slum clearance schemes became largely based on housing conditions themselves, rather than on evidence of mortality or disease. Moreover, in the 1930s the publications of McGonigle, Orr, and Titmuss made it clearer than ever that poor health was a product of poverty, as reflected in poor diet and other matters as well as housing.[122] Nonetheless, housing played its part, and there was still much emphasis on the general effects of slums on mortality, and on tuberculosis, rheumatism and respiratory diseases. The standardised death rates and infant mortality rates for London over the period 1928–37 emphasise the relative healthiness of the outer districts. However, whereas the Inner East had the worst general death rate, the Inner West was worst in terms of infant mortality. Poor boroughs like Bermondsey and Poplar had rates about the London average, whereas the Boroughs with the worst record were Paddington (84.8) and Kensington (81.5).[123] Amongst the various factors that account for this, multi-occupation, overcrowding and relatively high rents must be included. In Paddington, infant mortality figures by ward showed a clear variation according to social class. Clarendon Street was singled out by the medical officer for special attention, and reported an average infant mortality rate of 141 per 1000 between 1926 and 1934, when it was reconditioned.[124] By 1951–52 no statistical relationship between infant mortality and overcrowding was discernible in London at the borough level, and this no doubt reflected the improvement in housing occupancy as well as other changes.[125]

Whilst census statistics cannot portray the actual and everyday experience of overcrowding, they are indispensable in providing some

Table 4.12 Overcrowding in London, 1931

A The percentage of persons overcrowded at each standard
B The percentage of persons overcrowded in given household sizes

		Household Sizes (persons)			
	1–2	3–4	5–6	7–8	over 8
i) At over 3 persons per room					
	A	B	B	B	B	B
	A	B	B	B	B
Inner East	7.2	nil	3.6	3.8	18.6	23.8
Inner West	3.3	nil	1.6	2.0	13.7	11.1
Mixed	3.7	nil	1.9	2.4	13.1	17.9
Outer	1.6	nil	0.8	0.9	5.1	9.5
London AC	3.6	nil	1.9	2.4	13.1	17.9
ii) At over 2 persons per room					
	A	B	B	B	B
Inner East	23.4	nil	9.6	26.0	46.6	70.4
Inner West	11.5	nil	4.5	19.0	31.6	30.0
Mixed	11.0	nil	4.5	11.6	32.2	51.9
Outer	9.2	nil	2.6	10.9	23.9	53.3
London AC	13.1	nil	4.6	15.6	33.3	54.8
iii) At over 1½ persons per room					
	A	B	B	B	B
Inner East	45.7	13.9	24.9	55.3	79.8	90.8
Inner West	26.0	10.2	15.7	42.2	51.4	38.3
Mixed	27.6	10.4	14.5	35.5	63.9	72.6
Outer	22.0	5.2	7.6	30.1	56.0	78.6
London AC	29.2	9.2	13.8	38.9	64.1	74.9

Source: General Register Office, Census 1931, Table 11

measure of its incidence. The Unhealthy Areas Committee emphasised the congestion of London in 1921 by pointing to the existence of 19 'black' wards with over 350 people to the acre, containing 295,860 persons with an average of 53 houses and 415 people to the acre. Wards with over 200 persons per acre contained 1,654,319 people. They used this to draw attention to not only the large amount of decentralisation necessary to relieve congestion, but also to the reduction in the number of dwellings per acre necessary to achieve town planning norms.[126] These aspects of congestion were taken up again in the 1943 County Plan.

However, during most of the inter-war period the greater emphasis was placed on the statistics of persons per room. The 1931 Census allows three measures of overcrowding by this means. The standard measure was occupancy at over two persons per room, whilst over three persons per room was used to indicate severe overcrowding. Lastly, occupancy at 1½ persons per room was thought by the Council for Research on Housing Construction (1934) to be a reasonable measure of housing

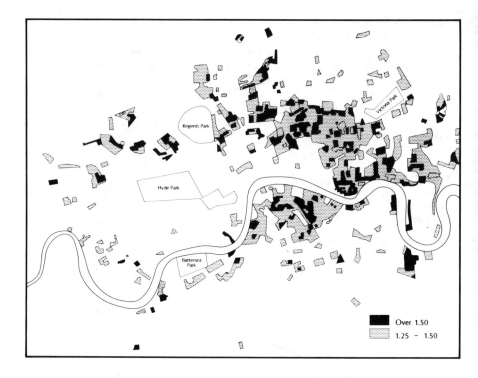

Figure 4.5 Overcrowding in London, 1931

shortage, and was so used by Massey and by Forshaw and Abercrombie.[127] Taking first the overall figures, Table 4.12 shows that in 1931 the Inner East was by far the most severely affected district, with 23 per cent of its population living at over 2 to a room and 46 per cent at over 1½ to a room. This was despite the fact that rents at any given dwelling size were 10 per cent below the County level. A map of enumeration districts compiled for the New Survey shows the geography of overcrowding in more detail (Figure 4.5). The map illustrates the empirical basis of the 'decentralisation area' of the 1943 Plan, including of course parts of the Mixed Boroughs. It also shows some exceptionally crowded enumeration districts in the inner West, particularly in Kensington, Paddington and St Marylebone.

A very striking feature was the extent to which overcrowding varied with the size of household. Except at 1½ persons per room, households with up to four members largely escaped overcrowding, but thereafter it mounted rapidly. This relationship accounts for some of the social and geographical variations in the incidence of overcrowding—for example pointing up once again the high average household sizes in the Inner East. It also indicates the existence of wide variations in overcrowding within similar social groups or social areas according to family circumstances. Finally, changes in household size underlay much of the improvement in overcrowding of rooms which was perhaps the most

Table 4.13 Overcrowding: Persons per Room, 1921–51

A Persons per room
B Persons per room in working-class households

	Census 1921 A	New Survey 1929–31 B	Census 1931 A	Census 1951 A
Inner East	1.41	1.42	1.31	0.94
Inner West	0.86	1.25	0.83	0.81
Mixed	1.09	1.15	1.03	0.86
Outer	0.93	1.07	0.88	0.79
London AC	1.05	1.21	0.98	0.83
Middlesex	0.87	–	0.80	0.74

Sources: General Register Office, Censuses 1921, 1931, 1951, Table 11. Smith, H. Llewellyn, The New Survey of London Life and Labour, London: 1931–35. Figures are the mean of those for the boroughs included in each group, as reported in vol. 3, 227 and vol. 6, 56.

Table 4.14 LCC Clearance Scheme: Densities

	persons per household	persons per acre	persons per room
1922–28	4.23	293	1.71
1931–34	4.20	249	1.58
1935–38	3.71	183	1.23

Source: calculated from London County Council, London Statistics (annual)

positive feature of housing experience during our period (Table 4.13). Between 1921 and 1931 improvement was achieved almost entirely by shifts in household size, and the number of rooms occupied by households of a given size remained remarkably stable. However, conditions probably improved from 1932 with the fall in unemployment, continued reduction in household size, and increased suburban house-building. The results of the Overcrowding Survey of 1935 were generally thought by contemporaries to show an improvement, but the standard adopted is impossible to compare precisely with other measures.[128] The major reduction in overcrowding by 1951, and particularly the marked narrowing of regional differences, owed much not only to social changes but also to the outflow of population from the Inner East, a process already beginning to accelerate before the war (Table 4.1). Overcrowding as it existed in the inter-war period was not to be seen again.

Some idea of the position of clearance areas in relation to overcrowding can be obtained from the published LCC statistics (Table 4.14). These show that, as expected, clearance areas had a high level of persons per acre and per room. However, densities are not spectacularly high if we relate them to the Unhealthy Areas Report, referred to earlier, or to the high densities shown over wide areas in Figure 4.5. Equally, it is clear from the absolute numbers involved that the great bulk of overcrowding occurred outside clearance areas. Within clearance areas, and indeed other blocks of high average density, there were very great variations in crowding between households, caused particularly by varying household size. This same factor of household size is the principal cause of declining densities, although these may also reflect the larger size of clearance areas in the late 1930s. It does seem possible, though, that by then the worst property was beginning to see the drop in demand that housing reformers had long awaited.

Slum life and culture

Joan Conquest in *The Naked Truth* (1933) wrote that:

The slum mind, a fungus kind of mental deformity bred from slum conditions, resignation to those conditions, and despair of ever rising above them, is spread throughout the slums as fungus spreads upon a dark damp wall.[129]

These 'shocking revelations' take to extreme one tendency of the literature of the 'slum mind', the conflation of behaviour and environment. The basic ingredients, however, ranged much more widely including, notably, moral condition, racial characteristics and intelligence. C. Martin, a public health inspector from Whitstable (Kent) wrote in *Slums and Slummers* (1935) that:

An appreciable percentage of the occupants of the slums . . . are born slum makers . . . This vicious class may be considered the core of the whole slum problem . . . drunkards, hooligans, loafing idlers down to the hardened criminals and moral degenerates.[130]

He goes on say that 'this class of people breed in lust', 'multiplying without restraint, their progeny not withstanding high infant mortality are very numerous'. 'Children grow up with warped bodies and minds, animalism and cruelty uppermost in their nature'. They were 'in constant moral danger'. 'They see white women living with coloured men and their half-caste children'. Indeed, crime and vice were 'particularly rife in those cities which possess comparatively large foreign quarters occupied by Chinese, Arabs, Negroes etc. The Irish labouring classes, with their ever-increasing families, are among the worst destroyers of property'. 'The habits of the lower class of Jewry are also filthy'.[131]

   B.S. Townroe, a former member of the Ministry of Health and chairman of the Housing Committee of Hampstead Borough Council, also found *The Slum Problem* (1930) in 'the slum mind as well as the slum dwelling'.[132] There were, of course, heroes and heroines even in the worst slums, but public opinion was misinformed by 'sentimental talk'. He quotes with approval Dr Hanschell who believed that 'the true slum making denizen is a valid sub-species of homo sapiens'. This was a parasitic class, the offspring growing up 'to repeat the parents uselessness all through life'. Some at least of these 'sub-species young' were 'hopeless and helpless by reason of stamped-in mental defect'. Townroe himself was particularly concerned that 'our slums are breeding grounds not only of physical disease but of mental rebellion'.[133]

Cyril Burt's *The Young Delinquent* (1925) is very different in character, perhaps the most carefully written book from the 1920s which has a bearing on our subject. However, whilst a multiplicity of related factors was stressed, the key question continued to be 'the relative importance of heredity and of environment, or more precisely of inborn or congenital factors on the one hand and post-natal influences on the other'.[134] According to Hearnshaw, Burt saw personality as a process of maturation rather than socialisation and 'conceived the person standing apart from the situation and capable of reacting independently of it'.[135] In Burt's case studies, attention was turned away from poverty and related factors, results being obtained by comparison with a control group drawn from the same social background. The principal question concerns the factors which, given identical social background, lead some children on to delinquency and others not.[136] These studies led Burt to emphasise the role of congenital factors, although he also concluded that 'the amount of delinquency coming from the lowest social strata is beyond question disproportionate; nevertheless in the higher and more prosperous ranks its frequency is still unexpectedly large'.[137]

Accounts such as those by Martin and Townroe were generally couched in general terms. They are clearly meant to apply, however, to the kind of 'patches of poverty and degradation' identified in the New Survey. Their general effect is to begin by constructing a group whose position lies right outside normal society. Very frequently, too, a second larger group of slum-dwellers was recognised whose general position was similar to that of Booth's Class B—one that was definitely an economic category, even if moral and other attributes also shaped their destiny. According to Martin 'if uncontrolled vice and criminal habits make the worst sector of the slum community, there is little doubt that poverty is responsible for the largest sector'. It was necessary to distinguish, however, between 'poverty caused by arrant selfishness amounting almost to vice' and that caused by 'misfortune, disease, ill-health and genuine unemployment'. 'Men and women affected in greater or lesser degree with the taint of idleness bulk largely in the slum community'. Moreover, 'the low standard of intelligence of the poorer classes is one of the cornerstones upon which the slum evil rests'.[138]

The accounts so far reviewed present an unattractive face, but in several cases, more sympathetic observers record confrontations that were clearly different from those they experienced normally in dealing with a wider section of the poor. Annie Barnes, as a Stepney Labour councillor going to inspect Wapping Wall for a slum clearance programme found that 'as we approached they came out like savages.

They came with broomsticks, even choppers . . . I had seen plenty of poor people, but I had never dreamed of anything as bad as this'.[139] Marie Paneth, encountering the children of Branch Street, records that they 'spat at us and tried to hurt us, and showered gross indecencies upon us with wild laughter'.[140] Paneth's study and Spinley's *The Deprived and the Privileged*, researched in 1949–50, were both located in the same area of Paddington 'at the lowest place on the social ladder'[141] with populations more transient than usual and including some Irish immigrants.

These two studies are both concerned with childhood development, and its consequences for later adult life. In both there is some breakdown of the separation of poverty and character, material and moral, by showing the importance of such factors as security, status, stigma and reward. Paneth believed that 'factors which human beings need for healthy growth and development are denied them'.[142] Children, especially girls, had adult responsibilities at an early age, but until they contributed to the income of the household they did not 'have meals served to them, either at a definite time, or properly at a table'.[143] There was a strong link with the mothers, who, it was recorded, 'are very rough with them, and rule severely with shouting beating and threats'. But in the case of accusation or attack from outside they offered 'unconditional protection'. Yet the children had parents 'whom they know are looked down upon and who are often prosecuted, cheating and being cheated . . . the children live in an atmosphere which, although outspoken and tough in many ways, is secretive and untruthful on essential points'.[144] The children had a feud of long standing with neighbouring streets. They behaved like 'disappointed and unhappy people'. 'A merciless world, full of danger and ill-will, barring them from every chance, that is the world as Branch Street youth must see it'.[145]

Spinley's account, written in a rather clinical fashion, emphasises basic insecurity, both emotional and material. "Neither the home nor the street provides a stable background . . . There is no routine or consistent line of behaviour mapped out".[146] Even in the play group, the child was 'always open to physical assault which he has to face alone'. In later life, 'his personality is such that he is unable to be sure of continuous employment'.[147] Aggression both arose from tensions and frustrations and was a response 'explicitly taught by older adults'. She mentions 'the very strong in-group out-group sentiment in the area which is often exaggerated when the members of a society are very insecure'.[148] Also characteristic was the habit of 'escaping from a situation when it is considered unpleasant or uninteresting'[149] Finally, she questions the effect of 'the tremendous amount of social work which is carried out in their midst', and 'the effect upon the slum child of learning of the low status of his family in the community outside his area.'[150]

During the inter-war period a notable polarisation is evident in writings about slum life, which persists into the post-war literature. A second stream emphasised the positive aspects of working-class life, but at the same time covered a much broader spectrum of that class.

Certainly, the debate on the slums was so structured that those who took a more sympathetic view usually chose the context of the 'wider slum' to express their views. Thus Marshall writes of the 'vigorous independent life' which would be recognised 'in Stepney or any other slum district'.[151] Similarly, Mrs Chesterton rejoiced that 'once over the frontier of the City you feel the surge of social independence that dominates East London right down to the docks'.[152] In the streets of North Southwark she encountered:

a vivid crowd, eager for simple fun and honest pleasure, there was a sense of life about these men and women that blew like a strong wind . . . the consciousness of the contrast between them and the foul holes in which they lived kept on recurring.[153]

This is a contrast to which she constantly returns. She had 'not before realised that self-supporting people, earning regular incomes, have to live in dens of this description'.[154] She thought that 'not only Hoxton but Shoreditch as a whole is very well dressed. The children are all clean and tidy, the boys are smart'.[155] Unemployment was not acute. She then went on to draw a contrast between workplaces and home life very different from that often used in explaining contemporary domesticity:

The difference between the finely planned and well-built factories of Shoreditch High Street and the miserable hovels behind their brave fronts . . . the cleanliness, floor space, ventilation, of the working hours—the decaying walls, depressing dirt, insanitation of the place reserved for sleep and leisure.[156]

A similar contrast is drawn by Horace Thorogood. For him the 'real slum' was 'hidden in remote back streets and courts and alleys'. Nonetheless, after describing an old block of flats in Bethnal Green, be continues:

smart young girls issue from these hideous places . . . to their jobs as typists or shop assistants in the City. You wouldn't suspect . . . that they had to keep those nice clothes wrapped up in paper all night to protect them from bugs.[157]

A much wider discussion takes place in Bakke's study of *The Unemployed Man* (1937), written about Greenwich. He underlines the difference between skilled and unskilled men, but his descriptions do not usually allow this distinction to be drawn. Instead, he emphasises the separateness of the working-class community. Workers rejected the idea that they were responsible for their own fate, but there was no strongly directed effort to escape from the insecurity to which this position gave rise. The emphasis was upon 'consolidating the position already occupied'.[158] Brightly polished brass door knobs, doorsteps whitened by daily scrubbing with chalk water, and lace curtains, were 'the necessary marks of distinction which separate the good and the bad housekeepers'.[159] More unusually, Bakke stresses the importance of the home to the male. The unemployed man's search for work was firmly linked to this base. 'His chief problem is protecting those elements around him, such as neighbourhood status, family relations, contacts with known firms and the like, rather than launching into new and untried fields'.[160] The most protective and secure environment was, however, the home and family life. 'The chief impression which I carry away is that of the ancestors looking down at one from the walls and the pride which even the poorest have in their homes'.[161]

In the accounts of post-war Bethnal Green the focus of attention is again on the absence of middle-class populations and values, producing a working-class 'subculture' which differed in significant ways from 'the "official" culture of the middle classes'.[162] Robb, working in 1947–49, reported that 'Bethnal Green is remarkably homogeneous as far as social class divisions are concerned'.[163] Glass and Frenkel (1945) pointed out some social distinctions—Bow, for instance, was a better area, and there were poorer parts, especially in the west. However, these geographical differences were 'not broad enough to disturb Bethnal Green's essential homogeneity. Everybody is poor and hence competition does not spoil personal relationships'.[164] The social distance between the best and worst housing areas was 'but a fraction of the gap which separates Bethnal Green from Bayswater or a municipal housing estate from its adjacent middle class suburb'.[165]

The society these authors depict is one strongly rooted in neighbourhood through long residence. Over three-quarters of the inhabitants of Bethnal Green were born in the borough, and they occupied particular houses and streets over long periods, often working nearby. According to Robb 'one consequence of this immobility is that everyone is surrounded by people very like himself, most of whom he has always known. Bethnal Green has many points of similarity with a village, or rather with a whole series of overlapping or interlocking villages'.[166] This local cohesion was further cemented by the neighbourhood play group, and later the boy gang, promoting associations which were often continued into later life, particularly in activities centred on local pubs. A further essential element was 'the amount of mutual aid, in the form of loans of goods and services, that goes on all the time among households in any neighbourhood'.[167]

The emphasis on locality and community often came from writers who supported redevelopment rather than a suburban solution to the slums. This was true of Glass and Frenkel, as of Mrs Chesterton before them. Glass likewise proceeded to contrast the physical nature of Bethnal Green with its social characteristics. Because of its physical make-up it was 'one of London's outstanding reconstruction areas'. But is was also 'a place where neighbours can rely on each other, where there is a general atmosphere of friendliness, of strength and independence'.[168] Indeed:

The outstanding feature of present day Bethnal Green is that, however aged, poor and shabby, it has solved one of the urgent problems of modern planning: how to create an urban community, the component parts of which are clearly distinct and yet integrated into a coherent whole'.[169]

Not only did physical and social environments not correspond, but community in this sense seemed to derive positive advantages from a certain lack of outside contacts, creating a relatively independent working-class world.

This was, however, a community which included hardly any of its teachers, or those in administrative posts. Glass recognised that Bethnal Green was 'drained of most of its best youth and there is a wide gap between officaldom and the people'.[170] Self, also writing in 1945, goes much further: 'the people have no faith in their power to effect changes'. Lack of wealth and lack of initiative meant a paucity of facilities so that 'in the social as in the economic sphere the means to lead a full and active life are lacking'. In terms of social services it was 'a community in which voluntary effort has been pumped from outside instead of growing up and circulating within'.[171] All the same, he agreed that the principal problem of the borough was its built environment: 'Bethnal Green is more a slum in looks than in pocket'.[172]

There were also other less attractive aspects of the community. For Robb, a central element in shaping social conditions in Bethnal Green was the importance of the male role in maintaining a steady income for the family. This 'seems to have become almost a test of manhood, of proper masculinity'. 'A man who for whatever reason is unable to carry out his breadwinning role, unless the failure is only of short duration, falls a great distance in the estimation of himself, his wife and children, and his fellows'.[173] The rather high possibility of failure in the inter-war period, which reinforced the significance of this test, was necessarily a problem at the individual level. The ease of insertion of an individual into the local group was also not an unproblematic matter. Robb also noticed that local group behaviour was characterised by 'very marked aggressiveness which is displayed in almost any circumstances and is nearly always masked by a display of joviality'.[174] He thought this enabled people to get rid of aggression, whilst leaving group solidarity unimpaired. Glass and Frenkel, too, were clearly worried by some aspects of local group behaviour, although they present as a thing of the past the 'street fights which were frequent until the early twenties and particularly so between the "Jewish" and the "Gentile" streets'.[175]

White's *The Worst Street* now enables us to locate the type of communities discussed by Paneth and Spinley much more accurately on the social terrain, and to understand more fully their historical development through the period. It is a richly textured book, drawing on oral histories and with much counterpointing of perspectives. It deals explicitly with a 'lumpenproletariat'—Campbell Road was coloured black on the New Survey maps, and had a notoriety comparable to only two dozen or so streets in the capital. Probably Paneth's and Spinley's accounts also apply mainly to the survey's blue streets, perhaps more to the black or black-lined. As such, a great many of the streets in clearance areas would already fall beyond that range.

Outside this social category, however, a greater vagueness prevails. The Bethnal Green accounts remain the closest approximation we have to the wider working-class world of inner London. However, none of those reviewed here was intended as a complete account of working-class life, and the sketches they present are obviously much affected by specific concerns. The intellectual and material effects of the war undoubtedly affected their descriptions, and one would expect social differences to be stronger in the inter-war period. Louis Heren's childhood Shadwell was 'not a homogeneous neighbourhood'. Alongside the native born cockneys were a majority of Irish immigrants and Polish Jews. 'There was no racial violence but religious prejudice was intense . . . I suppose we were all anti-semitic . . . the mutual antipathies of the catholics and protestants were constant'.[176] Despite this, he still insists that Shadwell was 'very much a village or hamlet'. Autobiographies of working-class childhood in the East End invariably stress the neighbourliness of the area, and the village theme is one that constantly recurs. What is required is a much richer view, incorporating individual and household variations as well as different social categories and social areas, for which the New Survey maps remain the best guide. Inter-alia this would also reveal some cross-patterning with the processes and effects associated with other social worlds, including that described by White and his predecessors.

Notes

NB: the records of the London County Council, including the Housing Committee Presented Papers (LCC HC) are housed at the Greater London Record Office.

1. White, J., *The Worst Street in North London: Campbell Bunk, Islington between the Wars*, Routledge, Chapman & Hall, London: 1986. I am grateful to Jerry for discussing these matters with me and for some useful references.
2. Barnes, H., *The Slum: its Story and Solution*, P.S. King & Son, London: 1931. Marshall, H. and A. Trevelyan, *Slum*, Heinemann, London: 1933. Quigley, H. and I. Goldie, *Housing and Slum Clearance in London*, Methuen, London: 1935. Townroe, B.S., *The Slum Problem*, Longmans, London: 1930.
3. Barclay, I. and E. Perry, *Report on a Survey of Housing Conditions in the Metropolitan Borough of Shoreditch*, Westminster Survey Group, London: 1928; also *Southwark* 1929, *Kensington* 1932, *Victoria Ward Westminster* 1927, *Ward 2 (Kentish Town) St. Pancras*, 1933.
4. Paneth, M., *Branch Street: A Sociological Study*, London: 1943. See also Klein, J., *Samples from English Cultures*, 2 vols., Allen & Unwin, London: 1965, vol. I, 3–40.
5. Clinard, M.B., *The Sociology of Deviance*, Holt, Rinehart & Davison, New York: 1968, 116.
6. Smith, Sir Hubert Llewellyn, *The New Survey of London Life and Labour*, 9 vols., London School of Economics, London: 1931–35, vol. 3, 109–10.
7. Duckworth, G., 'The making, prevention and unmaking of a slum', *Journal of the Royal Institute of British Architects*, 33, 1926, 328.
8. Burt, C., *The Young Delinquent*, London University Press, London: 1925, 74.
9. Clinard, op.cit., 116.
10. Recent studies of 'dreadful enclosures' also refer, in general terms, to areas of this scale, for example Damer, S., 'Wine Alley: The Sociology of a Dreadful Enclosure', *Sociological Review*, 22, 1974, 221–48.

11. Chesterton, Mrs C.E. (formerly Ada Jones), *I Lived in a Slum*, Queensway Press, London: 1937, 68.
12. Simon, E.D. and J. Inman, *The Rebuilding of Manchester*, Longmans, London: 1935, 56.
13. For Booth's views in relation to his analysis of the urban structure see Yelling, J.A., *Slums and Slum Clearance in Victorian London*, Unwin Hyman, London: 1986, 51-8.
14. Hansard 297, H.C. Deb., 5s., col. 368. Speech by the Housing Minister, Hilton Young.
15. Jacobs, J., *The Death and Life of Great American Cities*, Jonathan Cape, London: 1965, 18, 140.
16. Registrar General, Census of England and Wales 1921: Workplaces, London: 1925.
17. Hall, P.G., *The Industries of London since 1861*, Hutchinson, London: 1962.
18. As reported in LCC Minutes, *passim*.
19. Royal Commission on the Distribution of the Industrial Population, Minutes of Evidence, London: 1938, Day 19.
20. Hoyt, H., 'The valuation of land in urban blighted areas' (1942), reprinted in Hoyt, H., *According to Hoyt*, Washington 1970, 454-64.
21. Southwark Housing Association, *Report on Housing Conditions in the Metropolitan Borough of Southwark*, London: 1935, 29.
22. Smith, op.cit., vol. 6, 394.
23. Public Record Office HLG 52/792, Moyne Committee, Minutes of evidence.
24. Smith, op.cit., vol. 3, 144.
25. Ibid., vol. 3, 151, vol. 6, 133.
26. LCC HC 19 June 1935 (16).
27. Ibid, 29 April 1936 (6-70).
28. Chesterton, op.cit., 157.
29. LCC HC 2 May 1934 (52).
30. Forshaw, J.H. and P. Abercrombie, *County of London Plan*, London County Council, London: 1943, 21, 28.
31. Martin, C.R.A., *Slums and Slummers: A Sociological Treatise on the Housing Problem*, J. Bale & Co., London: 1935, 28.
32. Little reference is made to the City of London, which in a number of cases is excluded from the statistics. It was not covered, for instance, by the New Survey and contained only a small population—10,999 in 1931.
33. LCC Housing Committee Presented Papers (HC) Dec. 1911 (3 vols.).
34. White, op.cit., 226.
35. LCC HC 22 Oct. 1930 (9-23).
36. LCC HC 17 Apr. 1929 (96).
37. Ibid.
38. LCC HC 6 Dec. 1922 (7).
39. LCC HC 19 Feb. 1931 (5).
40. Ibid.
41. LCC HC 28 Jan. 1931 (6-8).
42. LCC Minutes 18 Oct. 1918, 912.
43. LCC HC 31 Oct. 1936 (6-175).
44. LCC HC 8 Nov. 1933 (16).
45. Barclay and Perry (1932), op.cit., 11.
46. LCC HC 20 Aug. 1919 (16-6).
47. LCC HC 6 Dec. 1922 (7).
48. LCC HC 6 Jun. 1934 (6-36).

49. Barclay and Perry (1929), op.cit., 17.
50. Ibid., 6.
51. Ibid., 20.
52. Ibid., 14; Southwark Housing Association, op.cit., 17.
53. LCC HC 16 Jul. 1919 (9).
54. Ibid.
55. Smith, op.cit., vol. 6, 187.
56. Calculated from London County Council, London Statistics (annual).
57. Bailey, D., *Children of the Green*, Stepney Books, London: 1981, 25-6.
58. Sinclair, R., *Metropolitan Man: The Future of the English*, Allen & Unwin, London: 1937, 177.
59. LCC HC 31 Jan. 1934 (25).
60. Marshall and Trevelyan, op.cit., 118.
61. LCC HC 28 Jun. 1933 (7).
62. Barclay and Perry (1929), op.cit., 3.
63. Smith, op.cit., vol. 6, 188.
64. Ibid., 189.
65. Massey, P.H., Survey of the slums of London, *Architects Journal*, 1933, 530. For rats see also Chesterton, op.cit., 27-8, 84; Thorogood, H., *East of Aldgate*, Allen & Unwin, London: 1935, 120.
66. LCC HC 7 Jul. 1937 (66).
67. See, for example, Foakes, G., *Between High Walls*, Shepheard-Walwyn, London: 1972, 67, and Linton, A., *Not Expecting Miracles*, Centerprise Trust, London: 1982, 52.
68. Blacker, H., *Just Like it Was: Memoirs of the Mittel East*, Valentine, Mitchell, London: 1974, 25.
69. Yelling, J.A., 'The Origins of British Redevelopment Areas', *Planning Perspectives*, 3, 1988, 282-96.
70. LCC HC 29 May 1935 (43).
71. LCC HC 1 Apr. 1936 (65); 21 Jul. 1937 (76).
72. Munby, D.L., *Industry and Planning in Stepney*, Toynbee Hall/Stepney Reconstruction Group, London: 1951, 88.
73. Forshaw and Abercrombie, op.cit., 83.
74. Smith, op.cit., vol. 3, 109.
75. Ibid., vol. 3, 8.
76. Rowntree, B.S., *Poverty and Progress: A Second Social Survey of York, 1936*, Longmans, London: 1941, 28.
77. The most valuable part of the Household Survey is the record cards deposited at the British Library of Political and Economic Science. However, no analyses of these could be attempted for the present essay which refers to the published material only.
78. Smith, op.cit., vol. 3, 138.
79. Ibid., vol. 3, 133.
80. Ibid., vol. 3, 141 quoting Booth, C., *Life and Labour of the People in London*, 17 vols., Williams & Norgate, London: 1889-1903, vol. 1, 70.
81. Ibid., vol. 3, 133, referring to Booth, op.cit., vol. 2, 41.
82. Booth, op.cit., vol. 2, 229.
83. Smith, op.cit., vol. 6, 431.
84. Ibid., vol. 3, 345.
85. Ibid., vol. 3, 256.
86. LCC HC 11 Jan. 1933 (11).
87. Phillips, G. and N. Whiteside, *Casual Labour: The Unemployment Question*

in the Port Transport Industry 1880–1970, Clarendon, London: 1985, 209–33.

88. Rowntree, op.cit., 152–5.
89. Calculated from Smith, op.cit., Borough Summaries, vol. 3, 345–88, vol. 6, 381–449.
90. Bowley, A.L., 'The Number of Children in Working Class Families in London 1929–30', *Journal of the Royal Statistical Society*, XCVIII, 1935, 363–75.
91. Calculated from Smith, op.cit., Borough Summaries, op.cit.
92. Gittins, D., *Fair Sex: Family Size and Structure 1900–1939*, Hutchinson, London: 1982, 99.
93. Holmes, A.R., 'Investigation into the effects of Rehousing by the London County Council', M.Sc (Econ.) London, 1947.
94. LCC HC 8 May 1935 (110).
95. Ibid., 11 May 1938 (80).
96. Abrams, M.A., 'The Housing of the Working Class, London 1937', *Agenda*, 1, 1942, 361.
97. White, op.cit., 198–218.
98. LCC HC 28 Jun. 1933 (7).
99. LCC HC 19 Jun. 1935 (44).
100. Marshall and Trevelyan, op.cit., 29.
101. Smith, op.cit., vol. 3, 357.
102. Massey, op.cit., 518; LCC HC 30 Oct. (30-7) and 16 Oct. 1935 (63); Bermondsey Medical Officer of Health Report 1938. The Ministry finally consented to clearance procedures in 1938.
103. Thorogood, op.cit., 123.
104. Southwark Housing Association, op.cit., 12–13.
105. Bennett, H.J., *I Was a Walworth Boy*, London: 1980, 60.
106. Abrams, op.cit., 361.
107. Southwark Housing Association, op.cit., 20.
108. Ibid., 23.
109. Crickmay, E.G., *Housing Conditions in a Selected Area of Paddington*, Paddington Housing Council, London: 1935, 8.
110. Southwark Housing Association, op.cit., 17.
111. Ibid., 22.
112. Abrams, op.cit., 361.
113. Smith, op.cit., 6, 314.
114. Spinley, B., *The Deprived and the Privileged: Personality Development in English Society*, Routledge & Kegan Paul, London: 1953, 41.
115. Barclay and Perry (1932), op.cit., 3.
116. General Register Office, Census of London 1931, xviii, 4, 22.
117. Smith, op.cit., vol. 3, 229–32, vol. 6, 59–61. The Manchester Standard required separation of the sexes over 10 (except married couples), and no more than 2½ equivalent persons per bedroom, children under 10 counting as a half.
118. Rice, M. Spring, *Working Class Wives: Their Health and Conditions*, Penguin, London, 1939 2nd ed. 1981, 219.
119. Barclay and Perry (1928), op.cit., 16.
120. Robb, J.H., *Working Class Anti-Semite: A Psychological Study in a London Borough*, Tavistock Publications, London: 1954, 58.
121. Spinley, op.cit., 80–1; see also Klein, op.cit., *passim*.
122. McGonigle, G., *Poverty and Public Health*, Victor Gollancz, London: 1936;

Orr, J., *Food Health and Income*, Macmillan, London: 1936; Titmuss, R.M., *Poverty and Population: A Factual Study of Contemporary Social Waste*, Macmillan, London: 1938.
123. Calculated from LCC London Statistics (annual).
124. Borough of Paddington, Medical Officer of Health Reports, 1930–39.
125. Martin, H.J., 'Vital Statistics of London 1901–1951', *Brit. J. Prev. Soc. Med.*, 9, 1955, 126–34.
126. Ministry of Health, Unhealthy Areas Committee, Second and Final Report, 1921, Appendix II, 21–4.
127. Massey, op.cit., 507; Forshaw and Abercrombie, op.cit., 150.
128. LCC, London Housing, London: 1937, 31–5; White, J., 'When every house was counted', History Workshop, 4, 1977, 186.
129. Conquest, J., *The Naked Truth: Shocking Revelations about the Slums*, T. Weiner Laurie, London: 1933, 106.
130. Martin, op.cit., 74.
131. Ibid., 75–7.
132. Townroe, op.cit., 5.
133. Ibid., 29 and quoting Hanschell 20–2.
134. Burt, C., *The Young Delinquent*, London University Press, London: 1925, 601.
135. Hearnshaw, L.S., *Cyril Burt: Psychologist*, Hodder & Stoughton, London: 1979, 316.
136. The same approach was used in later criminological studies in London, notably A. Carr-Saunders et. al., *The Young Offenders*, Cambridge University Press, Cambridge: 1942.
137. Burt, op.cit., 70.
138. Martin, op.cit., 82, 91, 95.
139. Barnes, A., *Tough Annie: From Suffragette to Stepney Councillor*, Stepney Books Publication, London: 1980, 42.
140. Paneth, op.cit., 14.
141. Ibid., 55.
142. Ibid., 121.
143. Ibid., 37.
144. Ibid., 122.
145. Ibid.
146. Spinley, op.cit., 80.
147. Ibid., 81.
148. Ibid., 89.
149. Ibid., 86.
150. Ibid., 143.
151. Marshall and Trevelyan, op.cit., 21.
152. Chesterton, op.cit., 223.
153. Ibid., 109.
154. Ibid., 90.
155. Ibid., 221.
156. Ibid.
157. Thorogood, op.cit., 123.
158. Bakke, E., *The Unemployed Man: A Social Study*, Nisbet & Co., London: 1933, 44.
159. Ibid., 157.
160. Ibid., 132.
161. Ibid.

162. Robb, op.cit., vii.
163. Ibid., 50.
164. Glass, R. and M. Frenkel, *A Profile of Bethnal Green*, Association for Planning and Regional Construction, Report no. 39, 1946, 10.
165. Ibid.
166. Robb, op.cit., 57.
167. Ibid., 61–3.
168. Glass and Frenkel, op.cit., 3.
169. Ibid., 12.
170. Ibid., 11.
171. Self, P., 'Voluntary Organisations in Bethnal Green', in Bourdillon, A.F.C., *Voluntary Social Services: Their Place in the Modern State*, Methuen, London: 1945, 240.
172. Ibid., 239.
173. Robb, op.cit., 56.
174. Ibid., 62.
175. Glass and Frenkel, op.cit., 7.
176. Heren, L., *Growing Up Poor in London*, Hamilton, London: 1973, 10–11.

Bibliography

1. The slum problem

Contemporary articles

Abrams, M.A., 'The Housing of the Working Class, London 1937', *Agenda*, i, (1942).

Allen, C.W., 'The Housing of the Agricultural Labourer', *Journal of the Royal Agricultural Society of England*, ixxxv, (1914).

Costelloe, B.F.C., *'The Housing Problem'*, *The Transactions of Manchester Statistical Society*, (1898–99).

Cowan, R., 'Vital statistics of Glasgow illustrating the sanitary condition of the population', *Journal of the Royal Statistical Society*, iii, (1840).

Duckworth, G., 'The making, prevention and unmaking of a slum', *Journal of the Royal Institute of British Architects*, xxxiii, (1926).

Duke of Bedford, 'On Labourers' Cottages', *Journal of the Royal Agricultural Society of England*, x, (1849).

Edgell, E.W., 'Moral statistics of the parishes of St James, St George and St Anne, Soho', in the City of Westminster, *Journal of the Statistical Society of London*, i, (1838).

Felkin, W., 'Moral Statistics of a District near Gray's Inn Court, London, in 1836', *Journal of the Statistical Society of London*, i, (1839).

Fletcher, J., 'The metropolis: its boundaries, extent and divisions for local government', *Journal of the Royal Statistical Society*, vii, (1844).

Jones, T., 'Labourers' Homes', *Quarterly Review*, c.vii, (1860).

MacVicar, J. Young, 'Labourers' Cottages', *Journal of the Royal Agricultural Society of England*, x, (1849).

Mann, H., 'Statement of mortality prevailing in Church Lane during the last ten years with the sickness of the last seven months', *Journal of the Royal Statistical Society*, xi, (1848).

Massey, P.H., 'Survey of the slums of London', *Architects Journal*, (1933).

Nicholls, G., 'On the Condition of the Agricultural Labourer with Suggestions for its Improvement', *Journal of the Royal Agricultural Society of England*, vii, (1846).

Rawson, R.W., 'Results of some Inquiries into the Condition and Education of the Poorer Classes in the Parish of Marylebone in 1858', *Journal of the Statistical Society of London*, vi, (1843).

Saunders, J., 'A parting glimpse of St Giles', *Illuminated Magazine*, iii, (1844).

Statistical Society of London, 'Report on 4,102 working-class families in Manchester', *Proceedings of the Statistical Society of London*, i, (1834–35).

Statistical Society of London, 'Report of the committee of the council of the Statistical Society of London on the state of the working classes in the parishes of St Margaret and St John Westminster', *Journal of the Royal Statistical Society*, iii, (1840).

Statistical Society of London, 'Report of the committee of the council of the Statistical Society of London to investigate the state of the inhabitants and their dwellings in Church Lane, St Giles', *Journal of the Royal Statistical Society*, xi, (1848).

Statistical Society of London, 'Investigation into the state of the poorer classes in St Georges-in-the-East', *Journal of the Royal Statistical Society*, xi, (1848).

Weight, G., 'Statistics of the Parish of St George-the-Martyr, Southwark', *Journal of the Statistical Society of London*, iii, (1840).

Weld, S.C.R., 'On the Condition of the Working Classes in the Inner Ward of St George's Parish, Hanover Square', *Journal of the Statistical Society of London*, vi, (1843).

2. The slum problem

Contemporary monographs

Adderley, J., *In Slums and Society*, London, 1916.

Adshead, J., *Distress in Manchester: evidence of the state of the labouring classes*, London, 1842.

Aronson, H., *Our Village Homes*, London, 1913.

Beachcroft, R.M., *Overcrowded London*, London, 1893.

Beames, T., *The Rookeries of London, Past, Present and Prospective*, London, 1851.

Besant, W., *East London*, London, 1901.

Bigland, J., *A Topographical and historical description of Yorkshire*, London, 1815.

Black, C., *Married women's work*, London, 1915.

Booth, C., *Life and Labour of the People in London* (17 vols) London, 1902–3.

Booth, W., *In Darkest England and the Way Out*, London, 1890.

Bosanquet, S.R., *The rights of the poor and Christian almsgiving vindicated*, London, 1841.

Bowmaker, E., *The Housing of the Working Classes*, London, 1895.

Carlyle, T., *Chartism*, London, 1840.

Carpenter, M., *Reformatory schools for the children of the perishing and dangerous classes and for juvenile offenders*, London, 1857.

Chadwick, E., *The Sanitary Condition of the Labouring Population of Great Britain*, London, 1842.

Chesterton, C.E., (formerly Ada Jones), *I Lived in a Slum*, London, 1937.

Chevassus, H., *Overcrowding in the City of London*, London, 1877.

Clark, E., *The Hovel and the Home; or Improved dwellings for the labouring classes and how to obtain them*, London, 1863.

Cochrane, C., *How to improve the homes of the people*, London, 1849.

Conquest, J., *The Naked Truth: Shocking Revelations about the Slums*, London, 1933.

Cooper, C.P., *Papers respecting the sanitary state of the part of the parish of St Giles in the Fields, London*, London, 1850.

Cranfield, T., *Social Survey of Courts and Alleys in the Borough District of Southwark*, London, 1824.

Crickmay, E.G., *Housing Conditions in a Selected Area of Paddington*, London, 1935.

Davies, M.L., *Co-operation in Poor Neighbourhoods*, Manchester, 1899.

Dickens, C., *Hard Times*, London, 1854.

Disraeli, B., *Sybil*, London, 1845.

Dodd, J.T., *The Housing of the Working Classes*, London, 1891.

Doré, G. and W.B. Jerrold, *London: a Pilgrimage*, London, 1872.

Engels, F., *The Condition of the Working Classes in England*, London, (new ed.) 1973.

Fallows, J.A. and F. Hughes, *The housing question in Birmingham*, Birmingham, 1905.

Fallows, J.A., *Facts for Birmingham—the housing of the poor*, Birmingham, 1899.

Faucher, L., *Manchester in 1844: its present condition and future prospects*, London, 1844.

Felkin, W., *Remarks upon the importance of an inquiry into the amount and appropriation of wages by the working classes*, London, 1837.

Garwood, J., *The Million-Peopled City; or, One-Half of the People of London made known to the Other Half*, London, 1853.

Gaskell, E., *North and South*, London, 1854.

Gaspey, W., *Tallis's illustrated London*, London, 1851-52.

Gavin, H., *Sanitary ramblings, being sketches and illustrations of Bethnal Green*, London, 1848.

Gavin, H., *The Habitations of the Industrial Classes*, London, 1851.

Gilbert, W., *Dives and Lazarus; or the Adventures of an Obscure Medical Man in a Low Neighbourhood*, London, 1858.

Girdlestone, C., *Letters on the Unhealthy Condition of the Lower Classes of Dwellings, especially in Large Towns*, London, 1845.

Gissing, G., *Demos*, London, 1886.

Gissing, G., *In the Year of the Jubilee*, London, 1894.

Gissing, G., *The Nether World*, London, 1889.

Godwin, G., *Another Blow for Life*, London, 1864.

Godwin, G., *Town Swamps and Social Bridges*, London, 1859.

Grant, J., *Lights and Shadows of London Life* (2 vols), London, 1842.

Grant, J., *Pictures of Life: The Dwellings of the Poor*, London, 1855.

Green, F.E., *The Tyranny of the Countryside*, London, 1913.

Greenwood, J., *Low Life Deeps: An Account of the Strange Fish to be found there*, London, 1876.

Guy, W., *On the Health of Towns*, London, 1846.

Haggard, H. Rider, *Rural England*, London, 1902.

Hatton, J., *Cruel London*, London, 1878.

Haw, G., *No Room to Live: the Plaint of Overcrowded London*, London, 1900.

Hill, O., *Homes of the London Poor*, London, 1875.

Hollingshed, J., *Ragged London in 1861*, London, 1861.

Howarth, E.G. and M. Wilson, *West Ham: a Study in Social and Industrial Problems, being the Report of the Outer London Inquiry Committee*, London, 1907.

Jaffray, J., *Hints for a history of Birmingham*, Birmingham, 1857.

Jay, A.O., *A Story of Shoreditch*, London, 1896.

Jay, A.O., *Life in Darkest London: a Hint to General Booth*, London, 1891.

Jerrold, D., *St Giles and St James*, London, 1851.

Jones, A., *The Homes of the Poor in Westminster*, London, 1885.

Jones, H., *East and West London*, 1875.

Kaufman, M., *The Housing of the working Classes and the Poor*, London, 1907.

Kay, J.P., *The moral and physical condition of the working classes employed in the cotton manufacture in Manchester*, London, 1832.

Knox, J., *The Masses Without! A Pamphlet for the Times, on the Sanitary, Social, Moral and Healthier Condition of the Masses, who inhabit the Alleys, Courts, Wynds, Garrets, Cellars, Lodging-Houses, Dens and Hovels of Great Britain*, London, 1857.

Langford, J., *The advantages of co-operation*, address to the members of the Birmingham Co-operative League, Birmingham, 1847.

Lhotky, J., *On cases of death by starvation and extreme distress among the humbler classes*, London, 1844.

Llewellyn-Smith, H.W., ed., *The New Survey of London Life and Labour* (9 vols), London, 1930–35.

MacCallum, H., *The Distribution of the Poor in London*, London, 1883.

MacCree, G.W., *Day and Night in St Giles*, Bishop Auckland, 1862.

Manchester Diocesan Conference, *Report on the Housing of the Poor*, Manchester, 1902.

Marr, T.R., *Housing Conditions in Manchester and Salford*, Manchester, 1904.

Marshall, H. and A. Trevelyan, *Slum*, London, 1933.

Martin, C.R.A., *Slums and Slummers: A Sociological Treatise on the Housing Problem*, London, 1935.

Mayhew, H., *London Labour and the London Poor*, London, 1851.

Mearns, A., *London and its Teeming Toilers, Who they are and how they live*, London, 1885.

Mearns, A., *The Bitter Cry of Outcast London*, London, 1883.

Miles, W.A., *Poverty, mendicity and crime*, London, 1839.

Millington, F.H., *The Housing of the Poor*, London, 1891.

Morrison, A., *A Child of the Jago*, London, 1896.

Morrison, A., *Tales of Mean Streets*, London, 1894

Morrison, A., *The Hole in the Wall*, London, 1902.

Nettlefold, J.S., *A housing problem*, Birmingham, 1905.

Nunns, T., *A letter to the right honourable Lord Ashley on the condition of the working classes in Birmingham*, Birmingham, 1842.

Parker, J., *On the literature of the working classes*, in Meliora, ed. C.J.C. Talbot, London, 1853.

Paterson, A., *Across the Bridges, or Life by the South London River-Side*, London, 1912.

Perrott, F.D., *Overcrowded London*, Smethwick, 1900.

Rawlinson, R., *The Social and National Influence of the Domiciliary Condition of the People*, London, 1883.

Reeves, M.S., (Mrs. Pember Reeves), *Round About a Pound a Week*, London, 1912.

Rice-Jones, Rev., *In the Slums: Pages from the Note-book of a London Diocesan Home Missionary*, London, 1884.

Rowntree, B.S. and M. Kendall, *How the Labourer Lives*, London, 1913.

Rowntree, B.S., *Poverty and Progress: A Second Social Survey of York, 1936*, London, 1941.

Sala, G.A., *Gaslight and Daylight, with Some London Scenes they Shine Upon*, London, 1859.

Sala, G.A., *Living London*, London, 1883.

Sherwell, A., *Life in West London: a Study and a Contrast*, London, 1897.

Simon, E.D., *The Anti-Slum Campaign*, London, 1933.

Simon, E.D., *How to Abolish the Slums*, London, 1929.

Sims, G., *Rogues and Vagabonds*, London, 1900.

Sims, G., *How the Poor Live and Horrible London*, London, 1898.

Sims, G., *My Life: Sixty Years' Recollections of Bohemian London*, London, 1917.

Sinclair, C., *London Homes*, London, 1853.

Symmons, J.C., *Tactics for the times as regards the condition and treatment of the dangerous classes*, London, 1849.

Timmins, S., *Birmingham and the Midland hardware district*, London, 1866.

Titmuss, R.M., *Poverty and Population: A Factual Study of Contemporary Social Waste*, London, 1938.

Townroe, B.S., *The Slum Problem*, London, 1928.

Tressall, R., *The Ragged Trousered Philanthropist*, London, 1914.

Tristran, F., *The London Diary of Flora Tristran*, London, 1842.

Valpy, R.A., *An Inquiry into the Condition and Occupations of the People in Central London*, London, 1889.

Vanderkiste, R.W., *Notes and Narratives of the Six Years' Mission principally among the Dens of London*, London, 1852.

Vaughan, R., *The age of great cities*, London, 1843.

Wakefield, E.G., *Households in danger of the populace*, London, 1831.

Walters, J.C., *Scenes in slumland*, reprinted from Birmingham Daily Gazette, Birmingham, 1901.

Whitburn, J., *The Housing Problem in Newcastle and District*, Newcastle, 1902.

Williams, R., *London Rookeries and Collier's Slums: a Plea for More Breathing Room*, London, 1893.

Woods, R.A., et al., *The Poor in Great Cities: Their Problems and What is being done to Solve Them*, London, 1896.

Wright, T., *The Pinch of Poverty*, London, 1892.

3. The slum in its historical perspective

Articles

Beresford, M., 'The back-to-back house in Leeds 1787–1937', in *The history of working-class housing*, edited by Chapman, S.D., Newton Abbot, 1971.

Carter, H. and S. Wheatley, 1979, 'Fixation lines and fringe belts, land uses and social areas: nineteenth-century change in the small town', *Transactions Institute of British Geographers*, iv, (1979).

Carter, H. and S. Wheatley, 'Residential segregation in nineteenth-century cities', *Area*, xii, (1980).

Dennis, R.J., 'Intercensal mobility in a Victorian city', *Transactions of the Institute of British Geographers*, ii, (1977).

Dennis, R.J., 1979, 'The Victorian City', *Transactions of the Institute of British Geographers*, iv, (1979).

Dennis, R.J. and S. Daniels, 1981, '"Community" and the social geography of Victorian cities', *Urban History Yearbook*, 1987.

Dyos, H.J. and D.A. Reeder, 'Slums and Suburbs', in *The Victorian City: Images and Realities* (vol. II), ed. H.J. Dyos and M. Wolff, London, 1973.

Dyos, H.J., 'Railways and Housing in Victorian London', *Journal of Transport History*, ii, (1955).

Dyos, H.J., 'The Growth of a Pre-Victorian Suburb: South London, 1580–1836', *Town Planning Review*, xxv, (1954).

Dyos, H.J., 'The Slums of Victorian London', *Victorian Studies*, xi, (1967-68).

Dyos, H.J., 'Urban transformation: a note on the objects of street improvement in Regency and early Victorian London', *International Review of Social History*, ii, (1957).

Flinn, M., 1974, 'Trends in real wages 1750-1950', *Economic History Review* second series, xxvii, (1974).

Gilley, S.W., 1973, 'The Garibaldi riots of 1862', *Historical Journal*, xvi, (1973).

Green, D.R., 'Street trading in London: a case study of casual labour 1830-60', in *The structure of nineteenth-century cities*, ed. J. Johnson and C. Pooley, London, 1982.

Green, D.R., 'A map for Mayhew's London: the geography of poverty in the mid-nineteenth century', *London Journal*, xi, (1985).

Harrison, B., 'The Sunday trading riots of 1855', *Historical Journal*, viii, (1965).

Kemp, P., 'Housing landlordism in nineteenth-century Britain', *Environment and Planning*, xiv, (1982).

Kemp, P., 'House property as capital: private rental housing in the late Victorian city', *University of Sussex, Department of Urban and Regional Studies*, working paper, xxix, (1982).

Kondratieff, N., 'The long waves in economic life', *Review of Economics and Statistics*, xvii, (1935).

Lawton, R., 'Population and society 1730-1900', in *An historical geography of England and Wales*, ed. R. Dodgshon and R. Butlin, London, 1976.

Lawton, R. and C. Pooley, 'David Brindley's Liverpool: an aspect of urban society in the 1880s', *Transactions of the Historical Society of Lancashire and Cheshire*, cxxv, (1975).

Lees, L., 'Patterns of lower class life in Irish slum communities in nineteenth-century London', in *Nineteenth century cities*, ed. S. Thernstrom and R. Sennett, New York, 1968.

Lees, L., 'Mid-Victorian migration and the Irish family economy', *Victorian Studies*, xx, (1976).

Malcolmson, P.E., 'Getting a Living in the Slums of Victorian Kensington', *The London Journal*, i, (1976).

O'Brien, P.K. and S. Engerman, 'Changes in income and its distribution during the industrial revolution', in *The Economic history of Britain since 1700*, vol. 1, ed. R. Floud and D. McCloskey, Cambridge, 1981.

Pooley, C., 'Residential mobility in the Victorian city', *Transactions of the Institute of British Geographers*, iv, (1979).

Power, M.J., 'East and West in early-modern London', in *Wealth and power in Tudor England*, ed. E.W. Ives, R. Knect and J. Scarisbrick, London, 1978.

Power, M.J., 'The social topography of Restoration London', in *The Making of the Metropolis*, ed. A.L. Beier and R. Finlay, London, 1985.

Richardson, C., 'Irish settlement in mid-nineteenth century Bradford', *Yorkshire Bulletin of Economic and Social Research*, xx, (1968).

Robb, J.G., 'Suburb and slum in Gorbals: social and residential change 1800-1900', in *Scottish urban history*, ed. G. Gordon and B. Dicks, Aberdeen, 1983.

Rose, M., 'Settlement, removal and the New Poor Law', in *The New Poor Law in the nineteenth century*, ed. D. Fraser, London, 1976.

Ross, E., 1982, 'Fierce questions and taunts: married life in working-class London 1870-1914', *Feminist Studies*, iii, (1982).

Ross, E., 'Survival networks: women's neighbourhood sharing in London before World War One', *History Workshop Journal*, xv, (1983).

Samuel, R., 'Comers and goers', in *The Victorian City*, ed. H.J. Dyos and M. Wolff, London, 1973.

Schwarz, L.D., 'Social class and social geography: the middle classes in London at the end of the eighteenth century', *Social History*, vii, (1982).

Shannon, H.A., 'Bricks—a trade index 1785–1849', *Economica*, i, (1934).

Sheppard, F., V. Belcher and P. Cottrell, 'The Middlesex and Yorkshire deeds registries and the study of building fluctuations', *London Journal*, v, (1979).

Smith, R., 'Housing History', *History Today*, xii, (1963).

Stokes, C.J., 'A Theory of Slums', *Land Economics*, xxxviii, (1962).

Taylor, I.C., 'The insanitary housing question and tenement dwellings in nineteenth-century Liverpool', in *Multi-storey living*, ed. A. Sutcliffe, London, 1974.

Thompson, E.P., 'The political education of Henry Mayhew', *Victorian Studies*, xi, (1967).

Thompson, E.P., 'Mayhew and the Morning Chronicle', in *The Unknown Mayhew*, ed. E.P. Thompson and E. Yeo, Harmondsworth, 1973.

Tucker, R., 'Real wages of artisans in London 1729–1935', *Journal of the American Statistical Association*, xxxi, (1936).

Vance, J.E., 'Housing the worker: determinant and contingent ties in nineteenth-century Birmingham', *Economic Geography*, xliii, (1967).

Wohl, A.S., 'The Housing of the Working Classes in London, 1815–1914', in *The History of Working Class Housing*, ed. S.D. Chapman, Newton Abbot, 1971.

Yeo, E., 1973, 'Mayhew as social investigator', in *The Unknown Mayhew*, ed. E.P. Thompson and E. Yeo, Harmondsworth, 1973.

4. The slum in its historical perspective

Books

Alexander, S., *Women's work in nineteenth-century London: a study of the years 1820–50*, London, 1983.

Allen, G.C., *The industrial development of Birmingham and the Black Country*, London, 1929.

Anderson, M., *Family structure in nineteenth-century Lancashire*, Cambridge, 1971.

Barnes, H., *The Slum: Its Story and Solution*, London, 1931.

Beresford, M., *Leeds and its region*, London, 1967.

Bramwell, W., 'Pubs and localised communities in mid-Victorian Birmingham', *Queen Mary College, Department of Geography*, occasional paper, 22, London, 1984.

Briggs, A., *History of Birmingham*, vol. 2, London, 1952.

Burnett, J., *A social history of housing 1815–1985*, London, 1986.

Bythell, D., *The sweated trades: outwork in nineteenth-century Britain*, London, 1978.

Cannadine, D., *Lords and Landlords: the aristocracy and the towns 1774–1967*, Leicester, 1980.

Chapman, S.D., *The history of working-class housing*, Newton Abbot, 1971.

Chesney, K., *The Victorian Underworld*, London, 1970.

Chilton, C., *Victorian folk songs*, London, 1965.

Clinard, M.B., *Slums and Community Development*, London, 1966.

Cullen, M.J., *The statistical movement in early Victorian Britain*, Hassocks, 1975.

Dennis, R.J., *English industrial cities of the nineteenth century*, Cambridge, 1984.

Dewsnup, E.R., *The Housing Problem in England: Its statistics, legislation and policy*, Manchester, 1907.

Dyos, H.J., *Victorian Suburb: A study of the growth of Camberwell*, Leicester, 1961.

Englander, D., *Landlord and tenant in urban Britain 1838–1918*, Oxford, 1983.

Finnegan, F., *Poverty and prejudice: a study of Irish immigrants in York 1840–1875*, Cork, 1982.

Flint, K., ed., *The Victorian novelist: social problems and social change*, London, 1987.

Foakes, G., *Between High Walls*, London, 1972.

Forster, C.A., *Court housing in Kingston-upon-Hull* Occasional Papers in Geography, Hull, 1972.

Fraser, D., *A history of modern Leeds*, Manchester, 1980.

Gaskell, S.M., *Model Housing*, London, 1987.

Gauldie, E., *Cruel habitations*, London, 1974.

Gayer, A., W. Rostow and A. Schwarz, *Growth and fluctuations of the British economy 1790–1850*, Oxford, 1953.

George, M.D., *London life in the eighteenth century*, Harmondsworth, 1966.

Gill, C., *History of Birmingham*, vol. 1, London, 1952.

Heren, L., *Growing Up Poor in London*, London, 1973.

Himmelfarb, G., *The idea of poverty*, London, 1984.

Holloway, J. and J. Black, *Later English broadside ballads*, London, 1979.

Humphreys, A., *Travels into the poor man's country*, Georgia, USA, 1977.

Johnson, P., *Saving and spending: the working-class economy in Britain 1870–1939*, Oxford, 1985.

Jones, G.S., *Outcast London: A study of the relationships between classes in Victorian Society*, Oxford, 1971.

Keating, P.J., *Into unknown England 1866–1913: selections from the social explorers*, Glasgow, 1976.

Kellett, J.R., *The Impact of Railways on Victorian Cities*, London, 1969.

Kerr, M., *The People of Ship Street*, London, 1958.

Lees, A., *Cities perceived: urban society in European and American thought*, Manchester, 1985.

Lees, L., *Exiles of Erin: Irish immigrants in Victorian London*, Manchester, 1979.

Lewis, O., *La Vida: a Puerto Rican family in the culture of poverty— San Juan and New York*, London, 1967.

Lloyd, P., *Slums of Hope: Shanty Towns of the Third World*, Manchester, 1979.

Mandel, E., *Long Waves of capitalist development*, Cambridge, 1980.

Meacham, S., *A Life Apart. The English Working Class 1890–1914*, London, 1977.

Needleman, L., *The Economics of Housing*, London, 1965.

Roberts, R., *The Classic Slum: Salford Life in the First Quarter of the Century*, Manchester, 1971.

Sponza, L., *Italians in nineteenth-century Britain: realities and images*, Leicester, 1988.

Stewart, C.J., ed., *The Housing Question in London, 1855–1900*, London, 1900.

Stride, L., *Memoirs of a Street Urchin*, ed. G. Davis, Bath, 1985.

Suttles, G., *The Social Order of the Slum*, London, 1968.

Swift, R. and S. Gilley, *The Irish in the Victorian City*, London, 1985.

Tebbutt, M., *Making ends meet: pawnbroking and working-class credit*, Leicester, 1983.
Townley, J.F. et al., *Dearth and disease in early modern Birmingham*, University of Birmingham, Department of Extra-Mural Studies, Birmingham, 1988.
Treble, J.H., *Urban Poverty in Britain 1830–1914*, London, 1979.
Valentine, C., *Culture and poverty: critique and counter proposals*, Chicago, 1968.
White, J., *Rothschild Buildings: life in an East End tenement block 1887–1920*, London, 1980.
White, J., *The Worst Street in North London: Campbell Bunk, Islington between the Wars*, London, 1986.
Williams, K., *From pauperism to poverty*, London, 1987.
Wohl, A., *The Eternal Slum. Housing and Social Policy in Victorian London*, London, 1977.
Yelling, J.A., *Slums and Slum Clearance in Victorian London*, London, 1986.
Young, M. and P. Willmott, *Family and Kinship in East London*, London, 1957.

Unpublished theses and reports

Green, D.R., 1984, *From artisans to paupers: the manufacture of poverty in mid-nineteenth century London*, Ph.D. dissertation, University of Cambridge.
Matthews, M.H., and A.G. Parton, *The geography of poverty in mid-nineteenth century Birmingham: a pilot survey*, Report to the Social Studies Research Council, 1982.

Index

(NOTE: Figures in italics indicate an article by the person annotated.)